A Century of Chinese Literature in Translation (1919–2019)

This book delves into the Chinese literary translation landscape over the last century, spanning critical historical periods such as the Cultural Revolution in the greater China region.

Contributors from all around the world approach this theme from various angles, providing an overview of translation phenomena at key historical moments, identifying the trends of translation and publication, uncovering the translation history of important works, elucidating the relationship between translators and other agents, articulating the interaction between texts and readers and disclosing the nature of literary migration from Chinese into English.

This volume aims to benefit both academics of translation studies from a dominantly Anglophone culture and researchers in the greater China region. Chinese scholars of translation studies will not only be able to cite this as a reference book, but will be able to discover contrasts, confluence and communication between academics across the globe, which will stimulate, inspire and transform discussions in this field.

Leah Gerber is Senior Lecturer and Course Director of the Masters in Interpreting and Translation Studies at Monash University. Leah's research focuses predominantly on the translation of Australian children's literature into German. She is the author of *Tracing a Tradition: The Translation of Australian Children's Fiction into German from 1945* (2014) and co-editor (with Prof. Rita Wilson) of *Creative Constraints Translation and Authorship* (2012).

Lintao Qi is Lecturer in the Masters in Interpreting and Translation Studies at Monash University. His research interests include all aspects of literary translation theory and practice, with a special focus on translation and reception of Chinese literature overseas and Australian literature in China through translation. He is the author of *Jin Ping Mei English Translations: Texts, Paratexts, and Contexts* (2018). Lintao is a NAATI-certified translator, National Education Committee member of AUSIT (Australian Institute of Interpreters and Translators), committee member of AALITRA (Australian Association for Literary Translation) and editor of *The Aalitra Review*.

Routledge Advances in Translation and Interpreting Studies

For more information about this series, please visit: www.routledge.com/
Routledge-Advances-in-Translation-and-Interpreting-Studies/book-series/RTS

A Century of Chinese Literature in Translation (1919–2019)

English Publication and Reception

Edited by Leah Gerber and Lintao Qi

LONDON AND NEW YORK

First published 2021
by Routledge
2 Park Square, Milton Park, Abingdon, Oxon OX14 4RN

and by Routledge
605 Third Avenue, New York, NY 10017

First issued in paperback 2022

Routledge is an imprint of the Taylor & Francis Group, an informa business

© 2021 selection and editorial matter, Leah Gerber and Lintao Qi; individual chapters, the contributors

The right of Leah Gerber and Lintao Qi to be identified as the authors of the editorial material, and of the authors for their individual chapters, has been asserted in accordance with sections 77 and 78 of the Copyright, Designs and Patents Act 1988.

All rights reserved. No part of this book may be reprinted or reproduced or utilised in any form or by any electronic, mechanical, or other means, now known or hereafter invented, including photocopying and recording, or in any information storage or retrieval system, without permission in writing from the publishers.

Trademark notice: Product or corporate names may be trademarks or registered trademarks, and are used only for identification and explanation without intent to infringe.

Publisher's Note
The publisher has gone to great lengths to ensure the quality of this reprint but points out that some imperfections in the original copies may be apparent.

British Library Cataloguing-in-Publication Data
A catalogue record for this book is available from the British Library

Library of Congress Cataloging-in-Publication Data
Names: Gerber, Leah, 1979– editor. | Qi, Lintao, editor.
Title: A century of Chinese literature in translation (1919–2019) : English
   publication and reception / edited by Leah Gerber, Lintao Qi.
Description: London ; New York : Routledge, 2020. | Series: Routledge
   advances in translation and interpreting studies | Includes bibliographical
   references and index.
Identifiers: LCCN 2020018218 (print) | LCCN 2020018219 (ebook) |
   ISBN 9780367321291 (hardback) | ISBN 9780429316821 (ebook)
Subjects: LCSH: Chinese literature—Translations into English—History
   and criticism. | Translating and interpreting—China—20th century. |
   Translating and interpreting—China—21st century.
Classification: LCC PL2274.2.E5 C46 2020 (print) | LCC PL2274.2.E5
   (ebook) | DDC 428/.040951—dc23
LC record available at https://lccn.loc.gov/2020018218
LC ebook record available at https://lccn.loc.gov/2020018219

ISBN: 978-0-367-54801-8 (pbk)
ISBN: 978-0-367-32129-1 (hbk)
ISBN: 978-0-429-31682-1 (ebk)

DOI: 10.4324/9780429316821

Typeset in Times New Roman
by Apex CoVantage, LLC

Contents

Illustrations

Figures

Tables

Contributors

Allan H. Barr, Professor of Chinese at Pomona College, is the author of a study in Chinese of a notorious literary inquisition in the early Qing, *Jiangnan yi jie: Qing ren bixia de Zhuangshi shi'an* (Zhejiang guji chubanshe, 2016), and has published numerous articles relating to Pu Songling (1640–1715) and other 17th-century authors. In recent years he has translated five books by the contemporary Chinese author Yu Hua, including the widely admired essay collection, *China in Ten Words*. His translations have appeared in *The Guardian, The Los Angeles Times, The New York Times*, and *The New Yorker*.

Will Gatherer is a Lecturer in Chinese within the University of Queensland's Master of Arts in Chinese Translation and Interpreting programme. Having completed his BA (Hons) from the School of Oriental & African Studies (SOAS) in London, Will worked in Beijing at the British Embassy and then subsequently completed his PhD at the University of Queensland. In addition to Will's academic role at UQ he is also a practicing NAATI-accredited professional translator between Chinese and English. Will is currently writing a literary studies monograph on the Chinese author Ma Yuan.

Qiang Geng is an Associate Professor in Translation Studies at the Institute of Corpus Studies and Applications, Shanghai International Studies University. His research interest in translation studies covers mainly modern Chinese translation history from 1949 to the 1980s. He is the author of the monograph *Translation and Transmission of Chinese Literature in the New Era: Panda Books Series and Chinese Literature Walking toward the World* (Nankai University Press, 2019), which explores the translation of Chinese literature into English that has been patronized by Chinese government institutes. More recently, his research has been on Chinese discourses on translation in contemporary times.

Leah Gerber is Senior Lecturer and Course Director of the Master of Interpreting and Translation Studies at Monash University. Leah's research focuses predominantly on the translation of Australian children's literature into German. She is the author of *Tracing a Tradition: The Translation of Australian Children's Fiction Into German from 1945* (2014), and co-editor (with Prof. Rita Wilson) of *Creative Constraints Translation and Authorship* (2012).

Nicholas Jose has published seven novels, including *Paper Nautilus* (1987), *The Red Thread* (2000) and *Original Face* (2005), three collections of short stories, *Black Sheep: Journey to Borroloola* (a memoir), and essays, mostly on Australian and Asian culture. He is co-editor, with Xianlin Song, of *Everything Changes: Australian Writers and China, a Transcultural Anthology* (UWAP 2019) and, with Benjamin Madden, *Antipodean China: Reflections on Literary Exchange* (Giramondo 2020). He is Adjunct Professor in the Writing and Society Research Centre at Western Sydney University and the Department of English and Creative Writing at The University of Adelaide.

Uganda Sze Pui Kwan is Associate Professor at Nanyang Technological University, Singapore. Her research interests comprise translation history of the 19th Century Sino-British relations, gender translation, and literary translation in Asia. She has written three monographs and (co-)edited one volume of articles on Global Asia. She is the recipient of several scholarships and awards, including the Hong Kong Biennial Award for Chinese Literature in 2019, and research scholarships at Cambridge and the University of Tokyo. Her visiting appointments at Princeton University and Harvard University reinforced her belief that translation theories can connect different fields.

Bonnie S. McDougall is Honorary Associate in Chinese Studies at the University of Sydney and Professor Emeritus at the University of Edinburgh. She first studied Chinese at Peking University in 1958–59. She returned to the University of Sydney in 1961 to continue with Chinese studies, leading to appointments at the University of Sydney, Harvard University, the University of Oslo and the University of Edinburgh. She has written extensively on modern Chinese literature and translated poetry, fiction, drama, letters, essays and film scripts by over fifty authors including Lu Xun, Mao Zedong, He Qifang, Bei Dao, Ah Cheng and Chen Kaige.

Lintao Qi is a Lecturer in the Master of Interpreting and Translation Studies at Monash University. His research interests include all aspects of literary translation theory and practice with a special focus on translation and reception of Chinese literature overseas, and Australian literature in China through translation. He is the author of *Jin Ping Mei English Translations: Texts, Paratexts, and Contexts* (2018). Lintao is a NAATI-certified translator, National Education Committee member of AUSIT (Australian Institute of Interpreters and Translators), committee member of AALITRA (Australian Association for Literary Translation), and editor of *The Aalitra Review*.

Carlos Rojas is Professor of Chinese Cultural Studies; Gender, Sexuality, and Feminist Studies; and Arts of the Moving Image at Duke University. He is author, editor, and translator of approximately twenty books, including translations into English of works by Yu Hua, Yan Lianke, Jia Pingwa, and Ng Kim Chew.

Ronald Schleifer is George Lynn Cross Research Professor of English and Adjunct Professor in the College of Medicine. From 1976 to 2000 he served as editor of *Genre: Forms of Discourse and Culture*; and from 1986 to 1999 he served as co-editor of The Oklahoma Project for Discourse and Theory (University of Oklahoma Press). In 1999 he was the Director of the Annual Convention for the Society for Literature and Science. In 2012 he served as Interim Editor of *Configurations: A Journal of Literature, Science, and Technology*. Prof. Schleifer now serves as co-editor of *Mariner 10: Cross-Disciplinary DVD-ROMS*, a series of electronic, interactive titles published by the University of Pennsylvania Press. Prof. Schleifer has written, translated, or edited twenty books.

Lu Shao is Professor of Translation Studies in the Department of English and Director of the Centre for China Studies Overseas at Sun Yat-sen University. She is Associate Executive Editor of the Chinese journal *New Perspectives in Translation Studies* and a member of the Editorial Board of *Translation Quarterly* (HK). She is the author of *Fuzzy Language in Literature and Translation* (Chi., 2011) and over 80 articles, most of them published in major international and national journals. Her research interests are in literary translation, fuzzy language in literature and translation, and narratology and the stylistics of fiction.

Jonathan Stalling is the Harold J. & Ruth Newman Chair of US-China Issues and Professor of International and Area Studies, and Co-Director of the Institute for US-China Issues, where he directs The Newman Prize for Chinese Literature, The Newman Prize for English Jueju, *Chinese Literature Today*, the *CLT* book series (University of Oklahoma Press) and the *US-China Poetry Dialogue*. He is also the founder and Curator of the Chinese Literature Translation Archive and an Affiliate Professor of English. Dr. Stalling specializes in Comparative US-China Culture, Literature, and Poetics as well as Chinese-English translation and interlanguage studies (and pedagogies). He is the author or editor of eight books. Stalling was the first non-Chinese Poet in Residence of Beijing University. Stalling's interlanguage work was the subject of two TEDx Talks.

Hongjuan Xin is a Professor of translation studies at the Faculty of Foreign Languages of Ningbo University. She obtained her PhD from Nanjing University, focusing on English translations of *Dao-de-jing*. Her academic interests also lie in translation studies of Yang Xianyi and his British wife Gladys Yang. She has completed a 2008–2009 Fulbright research project on translating *Dao-de-jing* and a research project on the Yangs' translated works funded by the Chinese Ministry of Education. Her monographs include *Translating Dao-de-jing: Theory Travelling and Image Reconstruction* (2008/2013/2016), *Dialogues of Chinese Translation Frontiers* (2016, co-authored) and *Translation Thoughts of Yang Xianyi* (2018).

Man Zhang is an Editor of the Journal *Comparative Literature in China* in Shanghai International Studies University, China. She has published two books in Chinese, *A Study of Lao She's Translated Literature* (2016, Shanghai Jiao Tong University Press) and *A Study of Lao She's Sino-foreign Literary Relations* (2018, East China Normal University Press) and articles in academic journals on translated literature. She is interested in the study of translated literature, Sino-foreign literary relations and comparative literature.

Introduction

Leah Gerber and Lintao Qi

Over 40 years ago, in his 1972 seminar paper "The Name and Nature of Translation Studies," James S. Holmes (1988, p. 72) claimed that one goal of product-oriented Descriptive Translation Studies "might possibly be a general history of translation studies." Before that goal could be realized, so-called "restricted" studies would have to be conducted, among which "area-restricted" refers to research limited to specific languages or groups of languages and/or cultures (1988, p. 74). In recent years, there has been a swing away from purely Eurocentric approaches to translation studies, towards research that explores LOTE (Languages Other Than English) cultures in translation. This shift is evidenced by a growing number of recent publications focusing on specific non-Anglophone cultures, such as edited volumes on Iran (Haddadian-Moghaddam, 2014), Japan (Curran, Sato-Rossberg, & Tanabe, 2015), Korea (Kang & Wakabayashi, 2019; Kim, 2019), Russia (Baer & Witt, 2018), and Turkey (Albachten & Gürçağlar, 2019; Tahir Gürçaglar, Paker, & Milton, 2015).

Within translation studies, research on the translation, publication and reception of Chinese works has grown exponentially in past years, yet there is a clear discrepancy between the volume of research published in Chinese and in English. Following the Chinese government's initiative of "Chinese Culture Going Global" at the beginning of the 21st century, a great number of Chinese-language journal articles and monographs on Chinese literary translation have been published. For example, a quick search using the key words "Chinese literature" and "translation" returned 645 results between 2000 and 2019 on the website of CNKI. By comparison, there are far fewer contributions in English. Moreover, a dedicated volume in English by an internationally reputable publisher remains absent from this body of scholarship.

Contributions that have been published in English with a focus on China (Chan, 2004; Han & Li, 2019; Luo & He, 2009; Qi, 2018) cover only limited aspects such as translation pedagogy, interpreter training, audiovisual translation (AVT), machine translation, etc., but there has been less focus on literary translation; those that do concentrate on literature may only present a single case study or focus on the work of one author/translator. A volume dedicated to the various facets involved with the translation of Chinese literary works is absent from international translation studies scholarship. This collection of papers presents an attempt to bridge this gap by showcasing quality research by outstanding scholars in the field and, in doing so, enriching the general corpus of translation studies from the perspectives of world literature and intercultural communication.

The following edited volume is distinctive in its diversity of contributors and topics. Scholars from a number of inter-disciplinary areas such as translation studies, literary studies, Chinese studies and area studies have contributed to it, some of whom are also prolific writers and/or translators. They come from different corners of the globe, including Australia, China, Singapore and the United States. Topics of concern vary from research on historical issues, to case studies of well-known translators and literary works, and reflections by translators. These papers embrace sociological, literary, linguistic, historical and archival methodologies of translation studies research. The diversity of papers will, we hope, enrich readers from translation studies as well as cognate areas by contributing more holistically to our understanding of Chinese literature in translation.

As the first scholarly volume to introduce the very broad theme of Chinese literature in English translation, we were selective in the timeframe chosen for analysis., Our contributors have limited their focus to the period between 1919 and 2019 (early 20th – early 21st century); 1919 references the historic May Fourth Movement, which heralded the beginning of the modern era for China. Arguably, this movement prompted more translation from other languages into Chinese, than from the Chinese language into others. Nevertheless, the responding flow of western thoughts, cultures, and literatures, as well as the increased movement of people from China to the West – which also generated greater interest in contemporary Chinese culture and literature – resulted in the translation and publication of many Chinese literary works in English in the first half of the 20th century.

Australian writer, translator and academic Nicholas Jose opens the volume, presenting *Lady Precious Stream* (1935), a text (re)written creatively by S. I. Hsiung. *Lady Precious Stream* is a modern Chinese text based on a traditional story, which was successfully adapted into a performance piece that was staged throughout the Anglophone world (and beyond) in the 1930s. Hsiung was also a translator of British drama into Chinese, during which process he grew acquainted with the theatrical tradition in English. Jose argues that this sensitized the translator to the possibility of adapting his work from the conventions of one theatrical tradition to those of the other. By examining the work's production and reception in Australia, Jose also claims that factors such as the requirement for a multitude of performers and costumes, and most interestingly, the historical contexts of the Sino-Japanese war, have all contributed to its global popularity throughout the 20th century.

Man Zhang's study of the English translation of Lao She's *The Yellow Storm* (1951) is just one of the papers to shed light on the complex relationships between agents in the translation process as well as the complex sociology that can surround author and translator. When Lao She discovered that his novel would be translated into English, he set about rewriting it. The translator Ida Pruitt, who was raised in China, deliberately opted for a technique of "unusual translation" to preserve the Chinese elements that resonated with her own memory of her childhood in China. Lao She disapproved, believing that this technique would hinder the reception of his work. The translator, with the intervention and support of other agents such as Pearl Buck, refused to make the suggested changes. The resultant "unusual" translation was very well-received by readers, thus contradicting the notion of polysystems (Even-Zohar) and the preference for domestication (Venuti): Chinese literary works held a secondary position in the American polysystem, which meant that usually, a domesticating translation would have been the norm. However, the success of this foreignized translation revealed that the phenomenon of literary translation is often more nuanced and complicated than first thought.

Archival research by Lintao Qi and Leah Gerber, based on the Allen & Unwin publishing archives, London, during World War II, also examines the complex social role of agents in the process of translation and publication of translated Chinese literature. Qi and Gerber coin the term "non-professional agents" to describe interventions by individuals with some degree of social, cultural, symbolic or economic capital These are people such as fellow authors, Chinese diplomats and family members, who influence the selection of texts for translation, the initiation and commission of a translation project and even the signing of contracts. In light of the significance of archival materials (framed here as part of the translation paratext) in the historical study of translation, the authors propose the possibility of an "archival turn" in translation studies.

By 1949, mid-way through the 20th century, the Communist Party of China had assumed power in mainland China. The ideological division between the socialists and capitalists meant that in the following decades, the Chinese reading market favored literary works from the other socialist countries such as the Soviet Union. The western world was, unsurprisingly, not interested in reading Party literature from China. The Chinese government did, however, gradually realize the importance of reaching out to the West and established an official department that would produce the English translation of Chinese literary works. A number of contributors have focussed on the period following, particularly on the impact of ideological factors in the translating and publishing sphere.

Qiang Geng labels the circulation of Chinese literature in the English-speaking world as "gift-giving": the Chinese government arranged for Chinese literary works to be translated into English and distributed the translations to the West free of charge. Geng approaches the topic of outbound translation, i.e. translation initiated by the source culture rather than sought out by the target culture, using the example of the Panda Books Series, produced by China's Foreign Languages Bureau since the early 1980s. The Party strictly controlled the translation process, from the selection of source texts and translators to the translation strategies and, most notably, to the distribution of published translations. Most of the translations were sent to western diplomats and various institutions free of charge, as an early way of exercising China's soft power. Geng scrutinises this act of "givism" in the political, economic and cultural contexts of China, highlighting that the government's implicit sinocentrism contributed to the eventual failure to acquire a wider Anglophone audience.

Bonnie S. McDougall writes from her experience as a translator in China's Foreign Languages Press for three years during the 1980s (in the period following the Cultural Revolution). McDougall discusses the multiple voices involved in literary translation within China's institutional translation movement. As in other chapters, her examples reiterate the complexity of the translation process in China, and the misconception that the translator's voice is monolithic in a literary work. McDougall also discusses the intervention of agents such as editors or publishers as well as the steps a translator can take when faced with the Party's censorship. This chapter presents a rare and fascinating insight into the process during this historical period.

During her period working at the Foreign Languages Press, McDougall claims that Gladys Yang and Yang Xianyi were the most well-known translators in China. By that time, the Yangs had translated a number of Chinese literary works, both classic and contemporary, including *Selected Works of Lu Xun* (1956). In Hongjuan Xin's chapter, Lu Xun is introduced as the "father of modern Chinese literature." His works, which have been widely (re)translated into many western languages, attract a great deal of academic attention in the English-speaking world. Hongjuan provides a chronological account of the translational history of Lu Xun's short stories into English, then presents an analysis of the Yangs' translation strategies through selective textual examples.

Uganda Sze Pui Kwan's chapter takes up the notion of world literature and the peripheral status of Hong Kong literature. Some westerners believe of Hong Kong that, in Kwan's words, "a colony could never produce literature since it is presumably a cultural desert." Kwan introduces a counter example, *Atlas: The Archaeology of an Imaginary City*, which won "the best translated work award: science fiction and fantasy translation awards" in 2013. The work was a product of what Kwan terms "self-collaborative translation," where the source text author Dung Kai-cheung self-translates and collaborates with two widely acclaimed English-speaking translators (one of them is Bonnie S. McDougall). For the edition of *Atlas* first published in Chinese in 1997, Dung produced a self-translation into English in 1998, and then a second one, collaboratively, in 2012. Here, Dung's freedom (as the source text author) to "authenticate, interpret and rewrite" his own text was inevitably constrained by the unique collaborative network within which the translation was produced; in which roles and boundaries were challenged and blurred. Kwan argues that such translations would "strategize minority literature such as that of Hong Kong to gain global visibility."

Will Gatherer explores the Avant-garde movement in Chinese literature in the 1980s, singling out the self-reflexive function of postmodernist texts written by established authors such as Ge Fei, Ma Yuan and Yu Hua. Translation is presented as a launching pad for Gatherer's in-depth discussion of literary expression; translation strategy is examined, not in terms of linguistic fidelity, but with regard to its impact and effect in context of the target language. The source texts examined in this chapter were all first published in the 1980s, but their English translations span more than two decades, with occasional retranslations, thus further enriching (and complicating) the area of study. Gatherer concludes that the translation strategies were employed in order to transfer the self-reflexive function in the Chinese novels, altering "their textual functions and in turn heavily altering the potential readings of the texts."

Historically, the Chinese government has acknowledged the importance of reaching out to the West and, as such, the internationally renowned Nobel Prize for Literature has always been highly regarded in China. In 2012, Chinese author Mo Yan won the award for his body of work that "with hallucinatory realism merges folk tales, history and the contemporary" (2012), and many believe that he is heavily indebted to his translators for the prize, particularly Howard Goldblatt. Lu Shao's article approaches Goldblatt's English translation of Mo Yan's *Life and Death Are Wearing Me Out* (2006) from the perspective of cognitive narratology. Lu explores the narrative shifts that occurred in Goldblatt's re-narration of Mo Yan's novels, which she believes have "contributed to their successful reception by the target readers." This chapter represents Lu's effort to demonstrate the mutually beneficial relationship between the disciplines of cognitive narratology and translation studies.

Clearly, since Mo Yan became the first Chinese laureate for the Nobel Prize in Literature, his work has been researched from different disciplinary perspectives, including literary studies and translation studies. In order to document the life and work of this important writer, Mo Yan archives have been set up in China and various parts of the world. In their chapter, Ronald Schleifer and Jonathan Stalling explore the Mo Yan archive hosted by the University of Oklahoma. Schleifer and Stalling propose, based on the Actor-Network Theory, a single general archival methodology, namely the Actor-Network Translation Studies. In their analysis, they draw on archival research to explain previously unexplored parts of the translation process, such as why Mo Yan was asked by his translator to rewrite the ending of one of his novels (to which he happily agreed). Like Qi and Gerber, Schleifer and Stalling's chapter illustrates the value of paratextual research in examining actors and their actions in the translation process, which textual analysis alone cannot reveal.

Indeed, a major component of research into translation archives is to document how translators make their decisions; this can be ascertained by analysing their commentaries on the translation process and product. Therefore, the third part of this volume includes contributions by two well-known Chinese Studies scholars who are also renowned translators of contemporary Chinese literature. Carlos Rojas has translated works by many renowned contemporary Chinese authors including Yan Lianke and Ng Kim Chew. In his chapter, Rojas reflects upon the challenges of "translating between languages" by drawing upon the example of the heteroglossic nature of 20th century German writer Thomas Mann's works, which he maps onto the Chinese language. He discusses the complexity of classical Chinese vs the modern vernacular (Rojas considers the switch between classical Chinese and modern vernacular Chinese a process of double translation), and he also considers issues of non-standard usage of the language, dialect and specialized vocabulary in translation.

The final contribution is by translator Allan H. Barr, who has been the sole translator of Chinese writer Yu Hua. In his chapter "Translating Yu Hua," Barr provides a vivid account of how he started learning Chinese and the beginnings of his translation enterprises. He introduces all five of his translations of Yu Hua's work, encompassing not only textual examples from the translation, but also first-hand record of these projects and academic reflections on the task of a translator.

This carefully curated collection of papers from all corners of the globe showcases China's diverse translation history between 1919 and 2019. The expansive scope of this volume provides both specialist and general readers with a comprehensive overview of contemporary Chinese literature in translation. We hope that Western readers accustomed to a Eurocentric perspective on translation studies will gain a more comprehensive and nuanced understanding of a very different translation culture.

References

Albachten, Ö. B., & Gürçağlar, Ş. T. (2019). *Studies from a retranslation culture: The Turkish context*. Springer Singapore.

Baer, B. J., & Witt, S. (2018). *Translation in Russian contexts: Culture, politics, identity*. Routledge.

Chan, L. T. (2004). *Twentieth-century Chinese translation theory: Modes, issues and debates*. John Benjamins.

Curran, B., Sato-Rossberg, N., & Tanabe, K. (2015). *Multiple translation communities in contemporary Japan*. Taylor & Francis.

Haddadian-Moghaddam, E. (2014). *Literary translation in modern Iran: A sociological study*. John Benjamins.

Han, Z., & Li, D. (2019). *Translation studies in China: The state of the art*. Springer Singapore.

Holmes, J. S. (1988). The name and nature of translation studies. In J. S. Holmes (Ed.), *Translated!: Papers on literary translation and translation studies* (pp. 66–80). Rodopi.

Kang, J. H., & Wakabayashi, J. (2019). *Translating and interpreting in Korean contexts: Engaging with Asian and Western others*. Taylor & Francis.

Kim, W. D. (2019). *Translations in Korea: Theory and practice*. Springer Singapore.

Luo, X., & He, Y. (2009). *Translating China*. Multilingual Matters.

Nobelprize.org. (2012). *The Nobel Prize in literature 2012 Mo Yan*. Retrieved February 21, 2020 from www.nobelprize.org/prizes/literature/2012/summary/

Qi, L. (2018). *Jin Ping Mei English translations: Texts, paratexts and contexts*. Routledge.

Tahir Gürçaglar, Ş., Paker, S., & Milton, J. (2015). *Tradition, tension and translation in Turkey*. John Benjamins.

Part I

Theoretical and historical reflections

1   Archival research as method

A study of "non-professional" agents of literary translation

Lintao Qi and Leah Gerber

Introduction

Translation as a social activity is interactive by nature. Not only are translations (re)created by translators, but the selection, commission, publication, circulation and reception of a translated work materializes via human interaction between various agents (Qi, 2018a). Whilst the sociological turn in translation studies recognizes the vital role of the translator as an active agent in the translation process (Milton & Bandia, 2009; Pym, 2006; Wolf & Fukari, 2007), there has been little analysis of interactions that take place between other agents within the literary system. The sociological approach recognizes, amongst other things, the field of social activity in which the act of translation takes place (Bourdieu, 1986); in this study, the publishing industry (field) becomes a site of power struggles among agents such as the author, commissioner, publisher, editor, reviewer, etc. The habitus (Bourdieu, 1986) of the individual translator (including family and education) is also acknowledged as adding considerable value to the way in which we consider the translation process, as are the notions of economic, social, cultural and symbolic capital (Bourdieu, 1986).

The analysis of paratexts in a translation context is often connected to the notion of visibility, reception and sociology of power networks such as the publishing industry (Munday, 215). Genette (1997) provided us with our working definition of a "paratext": a literary work or "text" that never appears in a "naked state," but which is accompanied by certain "productions" such as the author's name, a title, preface or illustrations that either feature in the text (peritexts) or outside the text (epitexts), such as letters, interviews with the author, etc. (Genette, 1997). Kathryn Batchelor, whose recent monograph comprehensively summarizes the various foci of research into paratexts in translation, claims that the most-studied feature is the translator's preface, followed by translators' notes, book covers, titles, etc. (2018, p. 26). Research, as Batchelor writes, "has primarily been in analysing peritextual material of translated texts, often in comparison with the peritexts of the original" (2018, p. 26). Although "paratexts have also been shown to offer extremely useful clues for literary historiographers, allowing them to reconstruct the publishing histories of particular authors or formulate clearer pictures of the flow of literary works across borders" (2018, p. 32), fewer studies have explored primary or archival materials in the form of interviews and correspondence; they can, of course, be much harder to access (Müller, 2013). Scholars such as Toury have, in the past, also questioned the reliability of such materials: interviews, surveys, letters and prefaces may present biases or subjective information (Toury, 1995).

Nevertheless, as Tymoczko writes, pure objectivity in research is a myth, and any study is necessarily subjective to some degree (2007, p. 146), whether in its design, its method, its data collection or its interpretation of data, and therefore in its conclusion. Adopting this view, we argue that paratextual materials (mainly from the epitext) should not be considered any more biased than our own interpretation thereof and, in keeping with recent trends in translation studies research (which extends the idea of translation far beyond the traditional notion of process or product), paratextual materials present scholars with important raw data on which the reconstruction and interpretation of that process can be based (Qi, 2018b).

Some very recent studies into paratexts that emphasize the vital link between paratexts and agency (Batchelor; 2018, p. 39) are particularly relevant to the arguments put forward in this paper. For example, adopting a sociological framework, Tahir Gürçağlar illustrates how preface writers are often "'more established' than the translators" (2013, p. 98); their intrusion in the peritext therefore endows the translator with more literary capital. Translator Nathalie Mälzer discusses the impact of invisible contributors (in her case, editors) in the translation process, suggesting that research should more keenly observe "the adaptations made by the various agents of the publishing industry" (2013, p. 170). Finally, Batchelor recognizes agency as a major feature of paratextual studies in translation, claiming that the very notion of paratexts "has also proved important to translation history and to discussions of agency in translation" (2018, p. 39).

The so-called "archival turn" took place in the humanities and social sciences in the last few decades of the 20th century (Adina Camelia, 2017). In order for translation studies to make similar evidence-based breakthroughs in historical research, an archival turn would make optimal use of epitexts such as archives and other primary material in order to enrich its corpus and empower its researchers in reconstructing how a translation product comes into being. Various researchers (e.g. Munday, 2013, 2014; Paloposki, 2017; Qi, 2016) have published studies on how scholars can use primary materials in the examination of the microhistory of translators or translations. Munday (2014), for example, employs archival materials to reconstruct a microhistory of translator Benard Miall and calls for more comprehensive use of primary materials in translation studies. Paloposki (2017) utilizes primary materials to unveil the "working practices of translators" and their interaction with publishers in the Finnish context. Qi (2016) rewrites the translational history of the classical Chinese novel *Jin Ping Mei* on the basis of extensive archival research, arguing that some target text features that are traditionally attributed to individual agents such as the translator or the publisher would most likely be the result of a complicated agential network consisting of other agents such as the copyeditor, the printer and literary censors.

Following the cultural turn, translation studies scholars began to approach the interpretation of translation products with particular regard to the socio-cultural contexts in which the translator was working and, in a similar same vein, Descriptive Translation Studies (DTS) pushed researchers to think of translation processes in a non-linear way. However, we are only now starting to learn how paratextual elements can assist us in reconstructing these processes (Qi, 2018b), especially by looking at the epitexts such as correspondence between the translator and the publisher, or the manuscripts of the translation that bears the traces of revision by the translators. The peritexts, which are always results of compromise between various agents, are usually "controlled" or "manipulated" in order to create harmony with the translated texts and the illusion of textual linearity. Epitexts, on the other hand, such as archival materials, though screened and curated by the archivists (Manoff, 2004, p. 12; Yale, 2015, p. 332) are largely "organic" in terms of content, and are therefore the most instrumental in uncovering the non-linear nature of the formation of translated texts.

This chapter endeavours to investigate the methodological implications of archival research in translation studies via examination of the Allen & Unwin archives in London dating from WWII (utilizing The Archive of British Publishing and Printing held at the University of Reading, U.K.) and including the years leading up to the war. Archives like this, which are believed to "bring to light new forms of knowledge that would otherwise have remained shrouded in obscurity" (Farge, 2013, p. 54), can contribute detailed information about various facets of translation history – at the micro-level in particular – and therefore contribute vital information to projects that aim to retrieve translation information. This research, based on those archives, attempts to explore the kinds of details that primary materials can offer in reconstructing the stages of pre-translation (e.g. selection of texts and translators), translation (e.g. agents and negotiations) and post-translation (e.g. reception and reversions). As well as adding to important work on translation paratexts, these studies, via the lens of sociology, contribute to a more nuanced understanding of agency in the translation process.

Non-professional and professional agents

In 2005, in her introduction to Latour's actor-network theory, Buzelin (2005, p. 203) observed that "the call for a more agent-oriented kind of research has been made repeatedly throughout the last decade." While network theory has gained currency in the field of translation studies (Hélène Buzelin & Folaron, 2007; Kinnunen & Koskinen, 2010), the notion of agency remains more fluid. Sager (quoted in Milton & Bandia, 2009, p. 1) defines an agent in translation as a person who is "in an intermediary position between a translator and an end user of a translation," however others (Milton & Bandia, 2009; Munday, 2012) include the translator within their definition of agent. Consequently, there is a range of agents "playing key roles in the preparation, dissemination and fashioning of translations," including "commissioners, mediators, literary agents, text producers, translators, revisers and editors" (Munday, 2012, p. 229). For Milton and Bandia, an agent could be any entity "involved in a process of cultural innovation and exchange" – a person, an institution, or even a journal (quoted in Hélène Buzelin, 2010, p. 6). In the same vein, Pym (2007, p. 745) considers agents to be "people, texts, or institutions." The expansion of the definition to include non-human agents has complicated the network, so much so that the discussion of agents now extends from the pre-translation stage through the actual translating process, and even well beyond the publication.

This chapter, however, is content to use the idea of human mediators: those who are involved in the various stages of a translation, from its inception to its reception. The notion of "professional" versus "non-professional" agent is equally important to dissect: in the process of literary translation, agents include, most commonly, those mentioned earlier: author, commissioner, publisher, editor, reviewer, etc. – people who are paid for their contributions to literary translation practice and products. In the discipline of translation studies, scholars also distinguish the practice of so-called "professional" translators and interpreters – those who are paid for the work that they do as linguistic and cultural mediators (Pérez-González & Susam-Saraeva, 2012, p. 150) – from the work of those who are untrained and unpaid. An increase in these unregulated acts of translation (such as volunteer translation, fan-subbing, collaborative translation, etc.) has meant that "the intrusion of unregulated outsiders into the translation industry remains rife" (Perez-Gonzales & Susam-Saraeva, 2012, p. 150).

As such, the terminology used to define a "professional" translator or interpreter has changed. The label "non-professional translators and interpreters" is used to describe "individuals not only without formal training in linguistic mediation but also working for free"[1] (Perez-Gonzales & Susam-Saraeva, 2012, p. 151). Following the development of special terms used to describe varying degrees of professionalism amongst translators/interpreters, the term "non-professional" agent has been coined in this paper. It describes intermediaries in the publishing process who are neither trained nor employed as publishers or editors, but who take on major roles in helping to publish translations. These non-professional agents all have other, major professional identities, such as diplomat, journalist, scholar, etc. and may also have some sort of familial relationship to the translator, as will be discussed later on.

Non-professional agents undertake roles of power or influence on an ad-hoc basis – they are either solicited by the "professional" agent such as a publisher, or they voluntarily enter the translation process – and can represent either party: the publisher or the author/translator. We have therefore termed the two types of non-professional agents (1) "volunteer" and (2) "solicited" agents. Therefore, the only "professional" agents in this discussion are the publisher, editors, etc. through whom a translation is initiated, commissioned, produced, published and promoted. The non-professional agents contribute to the translation enterprise by means of interaction with the author or publisher at various stages of the publication process (text selection, contractual obligations, payment, etc.).

The methodology employed in this study was to physically access the Allen & Unwin archives in the U.K. and to analyze the nature of the interactions between professional and non-professional agents, examining the impact these non-professional agents may have had on the translation process.

Solicited agents

In 1960, Sir Stanley Unwin, founder of the British firm Allen & Unwin, indicated that many publishing houses ran their own translation departments or employed personnel specifically tasked with the publication of translations (1960). Publishing personnel would often be in charge of texts from different languages that needed to be translated into English, and it was not unusual for some languages to fall outside of their own linguistic specialization. On such occasions, analysis of archival material suggests that external opinions then sought from "expert" acquaintances, such as long-time published authors or people with some form of recognized cultural capital (such as scholars working in universities).

One such expert was Arthur Waley, perhaps the most famous British Sinologists of the 20th century. Waley translated from Chinese into English, and almost all of his translations were exclusively released by Allen & Unwin in the U.K.[2] His social, cultural and symbolic capital was palpable and, as a long-time, best-selling author of Allen & Unwin, Waley had won the unconditional confidence and trust of the publisher. It was customary for writers who published with Allen & Unwin to be asked to act as readers, in the process providing their advice on texts considered for translation and commenting on the likeliness of commercial success – in fact, this was common practice in the publishing industry as a whole (Collin, 1996). Waley, however, enjoyed the added privilege of actually *deciding* whether a submitted translation should be accepted or not, and even how the translation should be edited for publication. Robert Payne's *The White Pony: An Anthology of Chinese Poetry from the Earliest Times to the Present Day, Newly Translated* (Payne, 1947) is a case in point.

Robert Payne had lived in Singapore and China and had married Rose Hsiong, the daughter of the former Chinese Premier Hsiung Hse-ling (Xiong Xiling) in 1942 (Mcdowell, 1983). Payne published over 100 books in his lifetime, yet his social, cultural and symbolic capital was, arguably, not nearly as strong as Waley's. In 1945, Payne submitted an English translation of Shen Congwen's *The Chinese Earth*, which he translated collaboratively with a Chinese translator Jin Di (further details will be provided in later sections) – which was eventually published in 1947.

In 1946, before *The Chinese Earth* was actually published, Payne submitted another translated work, *The White Pony*, to Allen & Unwin for consideration. But before deciding on whether to publish *The White Pony*, Allen & Unwin turned to Waley for an opinion: "As we are doing other work of [Robert Payne's] we should like to accept this one unless you advise strongly to the contrary" (Unwin, 1946, September 3). After a week or so, Waley returned his report to the publisher, who had assured him that "we shall act precisely on the lines you suggest and shall take care not to bring you into the matter" (Unwin, 1946, September 13). Apparently, Waley requested that his identity as the reader of *The White Pony* should not be disclosed; Payne's book was an anthology of Chinese verse, and as

Waley was also known for his translations of Chinese poems, there might have been a perceived conflict between the two translators' works.

Payne wrote back to Allen & Unwin to the effect that he was prepared to "meet the proposal" by "omitting the first hundred pages" of *The White Pony*, which was in itself a significant compromise and an eager gesture of cooperation. The publisher swiftly shared Payne's letter with Waley, and trusted him with a further decision on the destiny of the book: "Do you feel that we should accept this compromise or are there any particular additional poems which you feel ought to be omitted?" (Unwin, 1946, September 20). Allen & Unwin's act of first soliciting Waley's view on the text and then inviting further very specific suggestions about how the content of the book should be organised and edited allowed the non-professional agent to proceed far beyond the usual reader's role. Furthermore, when compared to the other non-professional agents that appear in the Allen & Unwin archives consulted for this paper, Waley seems to be the only author/translator who was so heavily relied upon (other non-professional agents include Hsiao Chien, George Yeh, and Chen Xiying), presumably because of his significant amount of cultural capital.

Not every reader was given such immense freedom to suggest changes directly to the publisher. Sometimes a publisher would engage a second reader before making a final decision about a book. The next example shows how a second reader had been carefully selected or "solicited" to consider Payne's other work of translation, *The Chinese Earth*, submitted a year earlier than *The White Pony*. On 26th June 1945, George K. C. Yeh (Ye Gongchao), the then diplomat of the Chinese Ministry of Information in London, received a letter from Allen & Unwin, which said:

> We are venturing to send another manuscript about China, viz., THE CHINESE EARTH by Shen Tseng-Wen [Shen Congwen]. We have already had one report on this book and shall be very grateful if you can give us the benefit of your opinion upon it also.
>
> (Unwin, 1945a, June 26)

The publisher's phraseology, "We are venturing to send another manuscript about China" implies the regularity of Yeh's service for Allen & Unwin. A Chinese diplomat working in London who later became the foreign minister of the Republic of China, Yeh had undertaken his undergraduate education in the U.S. and obtained his M.A. from Cambridge University in the U.K. He was thus very well-versed in both languages and cultures (Waggoner, 1981). Like Waley, he held a considerable amount of social, cultural and symbolic capital, so it is understandable that Allen & Unwin was keen to elicit his view on *The Chinese Earth*. Yeh soon gave his favorable opinion on the translation with his "highest recommendation for publication" (Yeh, 1945, June 29), to which the publisher soon responded:

> We are delighted that these interesting Chinese translations are reaching us, and have at once written to Stephen Payne saying how pleased we are to publish his son's translation of Shen Tseng-wen's [*sic*] work.
>
> (Unwin, 1945a, July 11)

Allen & Unwin's reply raises two important questions: first, how did Shen's work come to the publisher's attention in the first place? And second, why did the publisher get in touch with Payne's father, Stephen, rather than with Payne himself? These questions will be tackled in the ensuing sections.

Volunteer agents

Shen was, at the time, an established writer in China, who was yet to make his debut in the Anglophone world. The Allen & Unwin archives reveal that his former student, Hsiao Ch'ien (Xiao Qian), acted as a non-professional agent, bringing his name to the attention of the publisher.

Hsiao went to London in 1939, and first worked as a Chinese teacher at the school of Oriental Studies. He then moved to Cambridge University to pursue his M.A. After the outbreak of the Second World War, he became a war correspondent for the well-known Chinese newspaper *TaKungPao* (*Dagongbao*), which was the only outlet from China to cover the war in Europe. The London office of the newspaper was in Fleet Street, and Hsiao regularly socialized with Bloomsbury Group affiliates such as Bernard Russel and E.M. Forster (Gittings, 1999), attracting him considerable social capital amongst influential publishing figures in London. Moreover, his works were published by Allen & Unwin in English, so he was known to Western readers. In his letter to Allen & Unwin, which effectively introduced the publisher to Robert Payne's English translation of Shen's *The Chinese Earth* (1947), Hsiao (1945, June 11) wrote:

> As you will remember, I have mentioned Mr. Shen several times, first in "The Etching of a Tormented Age," and then in one of the lectures in "Dragon Beards versus Blueprints." . . . It would be presumptuous on my part to recommend the quality of the book and the significance of it to you knowing how very expert you are in judging books, but if there is anything I can do for you to facilitate publication of the book you may be assured that my services are always at your disposal.

Less than a fortnight later, he again wrote to Allen & Unwin: "I hope you will let me know the fate of [*The Chinese Earth*]" (Hsiao, 1945, June 19). When told that the book had been accepted, he immediately cabled the news to Shen, and then reported Shen's reply to Allen & Unwin:

> [Shen] wonders whether it is possible for you to have it published within this year or at least make it definite that it would be in the early part of next year. Naturally he does not know the difficulties of paper rationing but . . . since you are so enthusiastic about his books and judging from the letters you have written to Mr. Payne, perhaps you might have this under consideration.
>
> (Hsiao, 1945, August 8)

Despite knowing full well that there was an issue with paper rationing at the time, Hsiao still faithfully conveyed Shen's requests to the publisher, urging Allen &

Unwin to comply. Acting here as a "volunteer" agent, Hsiao did whatever he could within his power for the author he had chosen to "represent." Hsiao's contribution was not confined to a simple act of liaison between author and publisher; he moved one step further, constructively mediating between the two parties. The fact that Hsiao and Shen were friends certainly plays a role here, but even in the case of other lesser-known authors, Hsiao made many similar recommendations during his years of service in the U.K. On 10th December 1945, for instance, Hsiao wrote to Allen & Unwin to introduce the publisher to a Chinese play:

> I am writing this letter to recommend a manuscript which was sent to me from China and which will be presented to you by Professor Chen Yuan with his added opinion. It is a play by Mr. Chu Tung called "Muffled Thunder" based on a very well-known novel "The Dream of the Western Chamber." . . . It is a very ambitious scheme . . . and I think the playwright has achieved something that only a painstaking person could do.
>
> (Hsiao, 1945, December 10)

Here, Hsiao acts again not only as a volunteer agent, but introduces a second volunteer agent to the publisher: another Chinese intellectual with considerable capital, "Professor Chen Yuan" (Chen Xiying), who was working for the Sino-British Cultural Council in London at the time. Chen appears multiple times in the Allen & Unwin archives as an advocate for Chinese literature. Because of his job and responsibility as a staff member in the Cultural Council, Chen's social/cultural capital and influence could be said to be even higher than Hsiao's.

It is important to note here that both Hsiao and Chen used their social and cultural capital as well as their vantage points in London to vigorously present selected Chinese literary voices to the western world. They were, however, invisible agents in the translation process: for example, when books Hsiao had worked so shamelessly to recommend were eventually published under the visible moniker of Allen and Unwin, the peritext of which bore the name of author and translator, there was no trace of him. Epitextually, however, the work of volunteer agents like Hsiao and Chen could be said to have had more impact than the professional agents.

Contracts and agency

In the discussion about solicited agents, the question was posed: why did Allen & Unwin fail to contact Robert Payne about his translation *The Chinese Earth*, instead writing to his father, Stephen Payne? Robert Payne was an extremely prolific author, publishing more than 100 books during his life time (Mcdowell, 1983), of which translation accounted for an insignificant part. His literary capital was therefore high, but he did not enjoy quite the same degree of social and symbolic capital as Waley. When Waley was contracted to publish a book, for example, he would quickly receive a contract prepared by the publisher with munificent provisions. The story was different for Payne – he was never invited to be a reader for Allen & Unwin, and he had to go through a more complicated process with the publisher as regards the contract.

While Hsiao acted as a volunteer agent for Shen (the author of *The Chinese Earth*), Robert Payne's father, Stephen, stepped onto the scene as the translator's representative. When the English translation of *The Chinese Earth* was first sent to Allen & Unwin in 1945 (which Payne had co-translated with his student Ching Ti [Jin Di]), Payne was teaching at the National Southwestern Associated University in Kunming, China (Payne, 1945, June 3). He did not, however, approach the publisher himself; instead, Stephen Payne, his father, formerly Chief Naval Constructor at the Naval Base Singapore and the Constructive Manager of the big Dockyard at Devonport during the war (Payne, 1945, July 12), acted as a volunteer literary agent for his son by sending a letter to Allen & Unwin, in which he presented his son as follows in the opening paragraph:

> My son, Robert Payne whose Chungking Diary is being published by Heinemanns on June 18th, has written to me from Kunming, China asking me specially to send to you the enclosed manuscripts of his translations from a modern Chinese author of the first rank: Shen Tseng-wen, of a number of his short stories in the hope that you will find them worthy of putting before an English speaking public.
>
> (Payne, 1945, June 3)

It seems unusual for a established author, translator and university teacher in China to appoint his father as representative of his work but it is likely that Stephen Payne undertook correspondence with the publisher since he was based in the U.K (Robert was in China), which expedited the publishing process significantly. A little over a month later, the publisher decided, based on the reader report by Yeh, to accept *The Chinese Earth* for publication, and wrote back to Stephen Payne about the contract (Unwin, 1945b, July 9), to which the father replied:

> As regards the contract my son and Shen are perfectly willing to leave the matter in my hands. I have signed on behalf of my son and his other collaborators on all occasions and I am quite willing to sign a contract waiving my son's rights to a share in the royalties. . . . I will write to my son and ask him to let me have a formal letter of authorisation from Tseng [Shen Tseng-wen]. I do all my son's contracts automatically.
>
> (Payne, 1945, July 12)

Again, Stephen Payne's deep involvement in the contractual side of his son's translation – he signed legal documents on behalf of his son – was more than likely because his son was often overseas. Despite his deep involvement in both the text selection and contract, it does not appear that Stephen had any commercial interest in the publication – he was merely acting as a conduit between Robert and the publisher. It does seem unusual that Stephen offered to sign a contract waiving Robert Payne's "rights to a share in the royalties," An explanation for this, however, can be found in an earlier letter from Stephen Payne to Allen & Unwin, in which the father related Robert Payne's "Quixotic" view on money: "My son . . . has written to me to say that he renounces his share in the royalties and wishes Shan Tsang-wen [*sic*] to have them all" (Payne, 1945, June 3).

This leaves somewhat in doubt one other question: the compensation of Robert's co-translator, Ching Ti. Archival research suggests that Shen appears indeed to have received all the royalties paid by the publisher through Stephen Payne (1945, August 2), who did touch upon the involvement of Ching Ti in passing in one of his letters: "I know nothing of the co-translator Ching Ti but I suppose that he first put the rough draft of the English and my son did the final translation" (Payne, 1945, June 3).

In this case, Stephen Payne's role as a volunteer agent in the publication of *The Chinese Earth* reveals an important piece of its publication history. Although Stephen Payne did not contribute to the translation product, his presence in various parts of the translation process seems to have been instrumental in exposing Shen's work to Anglophone readers. It also reveals the unusual arrangement of Robert Payne waiving his right to royalties so that Shen Tsung-wen was given the full share. This tells us something about Robert Payne's character, and perhaps about Shen's financial situation during the war – Shen was known to be living a double life at the time, and needed money to raise two families.

Both Hsiao Ch'ien and Stephen Payne continued to act as agents in the publication of the English translation of *The Chinese Earth*. Soon after the contract was signed, Stephen Payne passed on a request from Robert to Allen & Unwin: "My son Robert has asked me to tell you that he hopes your American agent will be able to get *The Chinese Earth* accepted in America" (Payne, 1945, August 2). In a similar vein, Hsiao's role as a representative of the Chinese author Shen extended into the book's production:

> I have just received from Shen Tsung Wen, author of "The Chinese Earth" (a book you accepted last autumn) a woodcut which he wonders whether you could include in the book, either inside the cover or as a separate illustration. The author of the woodcut is Hsia Ming.
>
> Mr. Shen indicated that he would like the background to be yellow and the woodcut to be in dark brown but of course he has no experience of European book production, so I should leave the whole matter in your hands.
>
> Should you have any suggestions to make I shall be very glad to write to Mr. Shen on your behalf.
>
> (Hsiao, 1945, December 28)

As a mediator between the author and the publisher, Hsiao often acted in multiple roles, sometimes blurring the boundaries, trying to facilitate the production and publication of the book. In the three paragraphs of his letter from 28 December 1945 (quoted above), Hsiao implies Shen's lack of knowledge about the European market, and in doing so, he shifts the decision-making power to Allen & Unwin. The notion of leaving "the whole matter" in the hands of the publisher appears to be a deliberate, pre-emptive gesture to prevent the publisher from feeling patronized by Shen's request, thus restoring the mutual respect between the parties involved. In his closing statement, Hsiao switches his stance again, this time offering to represent the publisher: "I shall be very glad to write to Mr. Shen on your behalf." By indicating his willingness to mediate on behalf of both parties, Hsiao quite possibly sped up the publication of *The Chinese Earth* significantly. Through his literary capital, not only was he acting as an agent in the promotion of Chinese literature to the Anglophone world, but his voluntary interference and mediation more than likely expedited the publication process of texts such as these, which may otherwise have languished at the bottom of an editor's pile, or never seen the light of day.

Conclusion

The focus in this chapter has been on the epitext, which records – often in great detail – the power play that takes place among professional and non-professional agents. Agents carry a great deal of social, cultural and symbolic capital, as evidenced in these various exchanges; it is clear that none of these translations would have been published without the input (volunteer or solicited) by non-professional agents.

As we have seen in all of the case studies presented thus far, these acts of interference by volunteer agents were viewed very positively by the publisher. Arguably, these non-professional agents carried more literary capital than either the translator or the author; it appears that the capital amassed by Waley (symbolic, social and cultural), Hsiao (symbolic, social and cultural), Chen (social and cultural) and, to a lesser extent, Stephen Payne (social and cultural) had a significant impact on the selection of Chinese works to be translated and published in the English-speaking world. Furthermore, because the non-professional agents all physically resided in the UK at the time, their actions had a substantial impact on the speed with which Chinese works were published in the Anglophone market.

Interestingly, these non-professional agents were able to exert – through firm, targeted yet gently worded letters – considerable power over the publisher. In all of the cases presented in this chapter Allen & Unwin wholeheartedly accepted the suggestions or directives put forward by the non-professionals – in fact, they seem grateful for their input, volunteer or otherwise. Some nepotism can be detected, with agents such as Waley and Hsiao clearly promoting the work of their friends. Remarkably, though, all non-professional agents appear to have been motivated mainly by altruistic reasons[3]; the desire to promote Chinese literature appears to dominate in these exchanges.

Archival studies such as those presented in this chapter can play a vital role in the way that we understand the publication of translated texts. Archives that are accessible to readers and researchers make the retrieval and reconstruction of the micro-history around a translation or a translator possible. Research of this kind has both methodological and theoretical implications for translation studies; methodologically, archival materials act as paratexts to the translation product. They provide a retrospective instrument for research on the inception, commission, production, publication and reception of a translated text. Theoretically, archival research as a paratextual approach enriches the concept of agent – we have distinguished between professional and non-professional agents in this paper – and the discussion around sociology and the politics of translation.

Notes

1 We also, however, understand that some non-professional translators may be paid for their work, therefore the nuances of this definition need to be carefully considered.
2 Some of Waley's translations published by Allen & Unwin are *Shi Jing* translated as *The Book of Songs* in 1937, *Lun Yu* translated as *The Analects of Confucius* in 1938, and *Xi You Ji* translated as *Monkey* in 1942.
3 In terms of motivation, a very similar finding was reached in Haddadian-Moghadam (2014), who found that Iranian translators usually have altruistic and non-economic motives for their jobs; they want to provide a cultural service to their fellow countrymen by raising their awareness of other cultures.

References

Adina Camelia, A. (2017). *Beyond discipline(s): The thought of the archive in Foucault and Derrida* (Unpublished doctoral dissertation). Monash University, Clayton.

Batchelor, K. (2018). *Translation and paratexts*. Routledge.

Bourdieu, P. (1986). The forms of capital. In J. G. Richardson (Ed.), *Handbook of theory and research for the sociology of education* (pp. 241–258). Greenwood Press.

Buzelin, H. (2005). Unexpected allies: How Latour's network theory could complement Bourdieusian analyses in translation studies. *The Translator, 11*(2), 193–218.

Buzelin, H. (2010). Agents of translation. In Y. Gambier & L. v. Doorslaer (Eds.), *Handbook of translation studies* (Vol. 2, pp. 6-12). Amsterdam: John Benjamins.

Buzelin, H., & Folaron, D. (Eds.). (2007). Translation and network studies. *Meta: Translators' Journal, 52*(4).

Collin, D. (1996). Interventions of the publisher's reader. *English Studies, 77*(2), 133. doi:10.1080/00138389608599015

Confucius, & Waley, A. (1938). *The analects of Confucius*. Allen & Unwin.

Farge, A. (2013). *The allure of the archives*. New Haven, CT: Yale University Press.

Genette, G. (1997). *Paratexts: Thresholds of interpretation*. Cambridge: Cambridge University Press.

Gittings, J. (1999, February 18). Hsiao Ch'ien: The scholar who went back home. *The Guardian*.

Haddadian-Moghadam, E. (2014). *Literary translation in modern Iran: A sociological study*. John Benjamins.

Hsiao, C. I. (1945, June 19). [Correspondence from Hsiao Ch'ien to Allen & Unwin]. AUC 216/11, University of Reading, Reading, UK.

Kinnunen, T., & Koskinen, K. (Eds.). (2010). *Translator's agency*. Tampere University Press.

Mälzer, N. (2013). Head or legs? Shifts in texts and paratexts brought about by agents of the publishing industry. In H. Jansen & A. Wegener (Eds.), *Authorial and editorial voices in translation 2: Editorial and publishing practices* (pp. 153–176). Éditions québécoises de l'œuvre, collection Vita Traductiva.

Manoff, M. (2004). Theories of the archive from across the disciplines. *Portal: Libraries and the Academy, 4*(1), 9–25.

Mcdowell, E. (1983, February 22). Robert Payne, author, dies at 71. *The New York Times*, p. B6.

Milton, J., & Bandia, P. F. (Eds.). (2009). *Agents of translation.* John Benjamins. doi:10. 1075/btl.81

Müller, P. (2013). Archives and history: Towards a history of "the use of state archives" in the 19th century. *History of the Human Sciences, 26*(4), 27–49. doi:10.1177/0952695113502483

Munday, J. (2012). *Introducing translation studies: Theories and applications* (3rd ed.). Routledge.

Munday, J. (2013). The role of archival and manuscript research in the investigation of translator decision-making. *Target, 25*(1), 125–139.

Munday, J. (2014). Using primary sources to produce a microhistory of translation and translators: Theoretical and methodological concerns. *The Translator, 20*(1), 64–80.

Paloposki, O. (2017). In search of an ordinary translator: Translator histories, working practices and translator-publisher relations in the light of archival documents. *The Translator, 23*(1), 31–48.

Payne, R. (1947). *The white pony: An anthology of Chinese poetry from the earliest times to the present day, newly translated.* Allen & Unwin.

Payne, S. (1945, June 3). [Correspondence from Stephen Payne to Allen & Unwin]. AUC 234/4, University of Reading, Reading, UK.

Pérez-González, L., & Susam-Saraeva, Ş. (2012). Non-professionals translating and interpreting. *The Translator, 18*(2), 149–165.

Pym, A. (2006). On the social and cultural in translation studies. In A. Pym, M. Shlesinger, & Z. Jettmarova (Eds.), *Sociocultural aspects of translating and interpreting.* Amsterdam and Philadelphia: John Benjamins.

Pym, A. (2007). Cross-cultural networking: Translators in the French-German network of petites revues at the end of the nineteenth century. *Meta: Translators' Journal, 52*(4), 744–762.

Qi, L. (2016). Agents of Latin: An archival research on Clement Egerton's English translation *The Golden Lotus. Target: International Journal of Translation Studies, 28*(1), 39–57.

Qi, L. (2018a). *Jin Ping Mei English translations: Texts, paratexts and contexts.* Routledge.

Qi, L. (2018b). The Patrons' invisibility: A paratextual study of the first complete English translation of Jin Ping Mei. *Translation Horizons, 3*(2), 21–34.

Shen, T., Ching, T., & Payne, R. (1947). *The Chinese earth.* Stories. Allen & Unwin.

Tahir Gürçağlar, Ş. (2013). Agency in allographic prefaces to translated works: An initial exploration of the Turkish context. In H. Jansen & A. Wegener (Eds.), *Authorial and editorial voices in translation 2: Editorial and publishing practices* (pp. 89–108). Éditions québécoises de l'œuvre, collection Vita Traductiva.

Toury, G. (1995). *Descriptive translation studies and beyond.* John Benjamins.

Tymoczko, M. (2007). *Enlarging translation, empowering translators.* St. Jerome.

Unwin, S. (1945a, June 26). [Correspondence from Allen & Unwin to George K. C. Yeh]. AUC 216/10, University of Reading, Reading, UK.

Unwin, S. (1945b, July 9). [Correspondence from Allen & Unwin to Stephen Payne]. AUC 234/4, University of Reading, Reading, UK.

Unwin, S. (1946, September 20). [Correspondence from Allen & Unwin to Arthur Waley]. AUC 359/15, University of Reading, Reading, UK.

Unwin, S. (1960). *The truth about publishing* (7th ed.). Macmillan.

Waggoner, W. H. (1981, November 26). George K.C. Yeh, Taiwan Aide. *The New York Times*, p. D14.

Wolf, M., & Fukari, A. (Eds.). (2007). *Constructing a sociology of translation*. John Benjamins.

Wu, C., & Waley, A. (1942). *Monkey*. Allen & Unwin.

Yale, E. (2015). The history of archives: The state of the discipline. *Book History, 18*, 332–359. doi:10.1353/bh.2015.0007

Yeh, G. K. C. (1945, June 29). [Correspondence from George Yeh to Allen & Unwin]. AUC 234/4, University of Reading, Reading, UK.

2 Unpacking the Mo Yan archive

Actor-network translation studies and the Chinese literature translation archive

Jonathan Stalling and Ronald Schleifer

Introduction

For decades scholars have placed translators at the heart of translation studies but in very different ways. From the 1960s to the 1990s translation studies were understood as ways of reading, interpreting and recasting - in short something that translators do.[1] This early focus on translation studies and theory as an embodied decision-making process has continued to thrive in cognitive psychology, psycholinguistics, and related fields. In addition, its lasting impact can be seen in the radical scaling interest in algorithmic and neural-network deep learning machine translation processing. While it is problematic to overgeneralize intellectual history in this way, it is important to note the consistent way in which translation has been understood as the "product" of a given translator or a translation program's decision-making process.

However, translation studies in the Humanities from the late 1980s onwards shifted along with most literary scholarship toward what Fredric Jameson described in his groundbreaking work *The Political Unconscious* as "symptomatic reading," whose aim was to disclose "the absent cause that structures the text's inclusions and exclusions." Within this framework, "the critic restores to the surface the deep history that the text represses" (1981, p. 60).

In this context, for most translation theorists, symptomatic reading practices focus upon the historical site of translation, as the translator becomes a synecdoche for a culturally and historically specific moment. In this period, translation became a site that revealed uneven power differentials undergirded by hidden, repressed, deep structures that translation theorists could unearth.[2] For many translation scholars working in China since the 1980s, this remains a dominant mode of criticism where western translation is read as a Eurocentric erasure of the Chinese worldview, aesthetics, structures of feeling, and so on.

Yet over the last decade we have seen a pushback across literary studies more generally against modes of symptomatic reading. A new generation of scholars are seeking alternatives to the Jamesonian paradigm with so-called surface reading, distant reading, thin description, reading as a practice of acknowledgement, and reparative reading, among other terms. What we hope to demonstrate in this essay is that the creation/curation of Chinese literature translation archives is likely to make the most impactful challenge to earlier translation studies paradigms. The reason for this is straightforward: earlier approaches have assumed translation to be the outcome of individually constituted, historically and culturally (ideologically) pressurized site/locations, whereas Actor-Network Translation Studies, as we outline it here, demonstrates how translations are outcomes of far larger, diffuse network structures. Problems arise when we limit translation studies to the published source and target texts (even if this is across larger corpuses of editions and variations) since these works are marketed as being "authored" by single humans, when they are not, at least in the case where layers of participants – publishers, editors, literary agents, marketing departments – all make significant contributions to the processes of translation.

The problem lies, in other words, in the material scholars study. When we open translation studies to the full archive of drafts, notes, correspondence, contracts, and other translation ephemera, we find translation to exist within distinct network structures organized by what Complex System Theory describes as "degree of node," a notion we will clarify later in this essay. Given this, we find that translation is best understood not only in terms of linguistic, cultural, cognitive, and ideological terms, but as large-scale negotiations between distinct economies of action. The working of those negotiations, we argue, are hidden in plain sight in the translation archive.

Actors and actions

Archival research allows scholars to encounter, articulate, and analyze the complexity of what we are describing with the acronym ANTS:

Actor-Network Translation Studies.[3]

The complexity of network theory distinguishes ANTS from other sociological theories of translation insofar as this term situates translation as a property of larger complex systems made up of translators and organizational institutions that grow out of and govern the situations they work in.

ANTS focuses on "actors" who may function as agents yet without the volition of human actors: the term the semiotician Greimas (1983) uses to describe this situation is "actants." ANTS asks us to rethink the common-sense notion of action altogether. In developing speech-act theory, J. L. Austin (1970) powerfully articulates a concept of action as essentially conventional rather than volitional. "Before we consider what actions are good or bad, right or wrong," he writes,

> it is proper to consider first what is meant by, and what not, and what is included under, and what not, the expression 'doing an action' or 'doing something'. These are expressions still too little examined on their own account and merits, just as the general notion of 'saying something' is still too lightly passed over in logic. There is indeed a vague and comforting idea in the background that, after all, in the last analysis, doing an action must

come down to the making of physical movements with parts of the body; but this is about as true as that saying something must, in the last analysis, come down to making movements of the tongue.

(1970, p. 178)

In this essay, as in his wider articulation of speech-act theory, Austin suggested that "action" is a social institution, a convention, rather than a simple fact. As we shall see, such a conception of "action" – like the focus on adverbs Austin pursued in this essay – allows us to comprehend "action" as a phenomenon that includes value as constituent elements in its comprehension as an act altogether; it replaces the positivism of "fact" with the *networking* "activity" of comprehending value as a determining factor in grasping phenomena as a meaningful whole.

Later in his essay, Austin (1970) wonders "how far . . . are motives, intentions and conventions to be part of the description of actions?" (p. 102) and suggests that "we can generally split up what might be named as one action in several distinct ways, into different *stretches* or *phases* or *stages*" (p. 201). He defines these aspects of an action quite nicely:

1) the *stages* of a so-called action describe the "machinery of the act," such as "the planning, the decision, and the execution" of an act;
2) the *phases* of an action describe different ways of apprehending an action so that "we can say that he painted a picture . . . or else we can say that first he laid on this stroke of paint and then that"; and
3) the *stretches* of an action describe it in a single term so that the description of what is done "may be made to cover either a smaller or larger stretch of events" with the result that a person's "act" can be described "*either* as turning on the hot tap, which he did by mistake, with the result that Watkins was scalded, *or* as scalding Watkins, which he did *not* do by mistake."

(p. 201)

All three of these ways of describing – or "unpacking" – what is meant by an action offer us a significant framework for understanding what is meant by the "action" of translation. The unanalyzed notion of "action," against which Austin catalogues these distinctions, is "a stand-in for a verb with a personal subject," and conceiving action on this level of abstraction implies that "all 'actions' are . . . equal, composing a quarrel with striking a match, winning a war with sneezing" (1970, pp. 178–179). Such an unanalyzed – or positivist – notion of "action" governs the subject-focused understandings of translation we outlined in the first two translation theories (translator as the single actor and the Jamesonian paradigm) at the beginning of this essay.

Austin's description of the staged machinery of an action allows us to imagine that a community of agents, rather than a single translator, governs the *stages* of an "act" of translation. In fact, all three of Austin's categories of action are conventional:

1)   in the social "machinery" of translation, different actors (or now: "actants") accomplish the *stages* of translation;
2)   in the conventions of description different events (or now: networks of events) comprise the *phases* of translation, rather than the single uncomplicated or "black box" event of translation; and
3)   in an evaluative whole (or now: translation studies) translation theorists apprehend the social worth of translation altogether in the *stretches* of translation (its consequences, before and after).

Conceiving the so-called act of translation in these terms also allows us to frame an analysis of translation with the notion of "degree of node," a term borrowed from Complex Systems Theory developed long after Austin wrote. In Complex Systems a node situates the number of connections an actant has to other actants and how the distribution of these connections over the whole network affects outcomes. In such systems, the number of connections, the "degree of node," is of the utmost importance: it is the measure of the force and value associated with any actant within the complex system (see Figure 2.1).

As such, degree of node measures the "outcomes," which are, we are suggesting, the actions, events, and value that we comprehend in the networked action of translation. It is our contention that archival research provides the evidence necessary for understanding how translation arises\ within a system of actions and agents, even while it helps shape such complex systems.

To this end, our study of Actor/Actant-Network Translation Study in relation to The Chinese Literature Translation Archive analyzes the richly archived actions of the first English translations of Mo Yan's novels by focusing on the well-documented networks of linguistic and social systems that produced those

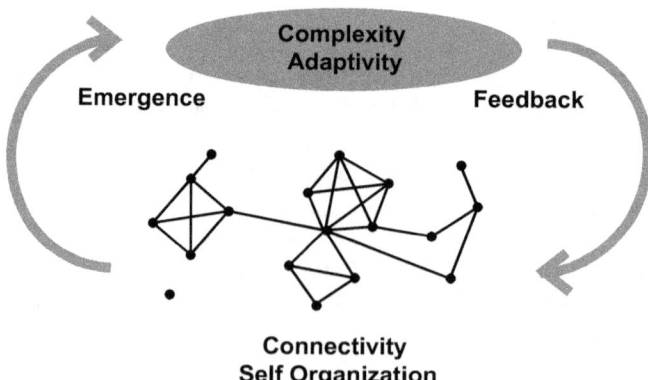

Figure 2.1 Degree of node in Complex Systems

translations. More specifically, ANTS uncovers the systematic ways in which those translations overcame many of the barriers to mainstream success that still plague Chinese literature today. The Mo Yan case clarifies crucial distinctions between Chinese and American literary networks embedded in linguistic and social systems. The surprising result of this analysis suggests that the Chinese language – the language system of Chinese – is individualistic while the American language system is more socially diffuse and collaborative. This is surprising because those linguistic systems arise, almost unintentionally, certainly complexly, within social systems that self-consciously emphasize the opposite value, collaboration in the Chinese social world, individualism in the American social world.

The Chinese literature translation archive case studies

There is something intuitive about the need for archival research in literary translation studies because the complexity of translation, as we mentioned earlier, is hidden in plain sight in the sprawling complexity of archives altogether. The example we describe here is the Chinese Literature Translation Archive (CLTA) at the University of Oklahoma Bizzell Library. The genesis of the archive was the formal gift of the Howard Goldblatt papers and personal library in 2014, followed soon by the acquisition of the papers of Wolfgang Kubin and of Wai-lim Yip, and then the acquisition of the Arthur Waley personal research library. Today the Chinese Literature Translation Archive houses a collection of well over ten thousand books from these personal libraries, so that upon entering the reading room of the CLTA, scholars walk into the sprawling, complex intellectual environments of arguably the two most influential English translators of Chinese literature in the twentieth and now the early 21st centuries.

The source and reference materials used by these translators now surround translation students and scholars and provide deep insights into the history of Chinese literature in translation. In addition to these source and reference materials (often including marginalia written by the translators), the archive also houses other important translation papers. In the case of the Howard Goldblatt Archive, the collection includes the letters written not only between him and dozens of authors from Mo Yan, Bi Feiyu, and Alai, to Chu T'ien-wen and many more, but also between the translator and his agents, editors, peers, and others.

Taken as a whole, these historical documents begin to reveal something beyond the "black box" of an achieved translation. "Black box" is a term Bruno Latour (1987) uses to describe an input-output model that does not analyze the processes that transform input to output (pp. 2–3). However, archived historical documents pry open the black box and allow a meditation on the social and linguistic complexity of translation that supplants the reductive limitations suggested by the simple self-evidence of a free-standing published translation, which stands before us as literally *authoritative* – with the author's name on the cover and the translator's name modestly set forth, usually in smaller font, on the title page. By unpacking the archive – by situating the social action of translation in the context of its own linguistic and social history – we can grasp the whole networking constellation that in aggregate reveals translation as a thoroughly historical field of production. We are no longer bound to the black box of published translations but can access a more fully-complex life-world replete with its intellectual environments and documentation. We hope that the CLTA can stand as a call to arms for other universities to begin the process of collecting, curating, preserving, and rendering translation materials discoverable to other scholars so that we can together initiate a new epoch of materialist sociology in Chinese literature translation studies.

Also worth noting is that the heart of the CLTA lies not only material, but also a new generation of Chinese Translation Studies scholars who are working hard to change the field for years to come.

Two CLTA case studies

Two visiting scholars have contributed to the cataloguing of the Howard Goldblatt papers at the CLTA from 2016–2019, and the contrasts between their work indicates the breadth of possible archival achievements. They are publishing research out of the collection and pointing to new ways of thinking through authorial and translative agency in the context of Chinese to English literature in translation.

Xu Shiyan's work has focused on translation networks in Hong Kong during the earliest part of Howard Goldblatt's career, and her work is illuminating the network pressures that undergirds agency/authority for a young translator within the Sinophone translation world. Yan Jia, on the other hand, has brought much needed attention to the editorial process in Goldblatt's career-long relationship with Mo Yan. Her work challenges us to think of the author as one actor-node (among many) in the translation network rather than simply assuming that the author – and the original (and originary) text – comprise the self-evident base upon which the superstructure of translation is built. In doing so, her work suggests that scholars adopt the idea of multivariate authorship to think through the questions of translative agency/authority.

These two projects nicely exemplify the complex interrelationships between the social and the linguistic in their very different starting points: that of the literary culture of Hong Kong and that of the translation-product culture of the United States, both of which can be examined in relation to the translation-product culture of China.

After reviewing these two CLTA case studies, we conclude this paper by arguing that translation studies can and should move beyond research centered upon authors as sovereign agents, with translators serving prior (antecedent) authors and prior texts. Rather, we want to analyze translation as *the emergent properties of translative networks*, which include but are not limited to final published translations and their reception. As we have already suggested, the translation networks that emerge from unpacking the archive are more than the social context of text production. More importantly, they necessarily include and designate all the organizational actors – agents/actors/actants, even the authority of authors – that determine the degrees of node and the complex "actions" of all agents, volitional and notable non-volitional, within a given network.

Case study 1: Xu Shiyan

The first case study to be published out of the CLTA was by Xu Shiyan, who was a visiting scholar at the CLTA in 2016–17. Her publications in relation to our Translation Archive have focused on a group of 82 letters between a young Howard Goldblatt and the editors at *Renditions* based at Hong Kong Chinese University, George Kao and Stephen Soong (Xu, 2016). The letters chronical a deep, sustained exploration of Goldblatt's translation of 干校六记 (*Ganxiao liuji*), a memoir of the Cultural Revolution by Yang Jiang. Xu explores a wide variety of the negotiations between these volitional actors, but these "network negotiations" can be best seen in the awkward translation of the work's title.

The decision to translate the title "干校" as "Down Under" was not made by the translator, but by the editor of *Renditions*, George Kao. Kao (1981) found problems with C. T. Hsia's translation of 下放 as "Downward Transfer" or "Transferred Down." The Chinese title referred to the history of twenty million intellectuals who were removed from their academic institutions and relocated to rural locations to be reeducated by the peasants during the Cultural Revolution. That reference would be readily grasped by the book's Chinese audience but not necessarily so by the foreign audience of a translation. The editors suggested, however, that one English title, "Down There," was too vague for the foreign audience, and that gave rise to Kao's suggestion to use "Downunder." While Goldblatt, a native English speaker, knew full well that "downunder" connotes "in Australia" to native speakers of English, he did not strongly assert his authority as a native speaker, but instead conceded the title to the editors (Kao, 1983).

To vet the idea further, the editors turned to John Minford, a then 36-year-old visiting fellow at the Research Center of Translation, Hong Kong Chinese University. He told the two editors, "Australians are no longer sensitive about the nuance of the word" (Soong, 1983). Then they made the decision: Kao (1981) wrote, "It might be misleading to a number of people but it did have an attractive ring of salability. Barring a better word, it should be retained." To make further clarification, quotation marks and a footnote were added when the word appeared for the first time in the Preface written by Jonathan Spence:

> "Downunder," of course, refers to Australia/New Zealand in English. Here it stands for the term *xiafang* (下放), literally "downward transfer." It applies more poignantly to the twenty million intellectuals uprooted from their academic and research institutions to live with the peasants in the countryside under military control during the Cultural Revolution.
>
> (Jiang, 1988, p. 2)

What remains so remarkable in this exchange, as with many others throughout the 82 letters, is the commitment of the editors to prioritizing fidelity to the original above all other concerns. They felt the need to find some English rendering that would maintain the notion of "downwardness" in the Chinese by a similar deictic expression in English. Still, the editors were also concerned about whether the strict linguistic rendering would create cultural misunderstanding. Thus, the editors were seriously concerned about whether the linking of "Downunder" and the "sent down youth" and "rustication regimes" during the Cultural Revolution would be offensive to those living in Australia. Even the clarification provided by Spence at the very beginning of the book is but a prophylactic effort to justify the idiosyncratic choice. Still, that choice seems doomed to fail precisely because of the powerful asymmetry between the title – catalogued, advertised, proclaimed in large font on the cover – and the prefatory note, even one by a person who possesses as much personal credibility and authority as Jonathan Spence, arguably the most well-known western historian in his field.

The point of Xu's research, and the characterization of it here, is not to point out that the title was a bad choice, which is inconsequential in terms of tracing the arc of intellectual history, but to show how translation network structures can radically differ from one another. The editors' passion to preserve the wit and nuance of Yang Jiang's Chinese prose in the English can be considered an antecedent factor of the Hong Kong literary network structure. Such a network structure is undergirded by the work and all-but-unconscious attitudes of the editors and their contemporaries like John Deeney, who together with others were in the midst of launching "the Chinese School of Comparative Literature." Within this network structure, actors participated in generally accepted cultural "attitudes" which were so habitual as to be unreflected upon, if not unconscious. Many years ago, Trilling (1950) described this under the category of "manners" in fiction, the "manners" or everyday *systematic* behaviors by which a culture manifests itself. He describes manners in this sense as

> all the buzz of implication which always surrounds us in the present, coming to us from what never gets fully stated, coming in the tone of greetings and the tone of quarrels, in slang and humor and popular songs, in the way children play, in the gesture the waiter makes when he puts down the plate, in the nature of the very food we prefer.
> [. . .] It is the part of a culture which is not art, nor religion, nor morals, nor politics, and yet it relates to all these highly formulated departments of culture. It is modified by them; it modifies them; it is generated by them; it generates them.
>
> (1950, p. 200)

Trilling's language seems uncannily like complexity theory in its narration of emergence and feedback. But more to the point here, its emphasis on "tone" is precisely what the editors of *Rendition* sought, almost non-volitionally, to express in the title of the book. That is, they were concerned about and energized by ideas of cultural translation and mistranslation and ultimately with the power-dynamics of translation, which can, and often did in their estimation, erase Chinese cultural particularity. Xu's work, by close reading of these 82 letters, shows how much what we are calling actor-networking went on behind the scene of Goldblatt's early career, and it points the way to understanding the impact of different network structures on translative outcomes.

Case study 2: Yan Jia

A second exemplary scholar who worked on and published research out of the CLTA, Yan Jia, like Xu Shiyan, participated in the cataloguing of the Goldblatt papers (2017–2018), where she undertook a study of the editorial agency and authority in American literary publishing. The network she describes is radically different from the one studied by Xu. Yan's work; she focused on how editors and literary agents in American literary publishing interact and lead to what she describes as the "multiple-authorship" or "multivariate authorship" of translated Chinese contemporary novels.[4] In her essay she argues that multi-authorship challenges the romantic notion of the author and the translator as solitary actors (Yan, 2020).

Her essay, "Multiple Authorship of Translated Literary Works: A Study of Some Chinese Novels in American Publishing Industry," argues that it is insufficient to study translation as a process executed wholly by a given translator, and she goes further still by claiming that translative network outcomes can actually extend in two directions: forward toward the target text but also backward in some cases toward the source text (Yan and Du, 2020). She therefore asserts that the term "multivariate authorship" (Stillinger, 1991, p. v) most accurately describe the translative process. As a case study, Mo Yan's second book in English, *The Garlic Ballads*, is exhibit A for her argument. In fact, this book, and specifically the translation of its final chapter, is arguably the most important moment in modern Chinese-English translation history.

> To make her case Yan points to the relationship between Mo Yan's literary agent Sandra Dijkstra and the publisher's editors, Nan Graham and Courtney Hodell, who had been responsible for the editing and publishing of Goldblatt's translation of both *Red Sorghum* and *The Garlic Ballads*. Yan cites several passages from letters among these actors, who were authorized by their positions within the system of publishing to be actors/actants in the network of translation. In her analysis, Yan cites passages from correspondence from Hodell including two pages of revision suggestions, where Hodell noted that in passages exhibiting "repetition and florid writing [which] slows the pace to the point where the narrative drive is lost" she had "cut" the text "judiciously so none of the atmosphere is lost" (Hodell, 1994). While such actions suggested the idea of multi-translatorship, Yan suggested that the next episode revealed the potential for what she called "multi-authorship." "The biggest issue," Hodell (1994) wrote, came with the end of the manuscript. Nan and I both felt that it didn't have the same power as the rest of the novel; Mo Yan seems to lay down all the threads he's tied together so carefully, and relies on the trick of the courtroom speech and newspaper article to make a tidy conclusion . . . . Let the characters show us what to feel, instead of having a speech tell us.
>
> (Hodell, 1994)

As it turned out the literary agent and both editors wanted Mo Yan to rewrite his novel, to literally change the way it ended by adding an entire new chapter. In her analysis, Yan Jia explores the meaning of the fact that Mo Yan did accede to their wishes and rewrote the novel by adding a new final chapter, Chapter 20. In this way, then, the evidence of the archive suggests that Yan Jia is fully justified in her claim that translation can be bidirectional, and therefore multivariate in its authorship, especially given the fact that subsequent Chinese publications of the text reveal that Mo Yan added the additional chapter in Chinese.

The two methodological approaches of these two scholars, focusing both on the social/cultural "hum" that surrounds and, indeed, gives rise to any translation project and also on the action and authority of publication systems that surround and give rise to any translation project, are nicely complementary. Moreover, taken together they challenge previous studies of Goldblatt's translation career by pointing to the interplay of actors/actants and to the emergence of authority itself in the larger network structure from which his published translations emerged.

Reading the scholarship that is emerging from the archive and, indeed, reading through the archive itself – including a new collection of nearly 100 letters from Mo Yan to Howard Goldblatt spanning their careers – has begun to pave the way to what we believe may be a common set of threads not only of their work, but a methodological approach that emerges from the presence of archival resources themselves.

ANTS: agent/actor/actant-network translation studies

As we have seen, the editorial agency/authority in the two case studies described in this paper outstrip the translator's agency/authority in the final stages of translation. Thus, Xu describes how the *Renditions* editors extracted agential power from the translator premised on their closer proximity to the source material's nuanced linguistic (deictic) meanings than the American translators, while in the case study by Yan, the Viking/Penguin editors and Mo Yan's literary agent and editors asserted agential and organizational power against the translator premised on their closer proximity to the targeted reader (their understanding of product-market fit). Xu's approach is purely archival and refrains from strong theoretical arguments, while Yan's approach finds the apprehension of multivariate authorship a benefit of the Chinese Literature in Translation Archive.

While each scholar has offered a viable critical framework to understand the nature of what we are describing as the layered complexity of translation, each has also offered an occasion for the unpacking of this layered complexity, the unpacking of the archive. Here, then, we are suggesting a single general archival methodology, Actor-Network Translation Studies (ANTS). To do this we are reframing the core terms of Actor-Network Theory as found in Bruno Latour and others so that such network theory, particularly in the complex context of the linguistic/semantic and the social/historical phenomena of translation, more precisely represents the relational configurations of the translation networks that are discoverable within archives such as CLTA.[5]

Here, then we contend that actor-network theory can be widened to encompass the actors and actants of discourse and impersonal social organizations, which function as agents of both social life and sentential grammar. This widening of actor-network theory takes up – but in its complex feedback system also conditions – the "networked labor" that we describe later in this essay, and it also manifests itself in the authority that emerges out of and shapes language systems and social systems, whose combination are manifest – hidden in plain sight – in the archive.

Unpacking the archive, uncovering ANTS: Mo Yan and Howard Goldblatt

In addition to Mo Yan and Howard Goldblatt, as we have seen, the CLTA scholars have shown how there are at least two other central volitional actors/actants who, one could reasonably argue, played more central roles than either the author or the translator in the success of the translation of Mo Yan. We are calling what they discovered the most important moment in modern Chinese-English translation history, specifically the translation of the final chapter in Mo Yan's novel *The Garlic Ballads*. That moment, as we have seen, is when Goldblatt abandoned a more scholarly attitude of fidelity and requested that the author rewrite the final chapter of his novel.

This is striking in many ways: after all, Goldblatt and Mo Yan had only in the last few months grown friendly through their extensive correspondence. The early years of their working relationship had been tense as they exchanged dozens of letters trying to weed out copyright infringements and a few loose ends, given earlier oral agreements that Mo Yan had made with others interested in translating his work. The question is: what were the circumstances – the systems of linguistics and culture organized around degrees of nodal connection – that allowed Goldblatt to push the author in this unprecedented way? In fact, he may very well not have pushed if Mo Yan had not himself already signaled his willingness to collaborate with his translator even if this meant changing the novel itself. So let us unpack the archive.

In a letter dated December 22, 1988, Mo Yan described the publication of the Chinese version of what would later become *The Garlic Ballads* in the well-known Chinese literary magazine *October*. In this letter he noted that

> The last chapter of the novel mainly consists of some abstracts of newspaper stories, which are almost copied from a daily newspaper. If you don't like it, you can cut it down a lot. I am totally respecting your decision.
>
> (Mo Yan, 1988)

Of course, it is one thing to cut back on the original, but quite another to ask for a totally new ending. Goldblatt felt empowered – through agency, authority or simply his position within the publishing industry – to forward the request or push back on it. In any case, some years after this note, after receiving the request from his editor and agent, on June, 15, 1994, Mo Yan wrote again to Goldblatt:

> I have received your fax. I rewrote chapter 20. Due to the limit of time, I scribbled and haven't given it enough time to mince the words. Without a doubt Chapter 20 is now much better than it was in my original ending, and more beautiful. I hope you can take the trouble to translate this part and you can revise what you deem inappropriate.
>
> (Mo Yan, 1994)

So happy was Mo Yan with his revised version that all subsequent publications in China included this changed ending. This personal correspondence – and more, which we are not presenting for want of space – reveals Mo Yan to be a deeply collaborative actor, one who, not unlike most American novelists writing today, believed in the added value others can bring to a literary work. But as we suggest in a moment, the degree to which the organizational/environmental context – functioning as an actant – gives rise to this quality is what is at stake in ANTS. Moreover, as we will see, Mo Yan is an anomaly because in his world, the world of Chinese literary network structures, authors do not share authorship with editors or "workshop peers."

It is therefore important to note that *The Garlic Ballads* stands as the first translation of a Chinese novel to have fully passed through the iterative value chain of the US publishing network in terms of both its English and its source text outcomes. As Yan Jia points out, other authors translated by Howard Goldblatt have not agreed to changes or have registered their severe displeasure with such requests. She cites the following examples when Goldblatt was asked to revise the first opening chapter of a novel by Li Rui. The author wrote back:

> Due to the huge cultural differences, I felt deeply that it is hard to be understood. However, I believe if it is a good novel, it is bound to move people and be understood by them – just as many European and American writers, despite how difficult or hard it is to read their works, thousands of Chinese are moved and understand them.
>
> (Li Rui, 1988)

Another example that Yan mentions comes from the novelist Bi Feiyu, who wrote to Goldblatt stating:

> I would like to reserve what you translated. I don't like cuts. I won't attract readers with stories. When you translated *Three Sisters*, you encountered the same problem, but we didn't give in. And the BBC journalist likes it. . . . We have our own literary aesthetics.
>
> (Bi Feiyu, 2014)

When compared to Bi Feiyu in particular, Mo Yan's engagement in the system in which his work is translated comes sharply into focus. Bi Feiyu's response suggests a more scholarly disposition, which likely sees translative and editorial interventions as symptoms of unequal power differentials rather than the complex workings of elaborate systematic nodal connections. At the time when Mo Yan was writing Goldblatt in the 1990s, the author clearly did not see being collabora-tive with his western counterparts as a sign or symptom of weakness in the face of unequal geopolitical power. For Mo Yan, as with most American authors of that time and now, the addition of another's labor, especially those with higher degrees of node, is seen to be an asset adding value to the text. The Chinese and English translation network structures are organized differently in relation to the meaning of agential/actantial assertion and negotiation.

Conclusion: American literary network structures, translation, and the future of "literature"

Let us conclude with a short discussion of the American Literary Network Struc-tures. If literature presents the "hum" of a community's culture in a manner that is more easily recovered than in everyday life – this, in essence, is Trilling's argument – then translation can be understood as the process whereby the source of a culture's "hum" is rendered particularly legible to the target community under its own (domestic) cultural norms. Understanding translation in this way, scholars seek to comprehend it in terms of a negotiation of "agency" between and among not only individuals, but larger epistemic structures, some on a global scale. This, in significant part, is why we have multiplied the terms "agency," "actors," "actants" and even "authority" in suggesting a complex accounting of linguistic/ social phenomena. Such multiplication, as we hope to have demonstrated, allows us to discern the networking of translation.

No wonder translation studies, and the sociological approach to translation studies in particular, continues to grow in importance, especially in China, where Chinese Literature and culture "going out" is a well-funded research topic. How-ever, many of the fundamental assumptions that undergird the distinctions drawn between "Chinese" and "Western" cultural assumptions quickly collapse under the weight of the evidence provided by ANTS archival research. For instance, Chinese and Western modes of sociality are generally understood on the basis of collectivist vs individualist tendencies. However, as we have already suggested, the principle distinction between the American and Chinese literary network structures can best be described as China's radically individualistic, producer-oriented literary network structure and America's radically collaborative and actor-diffused network structure. Chinese authors tend to be allergic to the idea of editorial meddling, and readers are so habituated to the idiosyncrasies of a largely unfiltered literary textuality that the Chinese market supports individualistic idiosyncrasy as normal. This is why the archival record of Mo Yan's exceptional position in this dichotomy is so enlightening. Still, the differences between these network structures are not due to inherent cultural differences, but the degree to which the American literary network has been transformed by the rise of value-added economics, which can be seen in the case of the structure of America's "literary publishing economy." The American literary network structure has existed within a modern economy for far longer than the Chinese literary network has, and as a result it has had more time to integrate itself into the larger systems that govern almost all other market dynamics.

We should begin with a commonplace observation: in the United States, literature by definition is always over-supplied. The vast majority of American fiction authors and poets do not earn their living from book sales or reading honoraria; rather they earn income from their validated capacity to provide "assessment-labor," as we might call it, for other writers: namely teaching, editing, publishing, marketing, designing, networking, etc.

This state of affairs in publishing began in the 1930s but exponentially grew from the 1980s onward, so that there are now over 300 creative writing degree programs in the US with an annual application rate of over 20,000; on the average, 3,000 new MFAs or creative writing PhDs are minted every year (Brady, 2019). While ostensibly creative writers enter creative writing programs to become successful writers, most will leave with another, more tangible outcome: their ability to assess and "improve" literary works written by others. Those who are just entering the literary market can increase their personal "degree of node" by providing other writers with assessment labor, different from (though networked with) the labor of writing. Such assessment labor includes presenting workshops, editing, reviewing, advocating, promoting, etc. Those who continue to provide positive assessment labor do it by teaching or consulting, while others will use their understanding of literary product-market-fit to provide negative assessment labor, which "filters" what gets published. They commonly start out as slush readers and gradually work up to literary agents or editors, capable of preventing the majority of writing from reaching an audience while promoting agency/authority in those authors who do make it through.

It is important to note that the value of literary intellectual property is not dependent upon the labor that goes into producing it, as one might argue in the traditional sense. In Marx and his predecessors, the "labor theory of value" presupposes that the economic value of a good or service is determined by the total amount of "socially necessary labor" required to produce it. But a literary work's value does not come from how much labor goes into creating it: such labor can be found in all the negatively assessed and unpublished literature that never enters the mainstream literary marketplace. Instead, the value of a work can be correlated with the amount of *networked labor* that is invested into it. *Networked labor*, unlike production labor, is provided by others, and therefore a work's success lies in how many other degrees of node have invested effort in it (such as literary agents, editors, marketers, reviewers, readers, licensees, adaptors, etc.).

Schleifer (2018) has argued that we can profitably distinguish between life-sustaining commodities, which form the basis of the labor theory of value, and life-*enhancing* commodities, products of the Second Industrial Revolution in the early 20th century in the United States, which are goods/services not *necessary* to life – not necessary to create the possibility of labor – but which "enhance" life. Such commodities by definition do not fit into the zero-sum system of value and surplus value that Marx and other "classical" economists analyzed. Instead, Schleifer argues, they are best understood in relation to complexity theory, where value is not simply the "base" of life, as are life-sustaining commodities, but emerges from the interplay outside the terrible calculus of absolute need (pp. 1–33). This analysis fits nicely into the "networked labor" described here. Perhaps the opposite of absolute necessity (and the labor theory of value, which is based upon necessity) is the relative need of nodal degrees, which *emerge* in systems/environments, both linguistic *and* social.

As we apply these ideas to translation studies, we can begin to discern the way such value-added economics, implicit in network theory (and in particular ANTS), affect the production, publication and reception of Chinese literature in English. Chinese authors and their English translators, as we have seen, work with high-level "networked labor." They can expect to discern authorial agency not as some quality of personality, but as *a quality of a system*. Those in the system with higher degrees of node base their agency, at least in part, on value that is *systematically* conferred upon actors (agents/actants). In the simplest terms, the more labor provided by networks of actors, agents, and actants, the more valuable intellectual property becomes.

In this, the value of intellectual property is a function of the "network economy" that we are describing. Such "value" is not inherent in individual labor, but emerges from the interplay of actants/actors – it emerges from the degree of node of its participants – which are diffuse and not readily identified with volitional "acts." For this reason, in order to discern the emergence and existence of "value" in the life-enhancing work of translation, we need to draw upon archival resources to study how actor networks function in relation to one another in the production/creation of inter-cultural translation. And when we study the value embodied in Chinese literature translated into English as an emergent property of the American literary/translation network structure – a value which, as we have suggested, is not "inherent" in the source text, but which emerges in the translated text – we can begin to understand "translation" no longer as the space of cross-cultural hermeneutics, but a larger set of more diffuse internetwork negotiations about the transition from one complex system to another. Once we begin to trace how actor networks are organized by these larger systems of networked labor, which themselves are organized by even larger exogenous forces, we can not only overcome the hagiographic impulse that traps translation studies within the simplistic history of sovereign actors (largely understood to be authors and translators), but also the reductive logic of cultural hermeneutics and poetics that reads the terms authors and translators as synecdoche for "epistemes" – that is to say, the "hum" – of culture.

When viewed historically, the rise of America's economy of networked labor has radically transformed not only literary norms, but the English language itself. Over the last half century, the exponential growth of the network economy has created a form of "consensus literary English" – this too is an instance of Trilling's "hum" – which we have not seen in literary Chinese. Not only does literary Chinese not have a Chicago Manual of Style or any other authoritative guides enforcing consistent literary norms across all publishing platforms, but more importantly the lack of a creative writing industry in China over the last fifty years means that the Chinese language has yet to undergo the same kind of an intensely competitive incubation process in which hundreds of thousands of creative writers receive feedback daily from programs and courses in creative writing.

Understood historically, the emergence of consensus literary English should not be seen as an advancement over literary Chinese. Nor does this mean that if the Chinese literary network system continues to develop into a full-blown economy of networked labor, Chinese literature would become more westernized. Actually, we may find that the rise of a Chinese literary network economy would have the opposite effect because it is driven by Chinese consumers; Chinese readers will determine literary norms, not English readers or those seen in other World literatures. Discussing the effects of a network economy on literary translation norms should therefore not be couched in the reductive logic of "east" vs "west" or "Chinese" vs "American" values, but instead in terms of the relationship between organizational and volitional actants/actors as these relate to one another within the context of intralingual and interlingual literary production and consumption. In any case, it is our hope that ANTS may shed light on how translation studies can stay current with changes in the systems and processes of literary publication as we explore these transformations of our field in real time. The ANTS oriented work being done by CLTA scholars is revealing far more about how actor networks in the 1980s and 1990s differed between the US, China, and Hong Kong. Scholars in the future will be able to use these resources and methods to uncover how new changes to Chinese and American network structures will change the meaning of "translation" itself in the coming years and decades.

Notes

1   This focus on translation as a personal agential process was succinctly summed up in Jiří Levý's article "Translation as Decision Process," in which translation was understood as a result of a decision tree structured by definitional instructions that define a given translation paradigm and selective instructions that narrow the translator's number of choices. According to Levý, the criteria applied in the process at each individual stage are semantic, rhythmical, stylistic and so on (1967). Later Sonja Tirkkonen-Condit and John Laffling elaborated on this idea by stating that "choice and decision-making are perhaps so fundamental in translation that almost any theoretical or research-oriented treatment is bound to relate to them in one way or another" (1993, 8f).
2   Translation studies from the 1990s through the 2010s were deeply informed by deconstruction, ideology critique, and the hermeneutics of suspicion as major theorists like Gayatri Chakravorty Spivak and Kwame Anthony Appiah turned toward translation while new figures like Lawrence Venuti and Douglas Robinson brought translation studies into the theoretical mainstream.
3   Later in this essay, we refer to the "Agent/Actor/Actant"-Network, taking up A. J. Greimas's notion of "actant," which describes an element of narrative which "acts" – which is to say, functions as a narrative agent – but is not necessarily an active agent (1983).

One example is the ring in *Lord of the Rings*. In *Structural Semantics* Greimas (1983) develops an actantial approach to language based upon the ethnological work of Vladimir Propp and Claude Lévi-Strauss (see also Schleifer for a detailed account of Greimassian "actants," 1987, pp. 87–110). In *Uses of Literature*, Rita Felski articulates the larger import of Greimas's neologism: "To be sure," she writes, "we can question the politics built into certain storylines, as feminist critics have done in relation to the Victorian novel, but our conceptions of politics, literature, human relations, the interaction between social structures and human agency, remain deeply beholden to the logic of narrative" (2008, p. 85). As we shall see, the interaction between social structures and human agency is of the utmost importance in analyzing translation.

4 We might note that it is a lucky accident that one of our networking terms, "agent," is explicitly inscribed within the American publishing system under the category of "literary agent." But, as we hope this essay will demonstrate, this is less an accident than an instances of the social/linguistic complexity of translation altogether.

5 Over the years, a growing number of translation scholars have employed Actor-Network Theory to explain the formation of translation networks. Tyulenev employs ANT to better understand how the central actors recruit other actors into their network. According to Tyulenev the process of translating-recruiting consists of four stages: (1) *problematization*, where the central actor conceives a project, identifies all other required actants (to use our term) and sets the network in motion toward an 'obligatory passage point' (OPP). (2) *Interessement*, where the Central actor recruits necessary actants into the project. (3) *Enrolment* where all the actants become actors by working toward their common project description. (4) *Mobilization* where the actual scope of the network fulfilling the initial task comes into being (Tyulenev, 2014, p. 166). Thanks to Zhang Wenqian for this reference. Others have employed ANT to accomplish other ends. See, for instance, Alvstad, C., Greenall, A.K., Jansen, H. and Taivalkoski-Shilov, K. (eds) (2017) *Textual and Contextual Voices of Translation*; Qi, L. (2016) *Agents of Latin: An Archival Research on Clement Egerton's English Translation of Jin Ping Mei*. Thanks to Zhang Wenqian for these references. These deployments of sociological ANT all remain largely indebted to Latourian concepts in doing so. Yet, as the present essay suggests, we see a need to frame a wider ANTS – in the context of Translation Studies (ANTS) rather than Theory (ANT) – as a set of concepts grounded more specifically in the material conditions of world literature in translation.

References

Alvstad, C., Greenall, A. K., Jansen, H., & Taivalkoski-Shilov, K. (Eds.). (2017). *Textual and contextual voices of translation* (Vol. 137). John Benjamins Publishing Company.

Austin, J. L. (1970). A Plea for excuses. In *Philosophical Papers* (pp. 175–204). Oxford: Oxford University Press.

Bi Feiyu. (2014). April 16th, 2014 paper. Howard Goldblatt collection, box 1, folder 10, CLT M1. Chinese Literature Translation Archive, University of Oklahoma Libraries, Norman, Oklahoma.

Brady, A. (2019, April 15). *MFA by the numbers, on the eve of AWP*. Retrieved from https://lithub.com/mfa-by-the-numbers-on-the-eve-of-awp/

Felski, R. (2008). *Uses of literature*. Malden, MA. Oxford: Blackwell Publishing.

Greimas, A. J. (1983). *Structural semantics* (D. McDowell, R. Schleifer, & A. Velie, Trans.). Lincoln: University of Nebraska Press.

Hodell, C. (1994). Papers, May 5th, 1994. Howard Goldblatt collection, box 7, folder 2, CLT M1. Chinese Literature Translation Archive, University of Oklahoma Libraries, Norman, Oklahoma.

Jameson, F. (1981). *The political unconscious: Narrative as a socially symbolic act*. Ithaca, NY: Cornell University Press.

Jiang, Y. (1988). *Six chapters from my life "downunder"*. University of Washington Press.

Kao, G. (1981). Letter to Howard Goldblatt and Stephen Soong, August 21st, 1981. Howard Goldblatt collection, box 10, folder 15, CLT M1. Chinese Literature Translation Archive, University of Oklahoma Libraries, Norman, Oklahoma.

Kao, G. (1983). Letter to Stephen Soong and Howard Goldblatt, October 5th, 1983. Howard Goldblatt collection, box 10, folder 15, CLT M1. Chinese Literature Translation Archive, University of Oklahoma Libraries, Norman, Oklahoma.

Latour, B. (1987). *Science in action*. Cambridge: Havard University Press.

Levý, J. (1967). Translation as a decision process. *To Honor Roman Jakobson: Essays on the Occasion of His Seventieth Birthday*, October 11, 1966, *2*, 1171–1182. doi:10.1515/9783111349121-031

Li Rui. (1988). March 8th, 1998. Howard Goldblatt collection, box 6, folder 5, CLT M1. Chinese Literature Translation Archive, University of Oklahoma Libraries, Norman, Oklahoma.

Mo Yan. (1988). December 22nd, 1988 paper. Howard Goldblatt collection, box 28, folder 2, CLT M1. Chinese Literature Translation Archive, University of Oklahoma Libraries, Norman, Oklahoma.

Mo Yan. (1994). June 15th, 1994 paper. Howard Goldblatt collection, box 7, folder 2, CLT M1. Chinese Literature Translation Archive, University of Oklahoma Libraries, Norman, Oklahoma.

Qi, L. (2016). Agents of Latin: An archival research on Clement Egerton's English translation of Jin Ping Mei. *Target: International Journal of Translation Studies*, *28*(1), 42–60.

Schleifer, R. (1987). *A. J. Greimas and the nature of meaning: Linguistics, semiotics, and discourse theory*. Lincoln: University of Nebraska Press.

Schleifer, R. (2018). *A political economy of modernism: Literature, post-classical economics, and the lower middle-class*. Cambridge: Cambridge University Press.

Soong, S. (1983). Letter to Howard Goldblatt and George Kao, August 5th, 1983. Howard Goldblatt collection, box 10, folder 15, CLT M1. Chinese Literature Translation Archive, University of Oklahoma Libraries, Norman, Oklahoma.

Stillinger, J. (1991). *Multiple authorship and the myth of solitary genius*. Oxford: Oxford University Press.

Tirkkonen-Condit, S., & Laffling, J. (1993). *Recent trends in empirical translation research*. Joensuu: Joensuun yliopisto, Humanistinen tiedekunta.

Trilling, L. (1950). *The liberal imagination: Essays on literature and society*. New York: Doubleday.

Tyulenev, S. (2014). *Translation and society: An introduction*. New York: Routledge.

Yan, Jia, & Juan Du. (2020, March 16). Multiple authorship of translated literary works: A study of some Chinese novels in American publishing industry. *Translation Review*. Published online.

Xu, Shiyan. (2016). 基于翻译过程的葛浩文翻译研究－以《干校六记》英译本的翻译过程为例. 外国语 *(上海外国语大学学报)*, **5, 8**.

3 Intuition and spontaneity in multiple voice literary translation

Collaboration by accident or by design

Bonnie S. McDougall

Introduction

Intuition, spontaneity, creativity, imagination: all of these terms are associated with literary authorship, and all indicate high approval. Literary translators, however, are sometimes praised but are more likely to be criticized for displaying the very same qualities in their work. Multiple voice translation (MVT; signifying that more than one translator is involved) may be subject to even more disapproval, as if the single, individual voice must, almost by definition, be the sole source of these four qualities, while interventions by others, such as editors or publishers, are routinely accused of destroying them (translation partners, however, are usually not even mentioned). Here, I will argue that literary MVTs can indeed please readers with an abundance of intuition, spontaneity, creativity and imagination.[1]

I have no solid evidence on which to claim that multiple voice strategies encourage these qualities in literary translation. Yet there are grounds to believe that MVT can indeed have this function, just as the translation partnership may be the result of accident rather than design. A major element in my recent reflections on literary translation has been to acknowledge and celebrate the role that chance plays in translation. Here, my particular emphasis is on the likelihood that the high level of accident or chance that exists in MVT may actually serve to produce these desirable qualities.

Among the relationships that this paper will cover are co- or dual translators; author and translator collaboration; editors' and publishers' relationships (by established written or unwritten rules and regulations as well as personal intervention); team translation, whether in commercial translation factories or specialist institutions such as Beijing's Foreign Languages Press; translation of a text produced by multiple authors (for example, letter collections by two or more parties); and educational translation (collaboration between teachers and students in class, and the supervisor-student relationship). Multiple partnerships may include either native speakers of each of the two languages (with either knowledge of both languages and cultures at rudimentary or expert levels) or speakers of only one of the two languages at any level. Factors influencing or arising from MVT include the collaborators' ideological preferences, whether shared or diverse, acknowledged or not; positive and negative consequences of conflict between co-translators; and the role of peripheral voices (proof readers, layout artists and illustrators) as well as editors and publishers. Not covered in this paper are the usefulness of theories such as Bakhtinian polyphony, specific linguistic resources (e.g. onomastics) and the impact of multi-media and web-based genres.

I apologize in advance for what may appear to be undue emphasis on my own practice in the examples and arguments in this paper: I make no claim to exhibit any of the four prized qualities named above, but I include these examples to illustrate the kind of circumstances that lead to multiple voice strategies in literary translation from Chinese into English (McDougall, 2011, 2018, pp. 388–400).

Multiple voice translation research

It can be claimed that all published writing, literary or not, translated or not, is a product of multiple voices, but the topic of multiple voice translation has only recently begun to attract interest in English-language translation research. A survey of over 400 books with the Dewey catalogue number 418.02 at the University of Sydney's Fisher Library in November 2019 confirmed this observation. Of a dozen or so books with titles indicating either encyclopedic coverage of translation studies or special attention to professional practice, all published since 1990, the great majority had no index reference to any kind of collaborative or team translation: they include *In Other Words: a coursebook on translation* by Mona Baker (2011); *The Routledge Handbook of Translation Studies* edited by Carmen Millán and Francesca Bartrina (2013); and the *Routledge Companion to Translation Studies* edited by Jeremy Munday (rev. ed. 2009), which contains a 74-page section on key concepts. The *Routledge Encyclopedia of Translation Studies* edited by Mona Baker (rev. ed. 1998) contains no entry on teamwork or co-translation, although the entry by Peter Bush on literary translation contains fleeting references to author-translator collaboration and to editorial intervention. There are no entries on collaborative translation, team translation. or co-translation in the *Dictionary of Translation Studies* (1997) by Mark Shuttleworth and Moira Cowie, even in an entry on multiple-stage translation. The *Oxford Handbook of Translation Studies* edited by Kirsten Malmkjaer and Kevin Windle (2011) has 17 references to team translation but nothing on other forms of collaborative translation. Most recently, *The Routledge Handbook of Chinese Translation* (2018) overlooks MVT altogether as a subject of interest for research.

Monographs dating from the late 20th century also neglect this issue. The last chapter in André Lefevere's classic *Translation, Rewriting and the Manipulation of Literary Fame* (1992) gives an excellent analysis of re-writing through editorial intervention but is silent on collaborative translation. The final chapter of *Contemporary Translation Theories* by Edwin Gentzler (1993), on newly emerging trends in translation studies, is also free of any mention of collaborative translation, an indication that although the practice is certainly known to be in existence, it holds no theoretical interest.

There is better news in some recent works. An essay by Li Defeng, at the time of publication a lecturer in the Department of Translation at the Chinese University of Hong Kong, writes of the need for translation training to include "real world" situations such as teamwork or collaborative translating, although it refers chiefly to the notorious "translation factories" that operate in Hong Kong but more especially on the Chinese mainland (Li, 2001, pp. 85–89). There is a brief section on the need for classroom instruction on team translation in *Pathways to Translation: Pedagogy and Process* by Donald C. Kiraly (1995) but nothing on collaboration. Daniel Gouadec's *Translation as a Profession* (2007) includes a comprehensive treatment of current practice in collaborative translation, and his notes on literary translation are well informed, but there is nothing as such on collaboration in literary translation (Gouadec, 2007, pp. 85–89, esp. 90–91).

Although I have not been able to track down the first mention of the term MVT, it is unlikely that I invented it. The term "multiple translatorship" may have been inspired by Jack Stilliger's *Multiple Authorship and the Myth of Solitary Genius* (Stillinger, 1991) but Stillinger does not consider the role of chance or accident in writing partnerships. In *Authorial and Editorial Voices in Translation*, edited by Hanne Jansen and Anna Wegener (Jansen & Wegener, 2013, p. 4), however, the partnerships analyzed by contributors are those between a single translator and other agents such as authors, editors and so on.[2] A website Google search on 15 October 2019 showed no entry for the term "multiple voice translation" but presented instead entries on "multiple translatorship" (a single translator with cooperation from other interested parties such as authors and editors), and on translation projects using new technologies that encourage simultaneous collaboration of a non-literary nature.

I assume that it is generally accepted that literary translators have had a variety of experiences in collaborative translation. Now that research on translators (and not just on translations or translating) has become respectable, more information and discussion about their various forms of collaboration have become available (e.g. Sternberg, 2015). Why then this neglect of theories about or analyses of MVT? Is it seen as merely peripheral or inferior as a translation technique? Or is its very obviousness a deterrent to investigators? To a large extent, these are unanswerable questions, since it would be difficult (impossible?) to set up a controlled experiment to test their comparative effectiveness. However, a survey of the kinds of MVT that currently exist may give some idea of its advantages and disadvantages.

Translation types: collaborative, co-, team, in-house, educational

Multiple voice translation types are many and tend to overlap. In this paper, I discuss the five most common types to be found in literary translation. They include: collaboration between partners offering different skills or different levels of skill; translation of a source text written by multiple authors; team and in-house translation; educational translation; and editorial and publishing-related interventions. I should prefer to reserve the term "co-translation" for a form of collaboration where both parties contribute at a similar level, although I expect it will continue to be used loosely, as it is now. Except where otherwise indicated, Chinese is the source language and English is the host or translation language; the reverse partnership, from English into Chinese, operates in a vastly different context, while collaborative translation from Chinese into languages other than English would, I imagine, each have its own set of characteristics.

A well-established form of collaborative partnerships in literary translation is where one or more translators actively collaborate with the original author; some studies treat only such partnerships as collaborative translation. Many Hong Kong authors (the late Leung Ping-kwan and Dung Kai-cheung, for example) were or are fluent enough in English to play a valuable role in translation collaboration. At present, most Mainland Chinese authors do not speak English well enough to reach this level of partnership but will most likely become more linguistically adventurous before long. I regret I have no information on the comparable situation in Taiwan.

The lack of authors with a level of English that encourages collaboration is not as serious as it may seem: authors are not necessarily the best explicators of their own work. Some authors actively refuse to clarify ambiguity in their work; others may have proficiency in spoken English but do not know enough about the English language or European culture to perceive translation problems. Only a few cases have occurred in my own experience where the Chinese author was a fully participating collaborator. Apart from language skills, nevertheless, the main obstacle is not that contemporary authors are unwilling to collaborate; it is that they are unable to do so, whether through illness or death, distances that cannot be overcome or political or other barriers that seem, or are in fact, insurmountable.

Whether or not the authors are available, other Chinese partners are a good or even a superior source of information and expertise. Partnerships involving collaboration between a native Chinese speaker and a native English speaker may often be very successful. Native English-speaker translators living in China have an immense range of choice among Chinese people who are qualified in both Chinese literary style and proficiency in English. Also, given the massive temporary or long-term emigration of Chinese speakers to English-speaking countries, a native English speaker has a good chance of finding a Chinese partner outside of China. The number of native English-speaking translators with advanced skills in spoken and written Chinese is also growing, and many such people have been able to spend long periods in China, becoming familiar with Chinese culture, geography, history and so on – along with expertise in English language, literature and culture.[3]

The problems that exist in any kind of collaborative partnership are likely to be practical: the amount of time (for both drafting and consultation) each partner can allow; the amount of money each may hope to make from the transaction; and the different attitudes they may take in regard to the nature of the final product and its readership. The use of high-tech communication such as web-based publications and email enables partners to collaborate at a distance, although distance may also permit one partner be less conscientious than the other.

As we all know, there are also cases where one or even both collaborating parties are deficient in understanding the other language and culture – or even their own. It may happen that these deficiencies do not become apparent until after the work is published; the deficiency may also occur at any stage before publication as well, so that the project is aborted. Although such failures are rarely documented or publicized, word-of-mouth communications within the slender ranks of literary translators have given collaborative translation an awful reputation, not to mention souring personal relationships that should have been productive.

Another unfortunate outcome of some collaborative translation occurs when the contributions of each party are unequal. The imbalance may be related to gender or to the economic or political power of the partners' countries of origin. Whether or not the author is one of the translation partners, the imbalance may even include a failure to acknowledge the partnership itself. Power relations have presumably been less problematic in Chinese-to-English literary translation in the last two decades. In principle, either party could claim unfair discrimination; in practice, it has often been the native English-speaker (who may also be the agent in seeking and managing publication) who is in the stronger position to ignore or downgrade the partnership at the time of or after publication (McDougall, 2012).

A variation on collaboration between two parties is where there are three: for example, the author, who may or may not speak English, a native English speaker, and another translator who is not necessarily a native speaker of either language but has a high level of expertise in Chinese language and culture, maybe also with specialist knowledge appropriate to the text. Examples of this kind may be few, but three-way collaborations still have a lot in their favor.

A third kind of partnership may arise when a translator accepts a Chinese text that is jointly authored, as in an exchange of letters between two (or more) Chinese writers. Ideally, two (or more) English speakers should be paired as translators for these texts, although for practical reasons this may not be possible. Here the single translator is obliged to adopt two (or more) different voices, in which vocabulary, grammar, syntax, tone and so on are kept distinct, the translator keeping track through glossaries or other means. Translators routinely face these problems in translating fiction or drama, where having two (or more) partners offers an attractive alternative.

Regardless of the kind of partnership, collaborative translation usually consists of sequential drafting with intermittent or extensive consultation, where one partner is responsible for an initial draft that is then passed on to the other partner, the two parties working independently with pauses for exchanges about meaning, context, elegance and so on. Such discussions, "now explaining, now arguing, . . . enlivened many a day of toil" (to use James Legge's phrase; see below), are essential to a collaborative partnership. It might be thought that the Chinese co-translator (whether or not this person is also the author) would prepare the first draft, but the opposite also takes place. I have also taken part in an exercise where both partners made first drafts that were then compared: in this case, the Chinese partner was the author, an arrangement that happily imbued non-literal solutions with proper authority.

Team or in-house translation, as it occurs today, is rarely collaborative in the sense given above: whether in translation factories of the most exploitative kind or in more respectable translation companies and institutions, it typically takes place at different stages and in different locations, without contact among team members at the same level; further, the translation text may be divided into sections, so that none of the initial drafters have any knowledge of the complete text. Their drafts are then passed on for coordinating by higher-level agents without necessarily consulting the original translators; the revised draft may then be passed on in turn to a team of editors, each with their own special function.

Team translation is not new: in China, it can be traced back to the Tang dynasty translations of Buddhist texts. On the face of it, team translation today, with all the advantages of new technology, appears to be a highly reliable and cost-efficient method for translation in specialist fields of business, commerce, law, science and technology and so forth. It is not yet common in literary translation, however, except in the world of popular fiction such as the Harry Potter novels by J. K. Rowling. There is excellent coverage of team translation in Guoadec's *Translation as a Profession* and I see no need to expatiate on what he has written, except to point out that he excluded literary translation as one of the common genres.

It was my good fortune to spend three years as a full-time translator/editor at an in-house translation institution, the Books section of the Foreign Languages Press (FLP) in Beijing. In contrast to commercial translation factories, the ruling ideology there was political and patriotic, the organization bureaucratic, and the atmosphere at that time generally civil. The FLP's institutional teamwork, especially in the 1950s and resuming in the early 1980s, has produced a large body of works of an acceptable, sometimes inspired quality.

Team translation at the FLP has been standard practice for foreigners such as myself as well as the staff: juniors prepare rough drafts, middle-ranking staff correct them, and senior staff complete a final draft before handing a final version over to even higher-ranking staff. I was started off with English drafts prepared by junior Chinese staff but was eventually allowed to write my own drafts from the original texts, to be handed on to senior members of the Chinese staff. This early experience of team translation was on the whole benign, leaving me with a lasting appreciation of teamwork.

Actual working conditions were in many ways disagreeable, however, even apart from the dismal physical discomfort. One aspect of the job that many of my colleagues and I found irksome was the requirement to observe official national guidelines for translating Chinese terms into English. (China is not the only country to have issued such guidelines; it is also the practice in Turkey; I believe these guidelines have now been relaxed in China.)

A more serious problem was the routine censorship of the original literary texts, performed by the editorial staff before the material was passed on to the translation staff. It might be thought that since all literary texts were already subject to censorship on first (and sometimes later) publication, there was no need for further censorship before their translation. The examples that passed through my hands instead suggest that the FLP's censorship was based on the editors' expectations of responses to the texts by foreign readers: that is, it was references to shortcomings in Chinese society (and to a lesser extent in China's economy and politics) that should be excised (McDougall, 2012, pp. 1–15). At the FLP in the 1980s, these and similar editorial practices were too often the combined result of the editors' patriotism and their ignorance of foreign countries, in contrast to the translation staff (especially senior staff, who for obvious reasons, were better informed). It is possible that the editors were merely carrying out instructions from higher echelons, but I was able in a few instances to argue successfully that the censorship should be withdrawn (McDougall, 1993, pp. 73–90). Although I was not in a position to monitor more than a tiny handful of cases, there is every indication that the editors' role routinely included what I have called negative collaboration.[4]

The growing professionalization of literary translation in general, in China and abroad, has caused more attention to be given to the question of whether editorial voices, including related inputs from illustrators, layout designers and other ancillary staff, should also be considered as collaborative. Although it is possible for translators (as with other writers) to argue against editorial rulings, translators may be even more unsuccessful in appealing because their status is generally perceived as even more inferior; this at least was the case in the bureaucratic structure at the FLP when I was there. In the world of academic or commercial translation publication in English-speaking countries, the status of translators in some cases may be high, but we remain reliant on editors and publishers to get our work published. I recall one case, involving a reputable publisher, where I found the editorial revisions to my translation completely unacceptable. I wondered if my translation skills had suddenly and rapidly deteriorated; or could it be possible that the editor took a dislike to the original work . . . Who knows? In any case, I still accepted most of the changes.

It may sometimes be difficult to determine the fine line between extensive editorial intervention and collaborative translation, as in cases where one translator is handed a copy of a translation by another hand that the editors deem inadequate. Since in such cases revisions can be lengthy and time-consuming, it may seem only fair that both translators are listed as co-translators, although they may never have been in contact with each other; in other cases, the re-translator may consider herself lucky to find her name somewhere in the acknowledgements.[5] One translation passed on to me by an editor was so poor that I was obliged to re-translate from scratch, although in the final version the original translator's name was still listed as sole translator; in this instance, it was the editor who ruled an eventual admission of co-translation. A much better experience was when the original translator asked me to check her translation for errors: this was a demanding task that took several days, but I was paid for it, thanked handsomely in the acknowledgements, at no point identified as a collaborating translator, and remained wholly satisfied with the transaction.

In some cases, it is possible to draw distinctions in editorial attitudes between commissioned and self-submitted translations but I have not found them decisive. The time spent and the perceptible amount of change are also basically immaterial to distinctions between editorial contributions and re-translation: the distinction has to be related to the kind of changes that are made rather than their quantity.

There are editors whose interventions are welcome, and I am grateful to many of them for this. Peter Jay at Anvil Press in London, in particular, has saved me from public embarrassment. All changes, welcome or not, require formal acknowledgement, and it is only fair to acknowledge editorial and related staff as contributors to the overall translation. Nevertheless, it is rare for them to contribute as fundamentally or as creatively to the final product as in the kind of collaborative partnerships discussed above. In other words, the concept of MVT is an extremely valuable aid in understanding and evaluating any literary translation, but it is one that operates on many levels. An excellent summary of editorial and related intervention in general translation can be found in Gouadec (2007, pp. 163–165).

I have left educational partnerships to the last because of their potential importance in a translator's life as well as their special characteristics. Most native English-speaking translators of Chinese literature have learned most or all of their knowledge of Chinese language and culture in colleges and universities, many at doctoral levels: they may be familiar with supervising and being supervised for work that includes translation. My own supervisor, A. R. Davis, himself a noted translator of classical Chinese poetry, insisted on meticulous attention to the original poem's meaning in all its aspects: vocabulary, rhythm, grammar, context and allusion, accompanied by faithful renditions that drew attention to the original's excellence. Davis would also offer in class or in individual supervision brilliant solutions to our problems in all areas. As I recall, he was deeply suspicious of theory, including translation theory (which, to be fair, was not, in the 1960s and 1970s, a particularly attractive body of thought.) I also recall his claim that he consciously refrained from learning how to speak modern Chinese in case it might subvert his native command of English in his translations.

While the supervisory relationship is sometimes fraught, classroom translation may be easier on both teachers and students. Since I moved to Hong Kong in 2006 and then on to Sydney in 2010, the great majority of my translation students have been native Chinese-speakers, although there have been considerable differences in their level of understanding. Teaching and learning at best become simultaneous for all parties: we all learn a lot.

At a different level again was the Sino-British Literary Translation Course, the first of three translation workshops that took place in 2008, 2009 and 2014 for early and mid-career literary translators from English to Chinese and from Chinese to English. All three events were sponsored by the Penguin Group and support for the initial workshop came from the Arts Council England and the Chinese General Administration of Press and Publications (GAPP); the syllabus was provided by the British Centre for Literary Translation. The translations into English were led by Howard Goldblatt and Bonnie McDougall, and the Chinese translators of English texts worked with British writers Hari Kunzru and Bernardine Evaristo.

It was in these workshops that I experienced the kind of exuberance associated with the most productive translation partnerships, elevated by the intensity of the efforts of a small group of beginners and old-timers. In terms of professional translation, it was exhilarating but utterly unrealistic. It was through this experience, nevertheless, that I became more convinced than ever before of the benefits of collaboration in stimulating intuition, spontaneity, creativity and imagination as ideas were bounced back and forth. It was also here that I was struck by the realisation of how crucial was the role of accident, coincidence, chance and contingency in our work.

Interlude: accident, chance, opportunity, coincidence, contingency

The process by which a literary translator and a literary author or work come together is another area of translation studies that has not much been studied (I found no mention of it in any of the translation studies that I examined). A passage in Gouadec's *Translation as a Profession* lays out pathways open for adoption by literary translators (Gouadec, 163–165), but the ways and whys by which collaborators come together for literary translation seem to have escaped scholarly attention.

My own experience suggests that just as the way in which a translator and an author or work come together is likely to be happenstance, and the way in which potential collaborators come together is much the same. The budding translator may well follow Gouadec's advice (or observation) on how authors or works may be selected, but where is the advice (or observation) on how to select a collaborator? Below I describe two famous translation partnerships that have a common foundation in sinology. Since these translation partners are no longer alive and wrote rather little about their experiences, these are to a large extent guesswork based on experience about what may have been accident or chance about them.

Translation partnerships and sinology

The development of sinology in English-speaking countries was from its very beginnings closely connected with collaborative translation from Chinese to English. The first and one of the most famous such collaborations was that between James Legge (1815–1897), a Scottish missionary who later became the first professor of Chinese at Oxford (1867–1897), and Wang Tao (1826–1897), a prolific writer, publisher and reformist, described by Li Hongzhang as "a rare genius with encyclopedic knowledge" (Cohen, 1974, p. 67; Lu, 2007, pp. 25–27). Together they collaborated on the translation and commentary on the Confucian classics that had dominated Chinese civilization throughout its dynastic history. However, only Legge's name appeared on the covers and title pages (and in library catalogues) of the five-volume set of Legge's *The Chinese Classics*, as if he was its sole begetter; the authors of the Chinese source texts are unknown, and Legge worked alone on the first two volumes; his translation partner's name first appeared in the preface to Volume 3. The little that we know about their collaboration methods can be found in that preface.

The question has been raised whether or not Wang Tao can be counted as a scholar and as a sinologist. Paul Cohen seems to be uncertain: early in his book he described Wang Tao as a Chinese scholar "steeped in the learning of China" (Cohen, 1974, p. 67), but later he qualified this judgment with the comment that he could not be called "a scholar in the classical sense" (Cohen, 1974, p. 154). Legge himself could show more generosity:

> Nor must [the Author] fail to acknowledge gratefully the services rendered to him by Wang T'aou, a graduate of Soo-chow. This scholar, far excelling in classical lore any of his countrymen whom the Author had previously known, came to Hongkong in the end of 1863, and placed at his disposal all the treasures of a large and well-selected library. At the same time, entering with spirit into his labours, now explaining, now arguing, as the case might be, he has not only helped but enlivened many a day of toil.
>
> (Legge, vol. 3, p. viii)

From this passage, at least, we may imagine frequent consultations and friendly, genuine exchanges of opinion and judgment.

Wang first encountered Legge in Hong Kong in 1862 (not 1863) and was soon in Legge's employ; and when for reasons of health Legge returned to Scotland in 1867, he invited Wang Tao to join him there. Wang soon after made the trip from Hong Kong to Europe, landing in London in January 1868. He then went on to Scotland, where he stayed for two years before leaving for Hong Kong in Legge's company in January 1870. While in Scotland, he spent most of his time at Legge's home in Dollar, but he also travelled with Legge to visit John Chalmers in Aberdeen where he took the opportunity to discuss with Chalmers some problems to do with *Chunqiu* [Spring and autumn annals] (Cohen, 1974, pp. 67–73). Despite differences in age and experience between Legge and Wang, their partnership lasted for nearly a decade during which they became good friends.

Another famous Chinese-English collaboration, more literary in nature and closer to the present day, is the partnership of Yang Xianyi (1915–2009) and Gladys Yang (1919–1999).[6] Yang Xianyi enjoyed an excellent education during a privileged childhood and youth in Tianjin. He began translating English-language poetry into classical Chinese around the age of fifteen, further polishing his linguistic skills after leaving for Oxford via Japan, Canada and the US in 1934. More or less lightheartedly, having by now become fluent in Greek, Latin and French, he began translating classical Chinese poetry into English around 1936. By then he had made the acquaintance of Gladys Tayler, who soon after became the first student to enroll in the new degree of Chinese Studies at Oxford. A long career of collaborative translation was thus launched.

Dedicating themselves to the Chinese war effort, the young engaged couple returned to China in 1940 to face an uncertain future. Their first formal collaborative effort took place around 1943 at the Institute of Translation and Compilation outside Chongqing: it was a translation of *Laocan youji* [The Travels of Lao Can], later republished in the Panda Book series in 1983 and credited equally to both translators. The Institute moved downriver to Nanjing in 1946 but conditions were so chaotic that Yang Xianyi was obliged to take on several other jobs as well. In 1950, the Institute was disbanded, although the Yangs stayed on in Nanjing from where they contributed translations to the new magazine *Chinese Literature*. In 1951 they were invited to join the Beijing committee for translating Mao Zedong's collected works but declined. Eventually they decided to join the newly established Foreign Languages Press in Beijing in 1952 (it seemed the most attractive of several possibilities) and for the next few years enjoyed the esteem of Beijing's intellectual, cultural and political élites. Among their early collaborations for the FLP are *Selected Works of Lu Xun* (1956) and *The Scholars* (1957). Thereafter, their fame as a Chinese-to-English translation couple quickly spread among interested parties across the world.

When I arrived at the FLP in September 1980, Gladys Yang and Yang Xianyi were the most famous translators in China, respected and admired for the range of their achievements as a translation couple, and, not least, for having survived severe harassment, several years imprisonment (Gladys in solitary confinement) and family tragedy during the Cultural Revolution. By that time, however, they were in different sections of the FLP and no longer translated together. Gladys Yang had an office in the *Chinese Literature* section, turning up every morning for her work on modern and contemporary literature, mostly by women writers; Yang Xianyi was somewhere in senior management although still working on translations of Western classics into Chinese and occasionally the reverse. Gladys Yang was often grim and apt to rebuke foolishness; Yang Xianyi was more relaxed although he could also be distant: the tragedy in their lives could not be easily forgotten. In the afternoons and evenings, however, their flat in the FLP compound was crowded with locals as well as visitors from abroad, the atmosphere a vigorous affirmation of survival against the odds.

I have often wondered how the Yangs would have translated *Liang di shu*, the published love-letters between Lu Xun and Xu Guangping; around 1979 Gladys Yang had been allotted the task but gave it a pass on the grounds that she was too busy. It does seem a great pity that they chose (or were obliged) not to make this a crowning achievement of their long partnership. The Yangs never claimed to be scholars, and in later life they would mention institutional constraints on their professional judgments, but thanks to their profound knowledge and understanding of Chinese and Western cultures, their linguistic skills and meticulous industry, and (as in the case of Legge and Wang) their keenness to discuss and argue the point at length with each other, no other couple has so dominated Chinese literary translation.

We now know a lot about Legge and Wang and about the Yangs but not so much about more recent collaborations. The lively literary scene that emerged in the 1980s has encouraged the emergence of new collaborative partners. Some of these consist of couples, often but not necessarily married, in which the source translator is a woman and the host is male (Sternberg, 2015, p. 9). It is not clear, however, how much the native speakers of Chinese actually knew about Chinese language, literature and culture. Nor is it clear how much the native speakers of English knew about English language, literature and culture, although some of them are well-known Chinese studies scholars. It is reasonable to assume that each pair were able to communicate and share their opinions. It seems to be taken for granted, however, that each were also expert in their own language and culture.

No other studies have yet been made on contemporary collaborations, but there is every reason to suppose that other patterns are emerging and will continue to emerge, based on changing circumstances. One aspect that would be of interest is the question of who may be expected to be the dominant voice in multiple voice literary translation in a partnership consisting of a native Chinese speaker and a native English speaker: the source translator or the host translator?

In this context, it is useful to note that that the Yangs' partnership has been for several years a popular topic for Chinese students taking courses on translation in theory and practice, as well as academic studies by more senior scholars. Unfortunately, many of these attempts are flawed: that is, the translations are attributed only to Yang Xianyi, whose name precedes Gladys's in their publications. The role played by Gladys Yang is downplayed or wholly ignored. It seems as if in the case of female-male translation couples, married or otherwise, if the woman's name is placed second her achievement may be ignored. Is this due to discrimination against women, or is it ignorant racism? Or is it simply poor bibliographic practice in academic referencing and library catalogues? Whatever, it is deplorable.

The partnerships described above differ in several respects but have at least two obvious features in common: that is, both of the partners are at least to some extent familiar with both Chinese and English cultures, and each of the pairs consist of a native speaker of English and a native speaker of Chinese. The advantage of this arrangement is relevant to debates on whether translation into English of Chinese works should be undertaken by native Chinese-speakers or native English-speakers.

I have a vivid memory of belligerent statements made at the Forum on Translation from Chinese into Foreign Languages: A Bridge to the World, held in Beijing in 2007, to the effect that Chinese culture was owned by the Chinese and that it could therefore necessarily be translated into foreign languages only by Chinese. The proposition that a national culture can be "owned" is odd. Has it ever been asserted that English literature is owned by the English? (Or the British?) How can a country or nation own a language? Can it prevent outsiders from speaking it or reading it or translating it? By imposing a fee, or a licence, or a jail sentence?

The premise that underlies this, that Chinese literature and culture can only be understood by its natives, is ludicrous. Given China's huge geographical and demographic size, its long history and its complex social structures, it seems extremely unlikely that there is a single "literature" or "culture" for either native Chinese speakers or foreigners to encompass.

In the case of Chinese-to-English translation, given the recent history of China in the last hundred years or so, the stand taken by some speakers at this conference failed to take into account the uncertain understanding by native Chinese-speakers of the kind of things that the English readers of the translation would know about as part of their general cultural background or which they could absorb in their reading without particularly questioning them. (Not all readers require an absolute understanding of the cultural significance of each word, phrase or sentence as they turn the pages, whether it be an original text or a translation.)

The use of stealth gloss demonstrates this point quite nicely. In stealth gloss, explanations of terms, objects, events and so on from the source text are inserted into the host text instead of appearing in footnotes. Insensitive stealth gloss may leave the host reader puzzled as to why the source author would bother to explain details that the source reader would surely know. This is bad enough, but the more serious problem for native-speaker source translators is that they would not usually have a firm grasp on what the host readers would or would not need to have explained.

There is also a mountain of evidence that being a native speaker of any language is not enough to enable high-quality translation from or into that language; the ultimate judgment on the translation must rest with the reader of the translation. For this and other reasons, it seems to follow that a translation from Chinese to English by a highly qualified native English speaker would start from a position of superiority to one by a highly qualified native Chinese speaker. This belief leaves me open to attack for the same kind of nationalism embraced by some of the Chinese translators at that forum. Rather than take sides between native speakers of the source or host text, however, I now prefer to endorse a balance of collaborative partners.

Not all translation partnerships would want to claim the glamour and respect enjoyed by the first two eminent models I have described above. To repeat, one attribute each of the four participants has in common is a high degree of competence in sinology. Regardless of comments made at the time by the translators themselves or others, all four qualify as sinologists in the best and widest sense of the term. Beyond that, the partnerships are based on the pairing of two native-speakers, each representing one of the two languages in question. However, not all partnerships follow this traditional pattern.

In my early days I was a lone translator, under the naive assumption that this was the normal procedure for literary translation. It was only after I began to work for the Foreign Languages Press in Beijing in the 1980s that I achieved a kind of enlightenment. Since then, I have taken part in various forms of collaboration as well as in-house team translation: partnership with an author; partnership with a native speaker; classroom collaboration with students; and workshop collaboration with younger translators. The main advantages initially seemed to be practical: we could get through a long manuscript more quickly – sometimes; and there was less chance of serious errors in either direction – perhaps. It took me some time to acknowledge that there were other factors that made collaboration yield more than simply practical advantages. Matching linguistic talents are only part of the story.

The most unexpected development in my translation practice has been the recruitment of my husband, Anders Hansson, a linguist and historian who is not a native speaker of either Chinese or English. On the other hand, he is a fluent and precise speaker of both languages and possesses as well a wide-ranging knowledge of Chinese and European cultures. This arrangement began in the mid 2000s with the triangular translation of Dung Kai-cheung's (2011) novel *Ditu ji* [Atlas] by the author, Anders and me, a collaboration that happily turned out to be successful.[7]

Encouraged by this, I went on to include sketches from Dung Kai-cheung's *The Catalog* for classroom teaching at the University of Sydney, starting in 2011; as in my classes in Hong Kong, the students (almost all of whom were Mainland Chinese) were first puzzled and then keen to grapple with them. After this promising beginning, I began to translate the sketches for my own pleasure, consulting Anders when I got stuck. Gradually it occurred to me that Anders should be first translator (taking the place usually occupied by a native speaker) with me as second translator. Disputes between us are common but rarely rancorous. We continue to consult Dung Kai-cheung for his comments and corrections, which are duly incorporated. It has been and still is a long and sometimes frustrating but always highly rewarding task.[8]

To a much greater degree than *Atlas*, *Catalog* depends on familiarity with Hong Kong Cantonese language and culture, knowledge that I do not possess. Objects and events in popular culture such as evoked in 1998–1999 when Dung Kai-cheung was writing *Catalog* are almost by definition short lived, and there is little trace of them to be found even in internet searches in Chinese or English. Anders handled all of this research. Despite its accidental origins, this partnership has turned out well. Should I have married an expert in Aztec astronomy or marine biology, it would never have happened.

Studies have shown that writing and thinking in a second language can encourage a deliberate mode of thinking, while working in one's native language encourages fluidity; according to *The Economist*, a bilingual person can have the best of both (Johnson, 2017a, p. 68). How much more does this apply to multiple voice translation. A more recent article in *The Economist*, on global changes in the technologies and economics of translation, ends with the sombre words, "The loners of the field, in other words, may find it hard going" (Johnson, 2017b, p. 71).

Personally, I would guess that the lone translator will survive, but collaboration, I am sure, is the road ahead.

Conclusion

It is painful to reflect on the need for a reminder that Chinese-English literary translation still requires a high level of sinological knowledge. The effect of globalization in the modern world and the spectacular rise of China to a dominant world power may seem to many people to have diluted the systemic differences between the languages and cultures of the English-speaking world and of China. In truth, the difficulties of translating literature from Chinese to English are still formidable. In addition, at least one and preferably all partners in collaborative Chinese-English literary translation, in additional to sinological expertise, need to have an understanding of the literatures and cultures that English-speaking readers take for granted.

Trying to sort these experiences of multiple voice translation into categories has been an odd sort of task. It is a reminder of their variety, whether of the texts themselves, the translation voices they embody, or the translators' relationships with various other colleagues, including authors, collaborators, colleagues, teachers and students, editors and publishers. Which of the relationships are accidental, and which are by design, or even a mixture of both, perhaps in the end does not really matter. All the same, it might be worth speculating which of them is more likely to produce literary translation embodying intuition, spontaneity, creativity and imagination.

Notes

1 This paper is a revised version of my presentation under the same name at Beijing Languages and Cultures University, the full text was translated and published as "Qiaohe haishi guyi: fuheshi wenxue fanyi zhong de zhijue he zifa xing" [By accident or design: intuition and spontaneity in multiple voice translation] (McDougall, 2019, pp. 72–85). I have written about my experience as a literary translator in the chapter "The Personal Narrative of a Chinese Literary Translator" (McDougall, 2018, pp. 388–400) and specifically about my official and non-official translation in Beijing in the 1980s (McDougall, 2011); I have tried to avoid excessively repeating myself here.
2 See also the review of this work by Carole Birkan-Berzin in *Translation Studies*, January 2017, pp. 107–109.
3 The *Paper Republic* website http://paper-republic.org/resources/trans/faqs/3/ maintains an extensive list of people who offer themselves as Chinese-English translators.
4 I am grateful to Thomas Zimmer and Lauren P. Pfister for raising this aspect of editorial intervention at the Beijing Languages and Cultures University forum in Beijing in September 2017.
5 I am grateful to Josh Stenberg for this point.
6 Yang Xianyi's autobiography, published originally in Italian (as dictated in English) in 1991 and subsequently published in English under the title *White Tiger*, first appeared around 1999 or 2000 (my copy has no publication data); there is also an autobiography written in Chinese which is not identical to the English version. Gladys Yang refused a request from a British publisher in the 1980s to write an autobiography; no biography of her has been published to date, but obituaries appeared in the British press at the time of her death.
7 A description of our working methods can be found in my introduction to *Atlas*, pp. xvii – xxviii.
8 The translation of *Catalog* has been accepted for publication by Columbia University Press under the title *A Catalog of Stuff As Dreams Are Made On*.

References

Birkan-Berzin, C. (2017). Authorial and editorial voices in translation 1 – collaborative relationships between authors, translators, and performers; authorial and editorial voices in translation 2 – editorial and publishing practices. *Translation Studies*, *10*(1), 107–109.

Cohen, P. A. (1974). *Between tradition and modernity: Wang T'ao and reform in late Ch'ing China*. Council on East Asian Studies, Cambridge, MA: Harvard University Press.

Dung, K.-C. (2011). *Atlas: The archeology of an imaginary city* (K.-C. Dung, A. Hansson, & B. S. McDougall, Trans.). Columbia University Press.

Gouadec, D. (2007). *Translation as a profession.* J. Benjamins.

Jansen, H., & Wegener, A. (2013). *Collaborative relationships between authors, translators, and performers* (Vol. 1). Vita Traductiva.

Johnson. (2017a, February 4). The giant shoulders of English. *The Economist.*

Johnson. (2017b, May 27). Why translators have the blues. *The Economist.*

Li, D. (2001). Translator training in Hong Kong: What professional translators can tell us. In Chan, Sin-wai (Ed.), *Translation in Hong Kong: Past, present and future* (pp. 85–95). The Chinese University Press.

Legge, J. (1960). *The Chinese classics: With a translation, critical and exegetical notes, prolegomena, and copious indexes: The Shoo king* (Vol. 3). Oxford University Press & Hong Kong University Press. (Original work published 1893–1895)

Lu, S. H. (2007). *Chinese modernity and global biopolitics: Studies in literature and visual culture.* University of Hawai'i Press.

McDougall, B. S. (1993). Censorship and self-censorship in contemporary Chinese literature. In S. Whitfield (Ed.), *After the event: Human rights and their future in China* (pp. 73–90). Wellsweep Press.

McDougall, B. S. (2009). CELT 09: The Suzhou experience. *In Other Words*, 33(Summer), 50–52.

McDougall, B. S. (2011). *Translation zones in modern China: Authoritarian command versus gift exchange.* Cambria Press.

McDougall, B. S. (2012). Ambiguities of power: The social space of translation relationships. *Journal of the Oriental Society of Australia, 44*, 1–15.

McDougall, B. S. (2018). The personal narrative of a Chinese literary translator. In C. Shei & Z.-M. Gao (Eds.), *The Routledge handbook of Chinese translation* (pp. 388–400). Routledge.

McDougall, B. S. (2019). *Qiaohe haishi guyi: Fuheshi wenxue fanyi zhong de zhijue he zifa xing* [*By accident or design: Intuition and spontaneity in multiple voice translation*]. Han Feng, pp. 72–85.

Sternberg, J. (2015). Chinese-English literary translation as an economic network: A freelance translator's experience-based perspective. *Perspectives on the Arts and Humanities Asia, 5*(2), 2–26.

Stillinger, J. (1991). *Multiple authorship and the myth of solitary genius.* Oxford University Press.

Yang, X. (approx 1999–2000). *White Tiger*, n.p.

4 Gift-giving

Panda Books Series and Chinese literature "walking toward the world"

Qiang Geng

Introduction

This chapter describes the Panda Books Series (PBS), a translation program initiated in 1981 by the Foreign Languages Bureau (FLB) to push Chinese literature to "walk toward the world." The uniqueness of the program is that it was outbound, which meant that the translation was initiated by the source culture into the target (Chang, 2015). Translations of this sort, not a predominant phenomenon in many cultures, was not included in Holmes' influential 1972 articulation that product-oriented research aims to describe "existing translations" (1972/2000, p. 176). Subsequently, outbound translation has attracted much less academic attention than translation initiated by the target cultures (Lonsdale, 2011, pp. 84–87), despite such translations having been widely practiced in several countries and regions including China.

In China, outbound translation as a social practice has been sponsored by government agencies on a large scale from 1949 to the present. This fact alone merits a reconsideration of the orthodox claim that translations are perceived primarily as "facts of the culture that would host them" (Toury, 2012, p. 18). Additionally, it is worth questioning whether the FLB, as a hierarchical agency under direct management by the Chinese central government, sponsored translation programs merely for exporting its ideology. This question still remains to be answered, especially considering the overhaul of politics, the economy and society in China of the 1980s, when official and unofficial actants began to reconcile with one another, superficially at least, on the grounds that both groups had been victims of the extreme leftist ideology prevalent at the height of Mao's era during the Cultural Revolution which ended in 1976.

Previous studies on FLB-sponsored outbound translation

A few studies have offered early partial analysis from different perspectives. The practice of government-run outbound translation in China, according to Xie Tianzhen (2014), Qiang Geng (2010) and Zheng Ye (2012), has been sustained by a simplistic view of translation as merely a linguistic transfer instead of as a communication across literary, cultural and political divides. As a result, the issue of reception of translation was barely considered, resulting in a failure to promote Chinese literature globally. The communication framework within those government-run outbound translation practices, indicative of target-orientedness, may have caused their failure, but cannot explain why the practice persisted for decades, despite being barely profitable economically. Ren Dongsheng and Gao Yuxia (2015, p. 93) regard this practice as a form of national translation, "a self-benefiting translation initiated by a sovereign state to realize certain strategies for its own interests." They seem to support a sinocentric imperative to such a practice, signifying a problematic but perhaps simplified vision of translation exclusively in service of the state's interests .

In addition, Bonnie S. McDougall argues that translation by the FLB was conducted within an authoritarian mode, with its hierarchical management lacking "any systematic and reliable information about its readers" (2011, p. 39), and so they were slow to respond to, if not dismissive of, their foreign readers' demands. By contrast, non-official translations, like the cases analyzed in McDougall's book, had a better performance in this respect, as they were produced within a gift exchange mode allowing free negotiation between participants over what and how to translate. However, I would like to argue that the gift exchange mode concept can also be applied to official translation programs like that of the FLB, with a little alteration to the conceptualization.

The notion of a gift-giving mentality is proposed to explain why the official programs have been sustained for decades, even though they barely made any economic gains. Similar to the notion of a mentality, Chang Nam Fung, in line with Polysystem theory, speculates about "a general sense of self-insufficiency" (2015, p. 102) as a norm governing Chinese government-run outbound translation, which was "initiated by and carried out in the source culture for its own consumption" (Chang, p. 103). Chang is partially right about the consumption rhetoric, but the fact of poor reception does not necessarily mean that outbound translation in China is not undertaken for foreign consumption. The misunderstanding of poor reception as an indication of "translation for its own consumption," I will demonstrate, can be corrected if we can figure out the reasons that such programs have continued despite being received ineffectively by their target readers.

Drawing on the above selective but representative research, and building on McDougall's notion of gift exchange, this article will explore what mentality has sustained programs like PBS in the specific Chinese context. That exploration will be preceded by a brief survey of what was translated and how the program was generally received by its English readership. Gift exchange, according to McDougall, implies equal, fair transactions and accessible communication between two parties. The concept of gift-giving, in contrast, highlights the giver's initiative and unilateral self-profit. Behind China's gift-giving in this situation lurks polymorphous values, some originating from Chinese traditional culture, some from modern politics and others from modern nationalism. Which values grow predominant is, to a large degree, dependent on specific contexts. Moreover, this article argues that PBS was part of a discourse of "walking toward the world" especially prevalent in the last two decades of the 20th century in the Chinese mainland. Central to the discourse is a conviction that China is entitled to give its excellent literature as gifts to others, sometimes asking for nothing in return, while at other times expecting an acknowledgement of its excellence in terms of literature, culture or other aspects. Gift-giving mentality can be part of a framework to understand how self-perception works in the case of PBS.

Production and reception of PBS

The Panda Books Series was modeled on Penguin paperbacks, and was proposed by Yang Xianyi, a distinguished translator of Chinese classics (Gittings, 2009). PBS was first initiated by the FLB in 1981 and ended in 2007. In the first six years of its circulation, it was under the direction of the editorial office of *Chinese Literature*. This was a monthly journal with English and French versions specializing in introducing Chinese literature and culture to foreign countries, first published during the turbulent years of the Cold War when China was engaged in ideological confrontations with many western capitalist countries, the United States of America foremost among them.

The FLB or Foreign Languages Bureau, now referred to as the China Foreign Languages Publication Administration, is a government-affiliated agency with a complicated history of restructuring since its inauguration on the day when the People's Republic of China was founded, 1 October 1949. The bureau was initially named the International Press Bureau of General Administration of Information of the Central Government of China. Two years later, the journal of *Chinese Literature* English version was in print. Yang Xianyi and his wife Gladys Yang, together with other Chinese and foreign staff members, were employed there. The French version began publication in 1968. In 1952, the International Press Bureau was reorganized into the Foreign Languages Press, which was then renamed the Foreign Languages Bureau in September 1963, under the direct leadership of the Publicity Department of the Chinese Communist Party; later in the 1970s the Ministry of Foreign Affairs took over its operation. In 1986, the Chinese Literature Press was set up as an independent branch to take full control of PBS. This continued until 2000, when the press was closed, and all the editorial work and translation was transferred to the Foreign Languages Press within FLB until 2007, when PBS's work came to a halt. The journal Chinese Literature, the Chinese Literature Press, and the Foreign Languages Press are all subsidiaries of FLB.[1]

During the years from 1981 to 2007, PBS produced about 200 titles in translation, 134 of which are in English, 66 in French, two in Japanese, one in German and one in a four-language version (Chinese, English, French and Japanese) (Xu, 2005, pp. 19–21; Geng, 2010, p. 46). Some titles were reprinted two times or more due to better circulation. If reprints are included, their English translations amounted to 219 items, 195 of which were published before 2000.[2]

Most of the translations in PBS were literary, including the primary categories of fiction, poetry and drama. In addition, other less popular categories encompassed prose, reportage, biography, travelogue and documentary writing. A few were practical texts related to Chinese culture in general, cuisines, costumes, buildings, Chinese comic dialogue, Taiji and arts in particular. The following table gives a general picture of the genres that were covered in PBS.

As Table 4.1 shows, what gets translated most into English is fiction, with 92 titles out of 134. Among the ten titles of poetry, only one is by a modern poet, Ai Qing, best known for his political lyrics popular around 1949 when new China was founded. The remaining nine are classical. Further analysis indicates that about 75% of the titles were modern and contemporary literature (Geng, 2010, p. 50), which demonstrates that Chinese literature of the 20th century is what PBS wanted most to spread to the outside world. Additionally, women writers in modern China were in PBS' favorite lists. A few women writers were selected for translation in the 1980s, even though by then most of them had not yet gained much literary fame in China. They included, among others, Wang Anyi, Chi Li, Zhang Kangkang, Fang Fang, Zhang Xinxin and Can Xue.[3]

How outbound translation like that of PBS was received in the target cultures is crucial to the realization of its publishers' intentions, whether they be political or poetical. According to Qiang Geng (2014), PBS was distributed through multiple channels, including subsidiary book dealers set up by FLB in the target cultures (UK & USA), some small local book shops, libraries listed in book exchange programs with their counterparts in China, gift-giving via personal contacts and Chinese embassies and consulates in the target countries. However, it failed to enter into mainstream distribution systems in the target cultures. Statistics, gleaned from target sources like book reviews (in professional and non-professional journals and newspapers), research articles, criticism, readers' responses, focused interviews and library collections, provide evidence that about 10% of the English titles from PBS won positive responses from professional readers or readers whose research was related to Chinese affairs. That 10% of well-received books included *At Middle Age* by the woman writer Shen Rong; *Heavy Wings* and *Love Must not Be Forgotten* by the woman writer Zhang Jie; a collection of short stories, *Seven Contemporary Chinese Women Writers*; and *A Small Town Called Hibiscus* by Gu Hua; these texts were reprinted from two to seven times before the mid-1990s and were welcomed among English readers (Yang, 2002, 266; McDougall, 2011, p. 42). Given the fact that almost 90% of FLB-published literature was unknown to English-speaking audiences, a gap existed between the FLB's intentions to push Chinese literature via PBS to "walk toward the world" and its real-life reception. This phenomenon cannot be fully explained until we have insight into why PBS was initiated in a post-Mao era.

Table 4.1 Diversified genres of PBS in English titles

Literature				Non-literature
Fiction	Poetry	Drama	Others (prose, report, biography, etc.)	16
92	10	1	15	

Gift-giving mentality behind outbound translation

It has been widely acknowledged that translation is produced within local contexts where participants, from individuals to institutes, always have some purposes to fulfill, whether they be to construct images of self or other, to consolidate the soft power of a state, or simply to introduce new items to renovate the domestic literary repertoire. Outbound translation in China has been highly mediated through strict systems and hierarchies whose ideologies were especially perceptible in the post-1949 years when a new national state adhering to Marxist and Maoist thought was established. Party ideology mediated the whole society vertically and pervasively in the first three decades before China reformed its economic system and adjusted its political apparatus in the final years of the 1970s. Even within the newly flexible political climate in the 1980s, Party ideology still informed the initiation of PBS and what could be selected for translation. However, even in a hierarchical organization like the FLB, we cannot simply conclude that the program is solely a product of Party ideology.

Gift-giving mentality: a definition

As will be illustrated, PBS was sustained by a gift-giving mentality, which here refers to a sense of necessity or responsibility felt by the contributors to give translated Chinese literature as gifts to foreign countries. As a social phenomenon, gift-giving itself has received sustained research by scholars including James Frazer (1918); Marcel Mauss (1966); Pierre Bourdieu (1986); in addition, Yang Lien-sheng (1981); and Mayfair Mei-hui Yang (1994) pointed out the logic of reciprocity behind the concept.

Gift-giving mentality in the context of FSB-published translations comprised three components. First was a perception, and sometimes even a taken-for-granted view, of the excellence of one's own literature and culture – at the very least, an understanding that the gifts are not inferior to their western counterparts. Second, a conviction that if givers favor a thing, recipients would be likely to find it enjoyable too and at least should not refuse the offer whether they like it or not. Givers, of course, can be individuals or agencies like the FLB. Third, gift-giving implies an act of *givism* in which the givers take the initiative to offer gifts, since recipients may not know enough about what's available to identify the texts that can best represent Chinese literature and culture.

Gift-giving: personal ethics and diplomatic assertion

Gift-giving changes its forms and meanings according to evolving contexts where restraints of politics and poetics, ethos and pathos mediate the interaction between givers and recipients across cultural boundaries.

Prior to China's direct contact with western powers in the mid-19th century, the enactment of gift-giving mentality was primarily concerned with personal ethics and then with cultural self-assertion in diplomatic contexts. In Book 15 of

The Analects of Confucius, Zigong, one of Confucius' disciples, asks his master if there is a single word that can guide a person's conduct throughout life. The Master suggested the word "reciprocity," explaining that "What you do not want others to do to you, do not do to others."[4] (Confucius, 2007, p. 109). "Reciprocity" implies benefits for both sides. But Confucius argued in the negative that if a person does not want others to do something to him, he should not do the same to others, indicating something bad and undesired.

If one favors something, however, is he right to expect others to like it in the same way? In the case of gift-giving, the givers prefer to offer gifts that they believe are good, high-quality, enjoyable items, which recipients would have no reason to refuse. However, this can be a self-centered kind of generosity, with no acknowledgement of a diversity of possible reactions from the recipients.

Self-centered generosity is visible in some notable historical diplomatic events. One such example occurred during the Qing Dynasty (1636–1912), when at the reception rite, Emperor Qian Long (1711–1799) ordered a jade scepter called a *ruyi* (symbolizing peace and prosperity) to be given as a gift to George Macartney (1737–1806). Macartney the special envoy from Britain who led the first official delegation to visit China in 1793, hoped to establish diplomatic relations, a necessary preparation for future trade between the two countries. The emperor's gifts, however, were not highly valuable in the envoy's eyes.[5]

This act of gift-giving bespoke the giver's self-perception of his own culture as superior. The Emperor gave gifts in accordance with state-to-state etiquette, because Macartney had also brought gifts to celebrate his birthday. But gift-giving was more an act of benevolence by the Central Kingdom to show conciliation[6] to its neighbors considered geographically and culturally marginal. In this case, gift-giving enacted an assertion of self-regard and the superiority of Chinese culture, which did not necessitate an exchange.

Grabbism as a provision in crisis

That strong sense of cultural superiority soon gave way to a "Century of Humiliation" (Scott, 2008, p. xi) inflicted by China's successive defeats in wars with western powers since the Opium War in 1840. Cultural confidence has been cast in shadow, and has made the re-evaluation of Chinese culture more urgent among Chinese intellectuals in the face of an influx of western products, thought and cultures. The gift-giving mentality was replaced by "grabbism," a term coined by influential modern Chinese thinker and fiction writer Lu Xun (1881–1936). One decade prior to Xun,

Liang Qichao (1873–1929), a well-known intellectual in the late Qing Dynasty, was among the intellectuals arguing the superiority of western cultures, advocating "to save China by observing the ways the west practices"(Liang Qichao, 1896/2002, p. 139). Yan Fu (1854–1921), a peer of Liang's who was known as a pioneer in introducing western political, economic and ethical thought to China, held a similar view that China was defeated not for lack of guns, canons or war ships but for a deficiency of intellectual learning from the west. In a similar attitude, Lu Xun, in the wake of the May Forth Movement of 1919, advised Chinese youth that Chinese books were replete with "zombie's optimism" (Lu, 1925/1941, p. 14), while foreign books were alive in their freshness, even with some descriptions of "decadence and weariness of earthly affairs."

It is unsurprising then that the first half of the 20th century witnessed a strong movement to rebuild Chinese culture by absorbing knowledge from foreign cultures, and as a result, Lu Xun proposed "grabbism" (na lai zhu yi) as a cultural strategy to "grab something useful to us, but according to our own judgment and visions" (Lu, 1925/1941, p. 14). The particular historical Chinese diplomatic gift-giving mentality had waned, but historical change would cause its return.

Translation as gift after 1949

The founding of the People's Republic of China in 1949 necessitated the return of a gift-giving mentality in translating Chinese literature into English. Two missions had grown urgent for new China: building a modern nation-state guided by Marxism and Maoist Thought; and navigating the global cold war between the two influencers of socialist and capitalist countries, the Soviet Union and the United States. Given these circumstances, translation was used, first and foremost, to facilitate unified thought to serve the economic, social and cultural re-construction of a nearly ruined China after the Chinese Communist Party defeated the Nationalists in 1949. Outbound translation was then designed to broadcast what new China was undertaking, to increase mutual understanding, to win sympathy and to create a friendly international environment that would be safe for the forthcoming domestic re-construction on a large scale.

Additionally, gift-giving was symbolic of cultural mastery with confidence and pride in China's own gifts. The *Chinese Literature* journal's English version directed by the FLB aimed to "reflect the current life in China via translations" (Chen Yi, 1959/1999, p. 160). Readers could

> learn about Chinese literature through the journal, understand that China is supportive of peace and a peace lover; they can see how China rises from the past misfortunes, and wears a new look. If they keep reading it for a long enough time, they would nurture a sympathy toward us.
>
> (Chen Yi, 1963/1999, p. 316)

Therefore, translated literature became "the wisest politics, the most powerful ideology, because it allures others into a political trap with impressive artistic images" (Chen Yi, 1959/1999, p. 160).

Within that gift-giving mentality, outbound translation of literature did not require a financial return, but aimed to create political effects by drawing sympathy from readers who might have had neutral political positions. Participants, including translators, worked not purely for economic gains but primarily for political gains and to foster cultural pride. Further, the gift-giving mentality echoed the policy of a "United Frontline" that was adopted by the Chinese Communist Party, the purpose of which was to win cultural approval from Chinese intellectuals, who had aspired to cultural independence via translating Chinese literature into foreign languages.

Gift-giving with social and cultural meanings in a new era

In the 1980s, the relationship between politics and literature underwent an overhaul as a result of official denial of the extreme leftism that had been practiced during the Cultural Revolution. The Third Plenary Session of the 11th Central Committee of the Chinese Communist Party in 1978 included an impetus to shift from class struggle during Mao's era to economic construction via "Four Modernizations" of industry, agriculture, national defense, and science and technology, a prelude to the policy of opening-up and reform. "The extreme leftism and revolutionary insanity of building a modern utopia gave way to a party line that featured a 'realistic' and economy-centered concern" (Hong, 2006, p. 225). According to the Marxist base/superstructure framework, socialist modernization was not only "a grand revolution in the fields of economy and technology, but also a grand revolution occurring to the whole superstructure with ideology as part of it" (Zhou, 1979).

The CCP took initiatives to adjust its policy concerning literature and art to soften its politically informed concept of "literature and art [being] subjected to and in [the] service of politics" (Mao, 1949, pp. 18–19). From that time, political intervention in literature and art decreased. As Deng Xiaoping (1979/1980, p. 7) stated in a congratulatory speech at the Fourth Congress of Chinese Literature and Art Workers held in Beijing in October 1979, "The Chinese Communist Party directs literature and art, not by giving orders; neither does it command a subjugation of literature and art to temporary, concrete and direct political missions." To Deng, literature and art had their own laws, which should be respected.

In that new climate, PBS translated Chinese literature, opening a window to allow foreign readers to perceive Chinese life and thereby to see a country ready to embrace the world, its people experiencing ups and downs, sorrow and happiness. As a form of gift-giving, authorities gave gifts not for free, but in order to correct the image that the west had about communist China in Mao's era and to ease the decades-long confrontation with western countries. A world with friendly neighbors would benefit China.

However, the Party did not change its strategy by which literature was utilized to serve the Party's current policies. The only difference was the imperative that the outbound translations were intended to serve: modernization instead of revolution. In order to project an image of China as open to reform, most literary works selected for translation were chosen to reflect how China had been undergoing great societal, political, and spiritual changes. During the decade from the late 1970s to the late 1980s, China's literary circles saw the emergence of "wound literature,"[7] "introspective literature,"[8] "reform literature,"[9] women's literature. Most of the translated titles were among the PBS translation lists. Authorities did not frown upon the choice of wound and introspective literatures, because their critique of extreme leftism, a mission carried out by intellectuals, fitted well into the Party's endeavor to correct its past wrongdoings.

However, the authorities' tolerance for dissident texts was at a relatively high threshold. Examples include the publication of the works of Bei Dao (pen name of Zhao Zhenkai, 1949–) as well as Lei Shuyan's "The Grass is Singing," a poem published in 1979 dedicated to the death of Zhang Zhixin (1930–1975), who was murdered in the Cultural Revolution because of her dissident ideas.

PBS status as a program controlled by a government agency could lead us to be suspicious of its relationship with Party ideology or to regard it as another example of government propaganda. This suspicion is understandable historically; however, the program was also part of a broader mentality of "walking toward the world" that prevailed in China in the 1980s, when phenomena such as women's volleyball in sports, the Yellow River rafting and the like were used to demonstrate Chinese people's excellence in body and spirit. In those new circumstances, a gift-giving mentality drove most traditional intellectuals to promote Chinese literature in international circles via outbound translation in order to gain acknowledgement of China's lost glory and to signal a revival of Chinese culture.

The freer political climate gave Yang Xianyi (1915–2009) much more freedom in selecting texts for translation (Yang, 2002, p. 265). Throughout the 1980s, when he was in charge of PBS, works revisiting the trauma inflicted by the Cultural Revolution on individuals and the state were in translation lists. This became possible because both authorities and intellectuals needed to be able to criticize the extreme leftism of the recent past to enable renewed thinking suitable for the "Four Modernizations." Works were increasingly selected because their aesthetic value was demonstrated by receiving the top domestic literary prizes such as the Mao Dun Literary Prize and the Lu Xun Literary Prize. For this reason, works by prize winners such as Gu Hua, Shen Rong, and Tie Ning were included in the program. The selections reflected a strategy of choosing works primarily according to their poetical values. But political concerns were also lurking behind the scenes. The case of Bei Dao's exclusion from the program attested to the political realities with which Yang Xianyi and his successor had to comply.

Givism with a strand of nationalism

Along with political, ethical and cultural concerns, the gift-giving mentality was also informed by a strain of nationalism. This was well illustrated in a series of articles published in China in the 1990s by Ji Xianlin (1911–2009), an influential Chinese philologist and intellectual. He proposed that China should adopt the policy of "givism" (song qu zhu yi) as a useful remedy to Lu Xun's "grabbism." In the words of Ji, "Today, in addition to the practice of 'grabbism,' we have ample reason to advocate the policy of 'givism,' which should be prescribed as our priority" (Ji, 1996/2006, p. 26). One of the motives for prioritizing "givism" was a strong belief in the values of the gifts. As Ji stated, "What are laid before us are pearls, but to other people, especially westerners, who just have no interest, what else we can do about it? We will give them as gifts to others if they do not come for it" (Ji, 2000/2006, p. 189).

The proposition of "givism," he further argued in another article, was based on the foundational contrast between western and eastern cultures' thinking patterns. Western culture, in Ji's words, is basically analytical, in that the world is broken down infinitely into its smallest components. This causes many problems in understanding the world. These problems could potentially be solved by listening to and considering contributions provided by Chinese culture, a culture featuring a mode of dealing with matters via synthesizing. Used together, Chinese thought and western thought can provide solutions to the problems facing the whole human race, from environmental deterioration to racial discrimination to western centrism and Eurocentrism.

Based on this argument, Ji made a bold prediction, confidently but also rather questionably, as to how power between the two cultures would be balanced in years to come:

> When entering the 21st century, western culture will inevitably make place for [its] eastern counterpart, thus ushering [in] a new era for humanity's cultures to develop. As the old Chinese saying goes, a river flows west-bound for the first thirty years, but will change its course to flow east-bound in the next thirty years.
>
> (Ji, 2006a, p. 11)

Ji's message is clear. Chinese culture is about to rise so as to best its western counterparts in the 21st century. Accordingly, the treasures of Chinese culture, including canonical works of Chinese thought, philosophy, literature and so on. shall be introduced to the outside world. The purpose of giving gifts is, as Ji argued, not for pursuing sinocentrism, but because "we do it for the benefits and future of the whole world, and will persist in doing it whether the west will accept it or not" (Ji, 1996/2006, p. 26).

Alongside that motive, another purpose that Ji ascribes to this giving of translations warrants attention. The gift-giving is also performed to realize "a utopia where all [the] human race enjoys prosperity" (Ji, p. 29). In another article, Ji argues that to give the best parts of Chinese culture to western countries is to fulfill our obligations in a spirit of internationalism. This spirit of internationalism and the perpetual pursuit of cosmopolitanism originates from a long-held conviction of "compatibility in diversity" (Yue, 1996, p. 22), a notion deeply ingrained in Chinese culture.

The gift-giving mentality includes the belief that to translate Chinese literature for the outside world is to realize a harmonious world, a world united by a common interest but also preserving diversity. This idea of translation contrasts with the framework of conflict, by which "the discursive negotiation of conflictual and competing narratives is realized in and through acts of translation and interpreting" (Baker, 2006, p. 1)

To summarize, political, cultural, ethical and national factors inform how a gift-giving mentality has sustained outbound translation. As Ji argued, gift-giving "has significance in both political and academic terms" (2000/2006c, p. 190).

Conclusion

Unlike target-oriented translation, Panda Books Series is source-initiated by the Foreign Languages Bureau, a government-affiliated agency, to promote Chinese literature to the world. The long history of outbound translation in China from 1949 onwards has offered us a chance to rethink assumptions about translation as necessarily initiated by target cultures. It is important to recognize that outbound translation serves the needs of the source cultures, as is illustrated by this case in the Chinese context, where politics and Party ideology have played dominant roles in determining the intellectual climate. Governmental insistence on mass-production of translation over decades necessitates serious and critical reflection on what has sustained programs of this sort, particularly when the reception is far from successful.

PBS was succeeded by much bigger programs: in 1995 by the Library of Chinese Classics and in 2004 by the China Books International, both of which are also run by government-affiliated agencies. But the gift-giving mentality behind those ambitious programs still motivates both agencies as well as intellectuals to offer Chinese literature as gifts to others. This mentality includes the beliefs that the gifts given are good quality and trustworthy. since the givers treasure the gifts; that the receivers have no reason to refuse them; and that the Chinese people are entitled to give their literature to foreign readers, who otherwise would be unaware of the value of Chinese literature for lack of access to it.

As the political, economic and societal milieus have changed over the course of history, the gift-giving mentality has, like a prism, reflected different facets of the thinking patterns of the Chinese people. Originally dominated by a sinocentric imagining of the world, gift-giving once displayed a strong sense of superiority over "uncivilized" neighbors and was given with no expectation of exchange. The century-long incursions by the west since the mid-19th century had suppressed gift-giving activity, fomenting advocacy of "grabbing" "spiritual food" from the west for cultural rebuilding. The founding of new China in 1949 renewed the Chinese people's confidence through socialism, simultaneously demanding a regaining of cultural superiority over western capitalist cultures. Because of that imperative, outbound translation of Chinese literature becomes indispensable to the agenda of nationalism. Gifts were then given in exchange for sympathy and support from the target readers, partly to raise support for domestic revolution and construction, and at the same time partly to satisfy the century-long pursuit of cultural excellence among intellectuals. In the 1980s, when political forces loosened their grip on literature, the new outbound translation program of PBS was initiated to allow foreign countries to have a glimpse into Chinese life and its impressive literatures. At that point in the evolution of the gift-giving mentality, authorities and intellectuals could cooperate in making Chinese literature greater again by translating and introducing it to the outside world, whether it is accepted or not. If the gifts are refused, more should be given, according to the gift-giving logic, until the imagined receivers come to realize their value.

Despite the changing contexts, the gift-giving mentality assumes an asymmetrical power relation between givers and receivers, contrary to McDougall's conceptualization of an equal and free gift-exchange. As China grows more visible in the international arena in proportion with its increasing economic and political powers, the gift-giving mentality is more likely to include concepts of changing balances of power in which it is time for China to be the decision-maker. The outbound translation programs in China will likely continue in the foreseeable future, despite the reception of most of the translations, which do not live up to the gift-givers' satisfaction. However, this does not mean that those translations are initiated merely for the satisfaction of the givers. The translations are intended for the foreign readers, even though they are not received exactly as intended according to the givers' mentality. It may be the right time to give serious reflection to the "reciprocity" in Confucius' rhetoric that is so central to Chinese culture, and ask if others truly want those gifts.

Notes

1 As to the history of FLB, sources of information are referred to the official website of China Foreign Languages Publication Administration, which is www.cipg.org.cn/jqgl/, visited on November 22nd, 2018.
2 Since English translations far outnumber French versions, unless stated otherwise, the following analysis will be only drawn from the English versions.
3 Most of them were born around 1950. Some of them have now gained more international visibility due to their works being translated into English, including Wang Anyi, a Shanghai-based writer who is known for her work *Song of Everlasting Sorrow* (2008) and Can Xue (a pen name of Deng Xiaohua), an avant-garde fiction writer in China.
4 All the quotes from Chinese sources, unless otherwise stated, are my translations.
5 James L. Hevia (1995, pp. 93, 106, 110), through his analysis of many sources including Macartney's diaries, demonstrates in his monograph *Cherishing Men from Afar: Qing Guest Ritual and the Macartney Embassy of 1793* (1995) that neither side brought enough curiosity and/or positivity to the gifts they received in the exchange.
6 In Emperor Qian Long's edict on the sixth day of August in the fifty-eighth year of his reign, he stated: if the English envoy shows respect and submission with sincerity to us, we shall conciliate them with act of benevolence. Archives of the Imperial Cabinet. (First Historical Archives of China, 1996, p. 13).
7 Wound literature, also called Scar literature, was designated from Lu Xinhua's short fiction *The Wound* (1978). The theme of Wound literature reflects a painfully emotional denouncement of the trauma caused by the Cultural Revolution to the Chinese people.
8 Introspective literature as a phenomenon was popular in China in the first half of the 1980s. Unlike wound literature, it goes farther into the history to rationally reflect on the absurdity of the Cultural Revolution.
9 Reform literature was produced as a direct reflection on the reforms that China initiated in 1978 and the subsequent changes to the country and its society.

References

Baker, M. (2006). *Translation and conflict: A narrative account*. Routledge.

Bourdieu, P. (1986). The forms of capital. In J. G. Richardson (Ed.), *Handbook of theory and research for the sociology of education* (pp. 241–258). Greenwood Press.

Chang, N. F. (2015). Auto-image and norms in source-initiated translation in China. *Asia Pacific Translation and Intercultural Studies*, 2, 96–107.

Chen, Y. (1959, June 9). Speech by comrade Chen Yi at editorial office of Chinese literature. In Dongyuan Zhou & Wengong Qi (Eds.). (1999), *Selected works and documentary of historical materials of China Foreign Languages Bureau Vol. 1 (1950–1981)* (pp. 160–165). New Star Press.

Chen, Y. (1963, August 3). Documentary of discussion hosted by comrade Chen Yi on behalf of Foreign Affairs Office of the State Council of the P. R. of China over the work of Chinese literature. In Dongyuan Zhou & Wengong Qi (Eds.). (1999), *Selected works and documentary of historical materials of China Foreign Languages Bureau Vol. 1 (1950–1981)* (pp. 310–323). New Star Press.

Confucius. (2007). *The analects of Confucius* (B. Watson, Trans.). Columbia University Press.

Deng, X. (1979, October 30). Congratulations by Deng Xiaoping on behalf of the Central Committee of Communist Party of China and the State Council at the Fourth Congress of Chinese literature and art workers. In China Federation of Literary and Art Circles (Ed.). (1980), *Collected papers of the Fourth Congress of Chinese Literature and Art Workers* (pp. 1–8). Sichuan People's Press.

First Historical Archives of China. (Ed.). (1996). *Collection of historical archives of English envoy of George Macartney's visit to China*. International Cultures Publishing.

Frazer, J. G. (1918). *Folk-lore in the Old Testament: Studies in comparative religion legend and law* (Vol. 2). Macmillan.

Geng, Q. (2010). *Chinese literature walking toward the world through literary translating: A study of English translation in Panda Books Series* (Unpublished doctoral dissertation). Shanghai International Studies University, Shanghai.

Geng, Q. (2014). Effect of government-sponsored translation model: A case study of Panda Books Series. *Comparative Literature in China*, 1, 65, 66–77.

Gittings, J. (2009, November 23). Yang Xianyi obituary: Distinguished translator of Chinese classics jailed during the cultural revolution. *The Guardian*. Retrieved from https:/// www.theguardian.com/world/2009/nov/23/yang-xianyi-obituary

Hevia, J. L. (1995). *Cherishing men from afar: Qing guest ritual and the Macartney Embassy of 1793*. Duke University Press.

Holmes, J. S. (2000). The name and nature of translation studies. In L. Venuti (Ed.), *Translation studies reader* (pp. 172–185). Routledge. (Original work published 1972)

Hong, Z. (2006). *A history of contemporary Chinese literature*. Peking University Press.

Ji, X. (2006a). 21st century: An era for cultures in the orient. In Xianlin Ji (Ed.), *Thirty years flowing eastward, afterwards thirty years flowing westward* (pp. 11–14). Contemporary China Publishing House.

Ji, X. (2006b). Advocation for compilation of *Cultures in the Orient Series*. In Xianlin Ji (Ed.), *Thirty years flowing eastward, afterwards thirty years flowing westward* (pp. 20–29). Contemporary China Publishing House. (Original work published 1996)

Ji, X. (2006c). We shall adopt the principle of *"Givism"*. In Xianlin Ji (Ed.), *Thirty years flowing eastward, afterwards thirty years flowing westward* (pp. 188–190). Contemporary China Publishing House. (Original work published 2000)

Liang, Q. (2002). On translating books. *Common logic of reform* (pp. 139–161). Huaxia Publishing House. (Original work published 1896)

Lonsdale, A. B. (2011). Directionality. In M. Baker & G. Saldanha (Eds.), *Routledge encyclopedia of translation studies* (pp. 84–87). Routledge.

Lu, X. (1925, Feburary 10). Books recommended for the youth: At the request of *Peking Newspaper Supplement*. Memorial Committee for Mr. Lu Xun (Ed.). (1941), *Huagaiji* (p. 14). Publishing House for Complete Works of Lu Xun.

Mao, Z. (1949). *Talks at the Yenan forum on literature and art* (2nd ed.). Liberation Press.

Mauss, M. (1966). *The gift: Forms and functions of exchange in archaic societies* (Ian Cunnison, Trans.). Cohen & West.

McDougall, B. S. (2011). *Translation zones in modern China: Authoritarian command versus gift exchange*. Cambria Press.

Reng, D., & Gao, Y. (2015). National translation program: A new concept. *Foreign Languages in China, 3*, 92–97, 103.

Scott, D. (2008). Preface: The "century of humiliation" as a retrospective icon. In D. Scott (Ed.), *China and the international system, 1840–1949: Power, presence, and perceptions in a century of humiliation* (pp. xi–xii). State University of New York Press.

Toury, G. (2012). *Descriptive translation studies and beyond* (revised edition). John Benjamins Publishing.

Xie, T. (2014). How Chinese literature going globally: Problems and solutions. *Comparative Literature in China* (1), 1–10.

Xu, S. (2005). A survey on Panda Books Series by Chinese Literature Press. *Everlasting Green Mountains* (4), 19–21.

Yang, L.-S. (1981). The concept of Pao as a basis for social relations in China. In J. K. Fairbank (Ed.), *Chinese thought and institutions* (D. Changguo, L. Renni, & Z. Yongtang, Trans., pp. 349–372). Linking Publishing. (Original work published 1957)

Yang, M. M.-H. (1994). *Gifts, favors and banquets: The art of social relationships in China*. Cornell University Press.

Yang, X. (2002). *White tiger: An autobiography of Yang Xianyi*. The Chinese University Press.

Yue, D. (1996). Cultural relativism and the principle of "compatibility in diversity". *Comparative Literature in China* (1), 22–28.

Zheng, Y. (2012). *The production and circulation of the translation of Chinese literature under the patronage of Chinese government: A case study of Chinese literature (English version, 1951–2000)* (Unpublished doctoral dissertation). Shanghai International Studies University, Shanghai.

Zhou, Y. (1979, February 2). On the issues of literature and arts during socialist new era: Talks at Guangdong forum on literature creation in December 1978. *People's Daily*, pp. 23–24.

Part II

Translations for the page and stage

5 Regarding *Lady Precious Stream*

A theatrical translation

Nicholas Jose

A Chinese play in English

The curious phenomenon of the play *Lady Precious Stream*, written originally in English by S. I. Hsiung and first published in 1934, has attracted fresh attention in recent years (Du, 2016; Ma, 2018; Ma & Xingzhong, 2017; Shen, 2006; Thorpe, 2016, pp. 103–133, 2019; Tian, 2017; Xiao, 2011; Yeh, 2014; Yeh, 2015; Zheng, 2015, 2017).[1] This comes after the decades of relative neglect into which Hsiung's "Chinese play in English" had fallen towards the end of the 20th century after its extraordinary triumph on stage in London in 1934 and then in New York and around the world. Diana Yeh described its worldwide success:

> Following its West End success, the production toured local theatres: the play, adopted as a staple by repertory and amateur groups, was performed throughout Britain. With the income from production rights, Hsiung bought back the family land – a half-mountain of tea-plants and rice fields – that his father had once squandered away. When *Lady Precious Stream* was republished in 1937 as a Methuen Modern Classic, it was adopted as a classroom text by hundreds of schools, shaping understandings of Chineseness in the minds of thousands of children. In 1938, Michael Barry produced it for the BBC; it was subsequently translated into several European languages – French, German, Dutch, Italian, Greek, Spanish, Polish and Romanian – and performed or broadcast throughout much of Europe as well as America, Israel and the British colonies from Hong Kong to Ceylon, from Trinidad to South Africa.
>
> (Yeh, 2014, p. 48)

It proved very successful in Australia, for example, where it was performed regularly into the 1970s.

The 21st century has given renewed visibility to Hsiung and his work, certainly as a subject of scholarly interest, if not yet a full-scale revival on the mainstream stage. That may yet happen in the unlikely career of this play. Ashley Thorpe, who mounted a workshop performance at the University of Reading and in London in 2011, calls it "without doubt, the most globally successful Chinese play" ever (Thorpe, 2019, p. 84).[2]

Lady Precious Stream faded from view at the same time as China stepped out onto the world stage following the Cultural Revolution (1966–76). New images of China replaced the old as access to and knowledge of Chinese culture improved. With more active cultural exchange between China and the West and a growing Chinese diaspora in many Western countries, there was a widespread determination to put an end to stereotypes that reflected the *chinoiserie* of earlier times, such as the haughty, inept patriarch and his long-suffering, constrained daughter.

Sha Yexin's absurdist drama *If I Were Real* (1983) and Chen Kaige's film *Yellow Earth* (1984) showed a tougher side of Chinese life with a more critical edge. It was easy to dismiss *Lady Precious Stream* as an unfashionable, embarrassing case of Orientalism that had served imperialist ends.

More recent ideas of hybridity, the transnational and the transcultural, however, together with a more nuanced understanding of the process, function and scope of literary translation, have complicated this picture. Work by theorists such as Susan Bassnett, *Translation Studies* (1980); Homi K. Bhabha, *The Location of Culture* (1994); Lydia Liu, *Translingual Practice* (1995); Naoki Sakai, *Translation and Subjectivity* (1997); and Douglas Robinson, *The Dao of Translation* (2015), to name only a few key texts, have enabled a new generation of scholars to revisit Hsiung's singular achievement with enhanced appreciation. *Lady Precious Stream* is a fascinating case. In the context of concern with the translation of contemporary Chinese literature, there are two questions to ask: Is *Lady Precious Stream* even a translation? Does it belong to modern Chinese literature? My answer to both questions is a qualified "yes." Then there is the further question of its unparalleled success. What is the work's secret? The answer to that lies partly in its timing, I will argue, but no less in its effectiveness in translating one great theatre tradition into another.

"The most globally successful Chinese play"

The reconsideration of S. I. Hsiung has been greatly assisted by Diana Yeh's biographical study *The Happy Hsiungs: Performing China and the Struggle for Modernity* (2014) which recovered the "lost histories" of the playwright Shih-I and his wife Dymia and supplied much valuable information about the author. Yeh also explores the larger issue of "their role in representing China and Chineseness to the rest of the world" (Yeh, 2014, pp. 4–5). Shih-I Hsiung (熊式一, Xiong Shiyi in standard pinyin, 1902–91) and Dymia Hsiung (蔡岱梅, Cai Daimei, 1905–87) were both born in Nanchang in Jiangxi Province, China. They had five children. The family moved between London, Beijing and Taipei; Dymia is buried in Hampstead Cemetery. Shih-I, an "anti-Communist all [his] life," returned after half a century to Beijing from Nationalist Taiwan, where he had lived since the early 1980s. On a second return trip to Beijing in 1992 he made the decision to stay there, only to die two weeks later (Yeh, 2014, pp. 143–144). Three of his children had returned to China from Britain in the 1950s, becoming involved in the making of the New China under Mao Zedong. One of them was Xiong Deni (熊德輗, 1927–2015), who taught translation studies at Beijing Foreign Studies University.

Lady Precious Stream begins on New Year's Day when Precious Stream's father, Prime Minister Wang Yun, orders a feast in the garden "to enjoy the snow (Hsiung, 1938, p. 7). His two elder daughters assemble with their unappealing husbands. All want the youngest daughter to please her father by making an acceptable match – the suitor who will catch the embroidered ball she throws from the pavilion. The gardener proves himself by besting the two sons-in-law in contests of strength and cultivation – then he gets the ball, as per Precious Stream's plan. Most of this is Hsiung's own embroidery on the basic plot line of the Chinese opera, with the snow scene a particularly enchanting touch, inspired by Chinese poetic tradition (Zheng, 2017, p. 30).

Act II jumps to the cave where the now-married couple are living in poverty. Hsieh is rewarded for killing a menacing tiger "with a red mane" by being made a captain and ordered to join an expedition to the Western Regions under the command of his hostile brothers-in-law. He must abandon his new bride. Precious Stream's mother comes to rescue her beloved daughter from this fate, but the virtuous young woman insists on staying in the cave.

Act III takes us to the Western Regions where Hsieh has been crowned king for the good service he has rendered the Princess there. She wants to marry him. But a wild goose flies by bearing a message from Precious Stream, who is still waiting for her husband in the cave, suffering as she has "for eighteen long years" of separation (Hsiung, 1938, p. 67). Hsieh responds to the wild goose's message by evading the Princess's marriage plans and gallops off to the frontier. There are three mountain passes to go through on the way back to China, which he manages cleverly and with much comedy, the feisty Princess in hot pursuit. At last she catches up with him. and he tells her about his wife who urgently awaits him. In the Chinese version, the Princess accepts the role of second wife. In Hsiung's version she somewhat implausibly agrees to accompany Hsieh to China as his "sister." In the end she is passed on to the Chinese Minister of Foreign Affairs. She asks him where he has learned his "charming manners." "In London," the Minister answers, in a line that surely got a laugh (Hsiung, 1938, p. 106).

The popularity of *Lady Precious Stream* in the 1930s is partly explicable in terms of sympathy for China in the face of Japanese militarism. The Treaty of Versailles in 1919 had favored Japan against China and led to the Japanese occupation of Chinese territory in the period that followed. This produced, by way of angry, passionate reaction, the patriotic New Culture Movement, of which Hsiung Shih-I was part. Japanese militarism culminated in the Sino-Japanese War (1936–45), of which the so-called Rape of Nanjing in 1937 is remembered as the worst among many atrocities. As Japanese depredations on Chinese soil, increased, in what marked the onset of world war in Asia and the Pacific, friends of China in the United States, Britain, Australia and elsewhere heeded China's call. Prominent Chinese figures in the West helped by advocating China's cause. and the political situation aroused sympathetic interest in Chinese culture. The 1935 Exhibition of Chinese Art at the Royal Academy was a major event in London. *The Good Earth* (1931), Pearl Buck's English-language novel of China, was an international bestseller, and she received the Nobel Prize for Literature in 1938. Hsiung and

Lady Precious Stream were enlisted in the "Aid China" campaign too; the play was seen as a product of an estimable culture that was under threat (Yeh, 2014, p. 69). Amy Dawson Scott, peace activist and the London founder of PEN, was an early admirer. Hsiung would become a Chinese delegate at the annual congress of the international organization of writers from 1934 on (Yeh, 2014, pp. 48, 70).

From London, *Lady Precious Stream* reached China too, where it was staged in Shanghai in 1935 by the newly formed International Arts Theatre, a collaborative venture of expatriate and local cultural figures. "The play was performed in English . . . with a cast of Chinese actors' (Bevan, 2016, p. 69). The lead was played by Tang Ying, who was described as "absolutely to the manner born" by the reviewer in the *North-China Herald* (Bevan, 2016, p. 69). She was approached for a New York production the following year and a film version that was under consideration by a Shanghai company, although neither project eventuated. When *Lady Precious Stream* opened on Broadway in 1936, the only part played by a Chinese national, on Hsiung's insistence, was the framing role of the Honourable Reader, which went to the daughter of the Chinese Ambassador to Washington, ensuring, in Diana Yeh's words, that the play served the interests of "the national Chinese subject (Yeh, 2014, p. 59)."

By the time W.H. Auden and Christopher Isherwood reached China in 1938, *Lady Precious Stream* was sufficiently famous for the director of China's Central News Agency to take the visitors to a performance of "the original Chinese version of the westernized play called *Lady Precious Stream*" (Auden & Isherwood, 1939, pp. 62–64). Again the play was felt to advance China's cause. The pair report vividly on the experience in *Journey to a War* (1939) in terms that closely echo Hsiung's introduction of the play for readers of the first English edition. For instance, Hsiung explains how: "when a player has . . . just finished [some long lines], [the property man] quietly presents to him or her a cup of tea to ease the throat (Hsiung, 1934, p. xvii). Auden and Isherwood make the same point in different words: "The stage-hands . . . occasionally coming forward to . . . offer a bowl of tea to refresh one of the singers after a difficult passage" (1939, p. 63). The play "has the marks of a fine culture," wrote another poet, Edmund Blunden (Hsiung, 1939, p. 165).

Lady Precious Stream in Australia: a brief stage history

The play spread rapidly through the Anglophone world. Its enthusiastic reception in Australia offers a pertinent case study, as the fate of Australia was perceived to be linked with that of China in a common experience of Japanese aggression. The earliest documented Australian production was in Sydney in 1936, featuring Doris Fitton and Sumner Locke Elliott. The cultural context of the play's staging was humanitarian and politically progressive. There was a Brisbane Repertory Theatre production later that same year, and another Sydney production. The play was performed at the University of Melbourne in 1943, produced by Mina Shelley and presented by the Australia-China Co-operation Association: "Proceeds for relief of the famine in China, where, in Honan province, millions of people are starving and dying daily through failure of the food crops and the ravages of war (Program ii, Figure 5.1).

The play also travelled beyond Sydney and Melbourne: there was a well-received production in Ballarat, Victoria, in 1948 directed by author Hal Porter, who made extravagant headgear for the production. The play was evidently a favorite of his. He had put it on at Prince Alfred's College, an all-boys school, in Adelaide, South Australia, in 1945, with "the School Captain in the title role": "*Lady Precious Stream* is very good," he later recalled. He produced it again in Tasmania at Hobart's Hutchins School the following year. By the time he got to Ballarat, Porter knew how to make it work: "I direct *Lady Precious Stream*, a chore, a habit I can perform with my back turned" (Porter, 1966, pp. 173, 226). Ballarat had a Chinese history and a resident population going back to the gold rush of the 1850s, which may have contributed to the popularity of the production. Porter was drawn to aspects of East Asian performativity like an addict, as he would claim later in *The Actors*, his book on Japan (Porter, 1968, p. 8). There was an all-girl student production from Star of the Sea Convent of Mercy in South Australia's Catholic Schools' Drama Festival in 1963, again in Adelaide.

There were no less than three productions of *Lady Precious Stream* in Sydney in 1961. A full production was directed by John Clark at the National Institute of Dramatic Art (NIDA). (For this and other information, see Ausstage: The Australian Live Performance Database. Clark had been a student at Hutchins School in Hobart and may have remembered Hal Porter's production.) NIDA's student cast included future luminaries of the Australian stage, among them Dennis Olsen, Anna Volska, Tessa Mallos, Barry Eggington and Rodney Fisher. Clark maintained his interest in

Figure 5.1 1943 Program of *Lady Precious Stream*

Asian performance in his subsequent role as artistic director of NIDA from 1969 to 2004, supporting creative exchanges with partner institutions in the Chinese world and encouraging greater diversity in the student population. Dennis Olsen, who helped backstage as well as playing the major role of the Prime Minister Wang Yun, had already acted in *Lady Precious Stream* in a production by the Therry Society at the Studio Theatre in Adelaide in 1959, where he played Second Attendant and the Minister of Foreign Affairs. The large cast of that production, directed by Mary O'Shaughnessy, included Patricia Pak Poy in the leading role. Pak Poy, born in Darwin in 1935, was Australian-born Chinese. Later, as a distinguished Sister of Mercy, she founded the Australian Network of the International Campaign to Ban Landmines. Dennis Olsen, born in Adelaide in 1938, went on to an illustrious stage career, with Ko-Ko in Gilbert and Sullivan's *The Mikado* as one of his signature roles. Perhaps his interpretation of that piece of Victorian *japanisme* was informed by *chinoiserie* memories of *Lady Precious Stream* in his youth.

Part of the appeal of *Lady Precious Stream* for community and school groups was its many roles. Another factor was the opportunity to play with Chinese elements such as costumes, props, make-up, music, movement – and sometimes people. There was little anxiety about "yellowface" in the period from the 1930s to the 1960s when *Lady Precious Stream* flourished on stages in the English-speaking world, performed by mostly non-Chinese actors. It was rumored that the Chinese-Australian star Rose Quong (1879–1972, born in Melbourne) might play the lead in the first London production, but that did not happen. The role eventually went to Maisie Darrell, a Caucasian actress. Another London Precious Stream, Australian-born Carol Coombe, was said to appear "thoroughly Chinese" and was photographed for the press using chopsticks (Woollacott, 2011, pp. 49–92; Yeh, 2014, pp. 42, 77).

The last documented production of *Lady Precious Stream* in Australia was in Melbourne in 1974 at the National Theatre Drama School under the direction of Joan Harris, though there may have been other school or amateur performances since (Cargher, 1974, p. 21). If a revival is overdue, Australia would be fertile ground for it, with its proximate and charged relationship with China in the present time, and forms of complicity, intimacy and wariness at all levels of society and government.

Lady Precious Stream as translation

S. I. Hsiung began as a translator, having studied English at high school and university in China. He soon dropped his academic aspirations for the new world of the movies – modern, cosmopolitan, entrepreneurial – and managed a few cinemas in Beijing and later, in Shanghai, the celebrated Pantheon Theatre. He translated "subtitles for silent movies and scripts for talkies" (Yeh, 2014, p. 21). But he was especially interested in spoken drama, a new art form imported from the West. Lu Xun admired Ibsen's power of social critique. Chekhov, Gorky and Eugene O'Neill provided further models of progressive drama. George Bernard Shaw, famously photographed with Lu Xun and educator Cai Yuanpei in Shanghai in

1933, was esteemed for similar reasons, along with British dramatists J M Barrie and John Galsworthy, all translated by Hsiung. Hsiung responded to the lightness of touch with which Barrie dealt with social issues, nowhere more so than in *Peter Pan* with its enduring mix of middle-class realism and escapist fantasy. Hsiung's Chinese translation was serialized by the Commercial Press in 1931 and enthusiastically received.

By the time he reached London in 1931, Hsiung had a practitioner's first-hand experience of adapting the foreign medium of spoken drama into a Chinese literary and theatrical context, including the conventions of the English stage that playwrights like Shaw and Barrie exploited so brilliantly. Rather than pursue spoken drama in vernacular Chinese, however, as his contemporaries Cao Yu (1910–96, author of *Thunderstorm*, 1933) and Lao She (1899–66, author of *Teahouse*, 1957) would do, Hsiung, encouraged by London friends, saw an opportunity to turn the tables and adapt Chinese theatre forms to an English stage.

Recent scholars have identified some of the many ways in which Hsiung's adaptation works: from a five or six hour *xiqu* (Chinese "opera") to a tight four-act play; the selective addition and omission of content to meet differing audience expectations; the cross-cultural substitution of comic effects; and the skilled use of paratexts (Ma, 2018; Ma & Xingzhong, 2016; Zheng, 2017). Da Zheng discusses a number of specific changes that helped to "ensure consistency, unity, and smooth flow" and revealed the "extraordinary . . . cultural sensitivity" evident in what he calls Hsiung's "re-creation" (Zheng, 2017, pp. 32, 33, 42). Thorpe attends to what happens in performance, off the page, as performers find a "hybridised performance style" to engage with the "self-conscious intercultural metatheatricality" of Hsiung's work. To put it another way, "the less seriously the actors took the text, the more the play came to life" (Thorpe, 2019, pp. 85, 90, 91).

Hsiung published a limited reading edition of *Lady Precious Stream* in 1934 with illustrations by two Chinese artist friends – four ink-and-brush paintings by Xu Beihong (1895–1953), ranked now among the greatest Chinese artists of the 20th century, and twelve wood-block prints by Chiang Yee (1903–77), author of the popular *Silent Traveller* series of books. The color plate image of the hero escaping from the Western Regions on horseback facing page 88 shows a typically dynamic Xu Beihong horse. A common name for the Chinese opera on which *Lady Precious Stream* is based is "The Red-Maned Fiery Steed" (*Hongzong Liema*).

Another name is *Wang Baochuan*, "Lady Precious Bracelet," the name of the heroine, which Hsiung subtly mistranslated to good effect. This reminds us that there is no original text, as such, of this work. Rather it was part of a continuing performance tradition, recited, sung, remembered, passed on, in changing styles and varying idioms and dialects (Cui, 2017; Hsiung, 1939, pp. 179–80). In that sense it was always contemporary as well as always traditional. That is what Hsiung does not tell us in his subtitle: "An Old Chinese Play Done Into English According to its Traditional Style." It is traditional *and* modern at the same time. Lin Yutang, reviewing the text in China in 1935, called it "eighty-five percent literal translation" (Lin, 1935, p. 107; Ma, 2018, p. 85). Hsiung reportedly chose *Wang Baochuan* to adapt because he saw the potential of the good woman at the centre of the drama to change the prevalent ideas of China and the Chinese in the Western imagination (Yeh, 2014, pp. 35–36). His re-creation fulfilled his purpose as a progressive, even patriotic entertainment that also promised – and delivered – commercial success.

Theatrical crossover

One factor in the success of *Lady Precious Stream* on stage was the evolution of the work through performance. After publishing the reading edition, Hsiung worked with Nancy Price as co-director on the production that opened in London's Little Theatre on 27 November 1934 and ran for a thousand nights. In 1938, an acting edition was published. The many changes made between these two editions reveal a process of sustained revision – a workshop process, in effect – as a Chinese-language original is creatively adapted into an English form that works with its audiences. Without knowing exactly who did what, we can conclude that the result was a highly attuned, mutually receptive collaboration between Hsiung, Price, the cast members and various offstage commentators to produce, in Thorpe's words, a "polysemic intercultural performance" with Chinese and English worlds working in partnership.

The major change was the introduction of a framing character called the Honorable Reader who ushers in each of the four acts with a courteously witty explanation of what is about to occur, interpreting the Chinese theatrical conventions in play. This character is the bridge between the stage world ("China") and the audience – an interpreter, a mediator. The words the Honorable Reader speaks come directly from the stage directions of the reading edition, which are elaborate and whimsical in the manner of Shaw and Barrie. The Honorable Reader represents the Chinese author/manager on stage. They are Hsiung's words in his authorial voice: the Honorable Writer.

In the London production, the part was played by a Caucasian male. In the New York production, it was played by a Chinese woman. Conventions varied thereafter. Thorpe regretted the "absence of an available actor of East Asian descent" for his 2011 staging, noting astutely that the framing presence of the Chinese author casts what was subsequently seen on stage as "imitation," a motley impersonation of China by actors who were not equipped with the full range of Chinese performance techniques (song, acrobatics, martial arts, etc.). In the 1934 reading edition, the stage directions had attempted to explain, for instance, how a horse is represented on a Chinese stage (with a horsewhip). In the 1938 acting edition, that convention was replaced with the sound of horses' hooves (the more familiar "clapping of coconut shells"; Thorpe, 2019, pp. 88, 91). Translation via theatre practice finds effective equivalents.

The sharpening of the repartee by making many small cuts is another feature of the translational changes from the reading to the acting edition. The formalities of farewell at the end of Act I, for example, are truncated when Precious Stream and Hsieh Ping-Kuei, the talented gardener she has chosen to marry in defiance of her parents, depart for their uncertain future. Instead there is a briefly stylized exchange of vows contrasted with equally taut denunciation:

HSIEH *(to audience)*. I will always honour you.

PRECIOUS S. *(to audience)*. And I will obey you.

HSIEH *(turns R. to* PRECIOUS STREAM*)*. I will protect you.

PRECIOUS S. *(turns L. to* HSIEH*)*. I will love you.

 (HSIEH *turns left and exits –* PRECIOUS STREAM *following.*)

WANG *(rising and going downstage –* MADAM *follows)*. Disgraceful!

WEI. Disgusting!

SILVER S. Scandalous!

WANG. Let us retire!

(Hsiung, 1938, p. 33)

The parallelism in these exchanges reflects the dramatic texture of Hsiung's re-creation throughout. Doubling, mirroring, mimicry, ironic reversals and repetitions with a twist characterize the bold dramaturgy with which he shapes the four-act version for the English stage of the 1930s. Hsieh Ping-Kuei and Precious Stream echo each other like Elyot and Amanda in Noel Coward's *Private Lives* (1930).

The second half of Act III includes the scene where the two lovers are reunited after long separation. In Chinese culture Wang Baochuan is an epitome of the loyal, long-suffering wife who waits for her husband's return over years of absence, infidelity, even reports of death: a Penelope figure to Homer's roaming Odysseus, "the man of twists and turns" (Fagles, 1996, p. 77). The reunion scene, known as "Wujia Slope," was popular with Chinese audiences as a stand-alone piece. It was part of the repertoire of Mei Lanfang, the celebrated Peking Opera performer who toured the world in the 1930s. The reunion involves recalling a riddle from the first scene, which the lovers repeat as a way of testing their true identity, despite the physical changes wrought by time. "Well, sir, do you understand riddles?" Precious Stream asks.

HSIEH. A little.

PRECIOUS S. Do you want to see Precious Stream?

HSIEH. Yes.

PRECIOUS S. Now, if you look far –

HSIEH. – she is a thousand miles away.

PRECIOUS S. Yes. And if you look near –

HSIEH. – she is before me. Am I speaking to Mrs. Hsieh, the famous daughter of the Prime Minster Wang?

PRECIOUS S. Oh, no, not the famous, but only the humble wife of Hsieh Ping-Kuei.

(Hsiung, 1938, p. 67)

The riddle's conjunction of distance and closeness takes on new meaning in the context of recognition across time and space and is a key instance of Hsiung's precise use of repetition with variation to develop the theme of perception and misperception.

In this scenario, the Western Regions are a proxy for the West, which includes the audience watching the play. The Royal Princess of the Western Regions can be imagined with her own "red mane" and green eyes: a Western performer who wears a dress instead of pants. The Honourable Reader sets up this two-way mirror at the start of Act III:

> HONOURABLE READER. We are now coming to a strange land known as the Western Regions. It is believed that the customs here are exactly opposite those of China. For instance, the women wear long gowns whilst the men wear short coats and have their trousers showing. Their appearance, too, is unusual. They have red hair, green eyes, prominent noses and hairy hands.
>
> The stage represents the magnificent court of the King of the Western Regions. Probably they have very queer furniture and very strange decorations. Indeed we would be quite at a loss to prepare the properties of this scene had we not the advantage of leaving the audience to furnish them according to their imagination.
>
> (Hsiung, 1938, p. 50)

A device from 18th-century *chinoiserie*, as exemplified in Olive Goldsmith's *The Citizen of the World* (1760–1761), by which an idealized China is used to satirize life in contemporary England, is reprised here. It achieves a simultaneous familiarization and estrangement. Bertolt Brecht would later advocate his more radical alienation effect in *Der gute Mensch von Sezuan* (*The Good Woman of Setzuan*, 1943 and *Der kaukasische Kreidekreis* (*The Caucasian Chalk Circle*, 1948), both retellings of Chinese tales, and in his influential essay "Alienation Effects in Chinese Acting," citing Mei Lanfang, whose performance in Moscow in 1935 he had witnessed (Bentley, 1966, p. 9; Tian, 1997, p. 201).

More broadly, Hsiung's dramaturgy works to find affinities in English plays familiar to his audience. The opening set-up with the domineering patriarch and his three daughters, the youngest of whom refuses to comply with his will, recalls *King Lear* in a different key, while the leap of eighteen years before the wayward husband can be wondrously redeemed has precedent in *The Winter's Tale*. The fourth act returns full circle to the scene of the first act after the pattern of Barrie's *The Admirable Crichton* (1902), which Hsiung had earlier translated into Chinese. Here the scene is the garden of the Prime Minister, "still the same old obstinate man" after the passage of years, but about to "have some unexpected shocks" (Hsiung, 1938, p. 80).

At the same time, the formulaic decorum of both Chinese and English societies are simultaneously mocked in the repetition of phrases such as, "Please don't stand on ceremony, but be seated," which makes for playful stage business (Thorpe, 2019, p. 90).

Conclusion

The larger significance of Hsiung's work as translation can be found in its sensitivity, as a light-hearted entertainment, to a pivotal phase of world history, the

dark clouds of which were already looming in East and West. The meaning –
or the meta meaning – of *Lady Precious Stream* lies in the mutual misprision it
dramatizes. This is one of the great themes of stage comedy – misidentification.
Here it not only operates at the level of character and plot, but is present in an
overarching conception, as two venerable cultures, each with long and strong theatrical traditions, misperceive each other. *Lady Precious Stream* is a staging of
misreading by a master stage manager. (For a parallel discussion, see Thorpe,
2016, pp. 103–133.)

If we consider the work in the long perspective of the understanding of the East
or Asia by the West over the three centuries from the Enlightenment to the first
half of the 20th century, we can share the conclusion reached by historian Jürgen
Osterhammel in his book *Unfabling the East* (2018). A felicitous mutuality of
esteem at the outset of the period gave way to a condescending sense of European
superiority by the end, which was a consequence of Western imperialism and
which produced the caricatures of Orientalism that Hsiung discusses in the After-
thought to his last play, *The Professor from Peking* (1939). As a translation by a
creative practitioner whose own fate hung in the balance then and thereafter, *Lady
Precious Stream* tips the balance back.

Hsiung understood what his compatriot Qian Zhongshu (Ch'ien Chung-shu,
钱锺书 1910–1998) observed as he reflected on these matters. The great Chinese
author and scholar studied in England and France from 1935–1938, experiencing
European attitudes to China at their most condescending. On his return to China
Qian recalled the craze for things Chinese in the 18th century, when the French
"admiration for China became excessive" and "the economies of entire regions of
China and India were geared towards the European export market" (Qian, 1941a,
p. 8; Osterhammel, 2018, p. 483). But the British were more ambivalent when it
came to the Chinese language, Chinese thought and literary production, and the
large civilizational question of China's capacity for modernity. Qian Zhongshu
magnanimously attributed this to an "inevitable loose-jointedness in generaliza-
tions about the spirit of the age." He saw the anti-Chinese attitudes expressed
satirically in 18th-century English literature as "a reaction against the popularity of
the Chinese taste in the English social life of the time" and judiciously concluded:

> Of course, free as they are from racial prejudices in their quest of wisdom
> and beauty, these writers do not see us as we in ourselves really are, and their
> views on things Chinese would furnish not a few significant examples to
> Samuel Butler's proposed "Essay on Human Misunderstanding."

He added: "To be so intelligently misunderstood is yet to be paid the compliment
of being worth understanding" (Qian, 1941b, pp. 8, 152). S. I. Hsiung might well
have agreed.

Notes

1 The author wishes to thank Ma Huijuan, who discussed *Lady Precious Stream* as a work
   of translation in a presentation she gave to the China Australia Transcultural Studies

(CATS) workshop at Beijing Foreign Studies University in November 2013. Thanks are also due to the Special Collections librarians at the Barr Smith Library, University of Adelaide; Julia Mant, archivist, National Institute of Dramatic Art, Sydney; Li Jianjun, Rodney Fisher, and Claire Roberts for their help. This research has been supported by the Australian Research Council Discovery Project 'Other Worlds: Forms of World Literature'.

2 Its only competitor, the Yuan dynasty play *The Orphan of Zhao*, translated into French in 1731 (the first Chinese play to be translated into any European language) and adapted by Voltaire as *Le orphelin de la Chine* in 1753, became popular in English in Arthur Murphy's version, *The Orphan of China* (1759). The Chinese original was adapted again for the Royal Shakespeare Company in 2012 by poet James Fenton. Yet *The Orphan of Zhao* has not enjoyed the wide international circulation of *Lady Precious Stream*. Orphan is a tragedy in lofty blank verse in which Chinese civilization is threatened by barbarian Tartars from the north. William Whitehead writes in his prologue: "On eagle wings the poet of to-night / Soars for fresh virtues to the source of light, / To China's eastern realms: and boldly bears / Confucius' morals to Britannia's ears"' (7–10). See also Thorpe (2016, pp. 25–50). Thorpe interprets the play in terms of its local British political context. Yet *The Orphan of China* also presents China as a civilizational counterpart to Britain (like Greece or Rome) in a way seldom seen again before the 21st century.

References

Auden, W. H., & Isherwood, C. (1939). *Journey to a war*. Faber & Faber.

Bassnett, S. (1980). *Translation studies*. Methuen.

Bentley, E. (Trans.). (1966). *Parables for the theatre: Two plays by Bertolt Brecht*. Penguin.

Bevan, P. (2016). *A modern miscellany: Shanghai cartoon artists, Shao Xunmei's circle and the travels of Jack Chen, 1926–1938*. Brill.

Bhabha, H. K. (1994). *The location of culture*. Routledge.

Cargher, J. (1974, December). New theatre for Melbourne. *Elizabethan Trust News, 13*.

Cui, H. (Trans.). (2017, June 1). Romance on an operatic stage. *Beijing (English)*, pp. 52–55. Retrieved from www.pressreader.com/china/beijing-english/20170601

Du Weihong. (2016). S.I. Hsiung: New discourse and drama in early modern Chinese theatrical exchange. *Asian Theatre Journal, 33*(2), 347–368.

Fagles, R. (1996). *Homer: The odyssey*. Viking.

Hsiung, S. I. (1934). *Lady Precious Stream: An old Chinese play done into English according to its traditional style*. Methuen.

Hsiung, S. I. (1939). *The professor from Peking*. Methuen.

Hsiung, S. I. (1971). *Lady Precious Stream: An old Chinese play done into English according to its traditional style* (Acting ed.). Methuen. (Original work published 1938)

Lin, Y. (1935). Review of the play *Lady Precious Stream*, by S. I. Hsiung. *T'ien Hsia Monthly, 1*, 106–110.

Liu, L. (1995). *Translingual practice: Literature, national culture, and translated modernity: China, 1900–1937*. Stanford University Press.

Ma, H. (2018). Hsiung's cultural translation of the Peking opera *Wang Baochuan*. In X. Song & Y. Sun (Eds.), *Transcultural encounters in knowledge production and consumption, encounters between East and West*. Springer Nature Singapore & Higher Education Press.

Ma, H., & Xingzhong, G. (2017). On the transcultural rewriting of the Chinese play *Wang Baochuan*. *Perspectives, 25*(4), 556–570.

Osterhammel, J. (2018). *Unfabling the East: The enlightenment's encounter with Asia* (R. Savage, Trans.). Princeton: Princeton University Press.

Porter, H. (1966). *The paper chase.* Angus & Robertson.

Porter, H. (1968). *The actors: An image of the new Japan.* Angus & Robertson.

Qian Zhongshu (Ch'ien Chung-shu). (1941a, December). China in the English literature of the eighteenth century. *Quarterly Bulletin of Chinese Bibliography* (New Series), *1*, 7–48.

Qian Zhongshu (Ch'ien Chung-shu). (1941b, December). China in the English literature of the eighteenth century. *Quarterly Bulletin of Chinese Bibliography* (New Series), *2*, 113–152.

Robinson, D. (2015). *The Dao of translation: An East-West dialogue.* Routledge.

Sakai, N. (1997). *Translation and subjectivity: On "Japan" and cultural nationalism.* Minneapolis: University of Minnesota Press.

Shen, S. (2006). S.I. Hsiung's *Lady Precious Stream* and the global circulation of Peking opera as a modernist form. *Genre, 39*(4), 85–104.

Thorpe, A. (2016). *Performing China on the London stage: Chinese opera and global power, 1759–2008.* Palgrave Macmillan.

Thorpe, A. (2019, Spring). After thought: Archiving absence through a practice-as-research production of Xiong Shiyi's *Lady Precious Stream. TDR: The Drama Review, 63*(1), (T241), 83–99.

Tian, M. (1997, Autumn). "Alienation-effect" for whom? Brecht's (mis)interpretation of the classical Chinese theatre. *Asian Theatre Journal, 14*(2), 200–222.

Tian, M. (2017). *Lady Precious Stream*: A Chinese *Chinoiserie* anglicized on the modern British stage. *Comparative Drama, 51*(2), 158–186.

Woollacott, A. (2011). *Race and the modern exotic: Three "Australian" women on global display.* Monash University Publishing.

Xiao Kairong. (2011). Cong jingju dao huaju: Xiong Shiyi yingyi *Wang Bao Chuan* yu Zhongguo Xiju Xi Zhuan [From jingju to spoken drama: Xiong Shiyi's translation of *Lady Precious Stream* and the turning West of Chinese opera]. *Xinan Daxue Xuebao (Shehui Kexue Ban), 37*(3).

Yeh, D. (2014). *The happy Hsiungs: Performing China and the struggle for modernity.* Hong Kong University Press.

Yeh, D. (2015). Staging China, excising the Chinese: *Lady Precious Stream* and the darker side of Chinoiserie. In A. Witchard (Ed.), *British modernism and Chinoiserie* (pp. 177–198). Edinburgh University Press.

Zheng, D. (2015). Performing transposition: *Lady Precious Stream* on Broadway. *New England Theatre Journal, 26*, 83–102.

Zheng, D. (2017). Creative re-creation in cultural migration. *Metacritic Journal for Comparative Studies and Theory, 3*(1), 26–44.

6 A descriptive study of Lu Xun's short stories in the English-speaking world – with focus on Yang Xianyi & Gladys Yang's translation

Hongjuan Xin

Introduction

Lu Xun, a Chinese literary giant, is renowned as the "Father of Modern Chinese Literature" for his pioneering contribution to promoting modern Chinese fiction. With his 34 short stories assembled in three collections including *Call to Arms*, *Wondering* and *Old Tales Retold*, Lu Xun is regarded as "the most translated and studied Chinese modern writer by western scholars" (Chan, 1975, p. 268). Over the past nine decades, his short stories have enjoyed some 20 English versions since the first publication of *The True Story of Ah Q* by George Kin Leung in 1926. English translations of Lu Xun's short stories have greatly contributed to the popularity of Lu Xun's works and modern Chinese literature overseas.

Based on Gideon Toury's Descriptive Translation Studies (DTS) approach, this article describes the English translation history of Lu Xun's short stories, focusing on the translation motives and strategies and their reception among readers. With a focus on Yang Xianyi and Gladys Yang's English translations of Lu Xun's works, it analyzes examples from one of Lu Xun's renowned short stories and discusses the translators' ideology, poetics and norms underlying the various translation strategies and methods used. By so doing, the author aims to explore and discuss the elements influencing the two translators' choices of their translation strategies and methods.

A diachronic description of English translations of Lu Xun's short stories

The history of English translations of Lu Xun's short stories can be divided into four stages by publication times and social influence:

- 1926–1936 (Lu Xun died in 1936);
- 1936–1949 (the People's Republic of China was founded in 1949);
- 1949–1981 (the final revised edition of the Yangs' translations was published in 1981);
- 1981 – present.

This section analyzes the translators' preface, publication statement, social background and the general reception of each stage, so as to reach conclusions on the translation strategies within different stages. Detailed information regarding year of publication, translated title, translator, translator's cultural background, and publisher of each is provided in Tables 6.1, 6.2, 6.3, 6.4 respectively: *The List of English Translations of Lu Xun's Short Stories* (1926–1936), (1936–1949), (1949–1981), (1981 – present).

The first stage: from 1926 to 1936

George Kin Leung, a Chinese translator born in the United States, was the earliest translator of Lu Xun's works into English. In the early 1920s, he returned to China, and started to translate Chinese literary works. Before translating *The True Story of Ah Q*, he wrote a letter to Lu Xun asking for permission, and later he continued corresponding with Lu Xun to exchange ideas regarding details of the work. When the translation was done, Leung sent it to Lu Xun for review. This version was published by the Commercial Press in Shanghai in 1926 and was aimed at foreigners in China and Chinese English learners. The main translation method used by George Kin Leung was word-for-word rephrasing, which Lu Xun commented on as showing great respect and loyalty to the original text, but with some mistranslations. Leung's version, despite having failed to achieve easy flow and natural expression, still received a relatively good reception among readers, and it was reprinted in 1927, 1929, and 1933.

E. H. F. Mills, a British scholar, was the second translator of Lu Xun's short stories. He translated *The Tragedy of Ah Qui, Con y Ki*, and *The Native Country* from the Chinese scholar J.B. KynYn Yu's French version *Anthologie des conteurs chinois modernes* into English. Mills' Mills's translation was later included in *The Tragedy of Ah Qui and Other Modern Chinese Stories*, published by Routledge in 1930 and by Dell Publishing House in 1931. This book marked the first publication of Lu Xun's short stories in the English-speaking world. Mills's English translation was generally loyal to Yu's French translation, which was later criticized for frequent reductions including of difficult phrases and paragraphs, even the preface. Therefore, Mills's translation featured a large reduction of Lu Xun's original text, especially the parts conveying differences between Chinese and Western culture.

From 1932 to 1934, George A. Kennedy, an American sinologist, translated six short stories entitled *K'ung I-chi, Medicine, A Gust of Wind, The Old Home, Remorse*, and *Diary of a Madman*. The stories *Medicine* and *K'ung I-chi* were first published in *The China Forum* in Volume I, 1932. Kennedy completed translating *A Gust of Wind* in 1932, and translated *Diary of a Madman* and *Remorse* in 1934. He published *The Old Home* in *the Far East*, volume 3, in 1940. With the exception of this 1940 version, the other five translated pieces were chosen by the American journalist Harold R. Isaacs for inclusion in his *Straw Sandals: Chinese Short Stories, 1918–1933* with forwards by Lu Xun and Mao Dun. Issacs finished editing this anthology in 1934, but for unknown reasons, it was not until 1974 that it was published in America by the MIT Press.

Also in this period, the American journalist Edgar Snow and the Chinese writer Yao Ke (also named Yao Xinnong) collaborated in translating some of Lu Xun's

Table 6.1 English translations of Lu Xun's short stories (1926–1936)

Year of Publication	Translated Title	Translator	Translator's Cultural Background	Publisher
1926	*The True Story of Ah Q*	George Kin Leung	Chinese American Translator	Shanghai: Commercial Press
1930	*The Tragedy of Ah Qui, and Other Modern Chinese Stories*	J. B. Yn-yuKyn (French version) E. H. F. Mills (English version)	Chinese Scholar British Translator	Routledge
1932	*K'ung I-chi Medicine*	George A. Kennedy	American Sinologist	Shanghai: *The China Forum*
1934 completed 1974 published	*Straw Sandals: Chinese Short Stories, 1918–1933*	George A. Kennedy (translator) Harold R. Isaacs (editor)	American Sinologist American Journalist	Cambridge, Mass.: The MIT Press
1935 1936	*Storm in the Village My Native Town The New Year Blessing*	Lin Yichin	Chinese Scholar	Shanghai: *The People's Tribune*
1935	*The Diary of A Lunatic*	G. N. Ling	Chinese Scholar	Shanghai: *The China Press*
1936	*A Cake of Soap*	Chiang Hsueh-tseng	Chinese Scholar	Shanghai: *The China Press*
1936	*Living China: Modern Chinese Short Stories*	Edgar Snow	American Journalist	London: George G. Harrap

Note 1. The list includes only indexed translations in the first publishing year;
Note 2. Some information in the list was collected from "Lu Xun in the English-speaking World" written by Li Jing.

Table 6.2 English translations of Lu Xun's short stories (1936–1949)

Year	Title	Translator	Role	Publisher
1938	*Looking Back to the Past*	Feng Yu-sing	Chinese Scholar	Shanghai: *T'ien Hsia Monthly, Volume 6*
1940	*The Old Home*	George A. Kennedy	American Sinologist	U.S.: *The Far East, Volume 3*
1941	*Ah Q and Others: Selected Stories of Lusin*	Wang Chi-chen	Chinese American Scholar	Columbia University Press
1941	*Short Stories by Lu Hsun*	George A. Kennedy (translator) Ku Tsong-nee (editor)	American Sinologist	Shanghai: Chinese British Publishing House
1944	*Contemporary Chinese Stories*	Wang Chi-chen	Chinese American Scholar	Columbia University Press
1945	Selected Stories By Lu Xun (English – Chinese Version)	Wang Chi-chen Liu Wugou	Chinese American Scholar	Beijing: Orient Press
1946	*Contemporary Chinese Short Stories*	Yuan Chiahua Robert Payne	Chinese Scholar British Writer	London: Noel Carrington Transatlantic Arts
1947	*Remorse*	Chen Limin	Chinese Scholar	Shanghai: World English Publishing House
1947	*The Comedy of the Ducks*	C.H. Kwock	American Translator	U.S.: *Journal of Oriental Literature*
1949	*At Dawn*	Joseph Kalmer	Austrian Translator	U.K.: *Life and Letters*

Note 1. The list includes only indexed translations in the first publishing year;
Note 2. Some information in the list was collected from "Lu Xun in the English-speaking World" written by Li Jing.

works entitled *Medicine, A Little Incident, K'ung I-chi, Benediction* and *Divorce.* All these translations were later compiled into *Living China: Modern Chinese Short Stories* edited by Edgar Snow in 1936. Snow and Yao consulted Lu Xun at times while translating his works, and they invited him to write a preface for the book. As Xiao (1983, pp. 1–10) commented in the preface of the Chinese version of *Living China,* Edgar Snow and Yao Ke chose to translate works that could give readers in the English-speaking world an authentic view of China at that time. They adopted the translation strategy of "prizing faithfulness to the original Chinese text over the quality of English."

In addition to the collected stories, there were independent translations of Lu Xun's short stories published in newspapers. Between 1935 and 1936, *Storm in the Village, My Native Town,* and *The New Year Blessing* were translated by Lin Yichin and published in *The People's Tribune.* G. N. Ling's translation of *The*

Table 6.3 English translations of Lu Xun's short stories (1949–1981)

Year	Title	Translator	Role	Publisher
1953	*The True Story of Ah Q*	Yang Xianyi Gladys Yang	Chinese Translator British Translator	Beijing: Foreign Languages Press
1954	*Selected Stories of Lu Hsun* (13 Stories)	Yang Xianyi Gladys Yang	Chinese Translator British Translator	Beijing: Foreign Languages Press
1956	*Selected Works of Lu Hsun Vol.1*	Yang Xianyi Gladys Yang	Chinese Translator British Translator	Beijing: Foreign Languages Press
1957	*Selected Works of Lu Hsun Vol.2*	Yang Xianyiw Gladys Yang	Chinese Translator British Translator	Beijing: Foreign Languages Press
1959	*Selected Works of Lu Hsun Vol.3*	Yang Xianyi Gladys Yang	Chinese Translator British Translator	Beijing: Foreign Languages Press
1960	*Selected Stories of Lu Hsun* (18 Stories)	Yang Xianyi Gladys Yang	Chinese Translator British Translator	Beijing: Foreign Languages Press
1961	*Selected Works of Lu Hsun Vol.4*	Yang Xianyi Gladys Yang	Chinese Translator British Translator	Beijing: Foreign Languages Press
1961	*Old Tales Retold*	Yang Xianyi Gladys Yang	Chinese Translator British Translator	Beijing: Foreign Languages Press
1970	*Modern Chinese Stories* (Kong Yiji; My Old Home; The New-Year Sacrifice)	W.J.F. Jenner (editor, translator for other authors except Lu Xun in this book)	British Translator	Oxford University Press
1973	*Silent China: Selected Writings of Lu Xun*	Yang Xianyi Gladys Yang	Chinese Translator British Translator	Oxford University Press
1974	*Wild Grass*	Yang Xianyi Gladys Yang	Chinese Translator British Translator	Beijing: Foreign Languages Press
1976	*Dawn Blossoms Plucked at Dusk*	Yang Xianyi Gladys Yang	Chinese Translator British Translator	Beijing: Foreign Languages Press
1981	*Call to Arms*	Yang Xianyi Gladys Yang	Chinese Translator British Translator	Beijing: Foreign Languages Press
1981	*Wandering*	Yang Xianyi Gladys Yang	Chinese Translator British Translator	Beijing: Foreign Languages Press
1981	*The Complete Stories of Lu Xun: Call to Arms; Wandering*	Yang Xianyi Gladys Yang	Chinese Translator British Translator	Indiana University Press

Note 1. The list includes only indexed translations in the first publishing year;
Note 2. Some information in the list was collected from "Lu Xun in the English-speaking World" written by Li Jing.

Diary of A Lunatic was printed by *China Press, 1st volume, 10th issue* in 1935, and Chiang Hsueh-tseng's translation of *A Cake of Soap* by was printed as the 2nd volume, 19th issue in 1936.

There are some noteworthy features of English translations of Lu Xun's short stories in this stage (1926–1936). First, direct correspondence between translators and the author Lu Xun, whom the translators admired, was a common practice among translators. Lu Xun's participation in the translations was evident, and this participation took on many forms. Some translators like George Kin Leung wrote letters to Lu Xun asking for permission to translate, some like Edgar Snow and Yao Ke sent the manuscript for revision, and some like George A. Kennedy invited the author to write a preface to the translation. Second, restricted in their translation practice by their great reverence for the original author, most translators chose foreignization as the translation strategy, adopting literal translation and even word-for-word translation methods. To some extent, this resulted in rough and rigid phrasing with little use of free-range expression on the part of translators. Third, translators were involved in one or more of the large collections of Lu Xun's short stories. This may explain why the influence of translation in the English-speaking world at this stage was limited.

The second stage: from 1936 to 1949

Wang Chi-chen, a Chinese scholar who taught Chinese language and culture at Columbia University, was a prominent translator of Lu Xun's works in this stage. Wang translated eleven of Lu Xun's short stories including *Our Story of Ah Q, Reunion in a Restaurant, The Divorce, The Story of Hair, The Diary of a Madman, My Native Heath, The Cake of Soap, The Widow, Remorse, A Hermit at Large* and *Cloud over Luchen*, and had them successively published in *China Today, Far East* (New York) and *T'ienhsia Monthly* (Shanghai) in the 1930s. All these 11 publications were compiled by Wang into the book *Ah Q and Others – Selected Stories of Lusin* (Lusin and Lu Hsun, were variant spelling of Lu Xun) that was published by Columbia University Press in 1941. Two years earlier, Wang had drafted the first English version of "Lusin: a chronological record, 1881–1936," and it was published in *China Institute Bulletin*, Volume III. In 1944, Columbia University Press issued *Contemporary Chinese Stories*, and two of Wang's translations, *What's the Difference* and *Peking Street Scene* were included. In 1945, *Selected Stories By Lu Xun* (English – Chinese version) was co-compiled and translated by Wang Chi-chen and Liu Wugou, and later it was re-published by the Orient Press. Works selected included *Professor Kao* translated by Wang Chi-chen and *A Happy Family* together with *Benediction*. both translated by Liu Wugou.

In 1938, *Looking Back to the Past* by Feng Yu-sing was printed by *T'ien Hsia Monthly* in Shanghai. In 1946, *Contemporary Chinese Short Stories*, edited and translated by Yuan Chiahua and Robert Payne, was published by Noel Carrington Transatlantic Arts. This book started with their co-translation of *The Wave of the Wind*. In 1947, *Remorse* translated by Chen Limin was published by World English Publishing House in Shanghai. Also in 1947, *The Comedy of the Ducks* by

C.H. Kwock was published in the *Journal of Oriental Literature, 1st issue*. In 1949, *At Dawn* translated by Joseph Kalmer was published in the *Life and Letters, 60th volume, 137th issue*.

There are notable features of the English translations of Lu Xun's short stories during this stage. First, English translations of story collections began gaining attention and interest overseas. Take *Ah Q and Others – Selected Stories of Lusin* by Wang Chi-chen for example: after the first edition was issued by Columbia University Press in 1941, the book was reprinted by Greenwood Press in 1971, gaining wide popularity in the English-speaking world. Second, compared with the previous translations, Wang Chi-chen's versions were better received than earlier translations by English-speaking readers due to Wang's mastery of idiomatic expressions and cultural notes. Motivated to spread Chinese culture and help Western readers gain further knowledge of Chinese literature, Wang adopted foreignization as his main translation strategy. Though Wang's translations made it possible for the targeted readers to learn about Lu Xun and his works, they were often criticized for excessive purposeful rewriting and over-interpretation. Third, English translations of Lu Xun's works, most of which derived from the translators' personal interests, had not attracted much attention until later decades. Seen within the broader historical context, this period was a time when Chinese literature held a marginal place among readers in the English-speaking world.

The third stage: from 1949 to 1981

Since the founding of the People's Republic of China in 1949, the Chinese central government has highly valued introducing Chinese classics to foreign countries. In 1952, the Foreign Languages Press was established as a major national facilitator of cultural exchange. That year, Yang Xianyi and Gladys Yang (to be referred to in this paper as the Yangs) were recruited by the Press as in-house translators.

The Yangs contributed considerably to introducing Lu Xun's works to the English-speaking world. They translated Lu Xun's 33 short stories into English between 1953 and 1981, including *Selected Stories of Lu Hsun* (13 stories; 1954), four volumes of *Selected Works of Lu Hsun* (1956–1961), *Selected Stories of Lu Hsun* (18 stories; 1960) and *Old Tales Retold* (1961). After the first publication of *Selected Stories of Lu Hsun* (16 stories) in 1960, the Press republished it in 1963 and 1972 respectively, followed by an English – Chinese bilingual version in 2000. *Old Tales Retold* was later republished twice in 1972 and in 1981.

The Yangs' translations over time also became popular among the Western presses. In 1981, Indiana University Press published *The Complete Stories of Lu Xun: Call to Arms – Wandering*. Major presses in Hong Kong and beyond continued to publish the Yangs' versions into the 21st century, as is further discussed in the fourth stage.

These are some features of the English translations of Lu Xun's works in this third stage. First, with support of the Chinese government, translation of Chinese modern literature in general has seen great yields, significantly promoted by the translation and spread of Lu Xun's short stories in the English-speaking world.

To increase the potential for modern Chinese literature to enjoy a wider audience in foreign countries, the Foreign Languages Press was established, and many scholars and in-house translators were recruited. Second, to ensure the spread of Chinese culture to the West, the Yangs adopted foreignization as their main translation strategy. Third, the Yangs' translations had an extensive reach and influence both at home and abroad. Their translations have been republished many times and have been well-received by both peers and reading audiences. Fourth, overseas presses during this stage increasingly started to publish translated Chinese literature. A number of foreign presses managed to acquire copyrights to the Yangs' *Selected Stories of Lu Hsun.*

The fourth stage: from 1981 to the present

Having dominated the market in the English-speaking world through to 1990, the Yangs' English translations of Lu Xun's works reached their heyday when *Diary of a Madman and Other Stories* by William A. Lyell, an American scholar and translator, was published that year by University of Hawaii Press. Lyell's version with abundant background notes, and taking domestication as the main translation strategy, vividly represented Lu Xun's writing style of mixing classical Chinese and the vernacular Chinese language *baihua*. However, his translation was criticized for lacking faithfulness to the source text, as evidenced by his seemingly casual additions to and deletions from the source. Lyell also added a great number of explanatory notes that may have discouraged some readers.

Another notable translator in this period was Julia Lovell, a British scholar and translator. She was the first to translate all of Lu Xun's 34 short stories. She translated *The Real Story of Ah-Q* and *Other Tales of China: The Complete Fiction of Lu Xun*, which was published by Penguin Books in 2009. Also adopting domestication, Julia Lovell's translation featured expressions that were more familiar and much better understood by average English readers of her time. When interviewed about her translation techniques by Wang (2013), she said "this translation is the result of my own understanding of Lu Xun's works." In 2014, Lu Xun's *A Madman's Diary* was again translated into English by a young Italian named Paul Meighan. It was published by Create Space Independent Publishing Platform. Meighan's *A Madman's Diary* appeared to have adopted the translation techniques – mainly diction and sentence structure – of the Yangs as well as those of Lovell.

During this period, the Yangs' translations were reprinted again and again. During the years from 2000 to 2006, Foreign Languages Press rolled out an English–Chinese series entitled *Echoes from the Classics*. Among the 30 books that made up the series, six were Lu Xun's works translated by the Yangs. Between 2002 and 2003, Chinese University Press in Hong Kong published the Yangs' *The New-Year Sacrifice and Other Stories, Wild Grass*, and *The True Story of Ah Q*. From 2009 to 2011, Capturing Chinese Publications together with CapturingChinese. com issued the series *Short Stories from Lu Xun's Nahan, Lu Xun's The Real Story of Ah Q*, and *Lu Xun's The New Years Sacrifice.*

Table 6.4 English translations of Lu Xun's short stories (1981 – present)

Year	Title	Translator(s)	Role	Publisher
1990	*Diary of a Madman and Other Stories*	William A. Lyell	American Translator, Scholar	Honolulu: University of Hawaii Press
2002	*The New-Year Sacrifice and Other Stories*	Yang Xianyi Gladys Yang	Chinese Translator British Translator	Hong Kong: Chinese University Press
2003	*Wild Grass*	Yang Xianyi Gladys Yang	Chinese Translator British Translator	Hong Kong: Chinese University Press
2003	*The True Story of Ah Q*	Yang Xianyi Gladys Yang	Chinese Translator British Translator	Hong Kong: Chinese University Press
2009	*The Real Story of Ah-Q and Other Tales of China The Complete Fiction of Lu Xun*	Julia Lovell	British Translator, Scholar	Penguin Books
2009	*Capturing Chinese: Short Stories from Lu Xun's Nahan*	Yang Xianyi Gladys Yang (translators); Kevin John Nadolny (editor)	Chinese Translator British Translator American editor	Capturing Chinese Publications; CapturingChinese.com
2010	*Capturing Chinese: Lu Xun's The Real Story of Ah Q*	Yang Xianyi Gladys Yang (translators); Kevin John Nadolny (editor)	Chinese Translator British Translator American editor	Capturing Chinese Publications; CapturingChinese.com
2011	*Capturing Chinese: Lu Xun's The New Year's Sacrifice*	Yang Xianyi Gladys Yang (translators); Kevin John Nadolny (editor)	Chinese Translator British Translator American editor	Capturing Chinese Publications; CapturingChinese.com
2014	*A Madman's Diary*	Paul Meighan	British Translator	Create Space Independent Publishing Platform

Note 1. The list includes only indexed translations in the first publishing year;
Note 2. Some information in the list was collected from "Lu Xun in the English-speaking World" written by Li Jing.

There are some notable features of the English translations of Lu Xun's works in this fourth stage. First, translations during this stage covered almost all of Lu Xun's works of fiction. For example, Julia Lovell translated all 34 short stories, and William A. Lyell translated 26 short stories. Second, the Yangs' translations continued to serve as an exemplary model for translators to follow. Many translators owed the success of their translations to the influence of the Yangs' translation style and techniques. For example, when hindered by sophisticated language features while translating Lu Xun's works, Julia Lovell made reference to *Selected Works of Lu Hsun* (1956–1960) and *Old Tales Retold* (1961), both of which had been translated by the Yangs. Third, owing to the reform and opening-up policy, translators during this stage enjoyed more freedom in translation than they had earlier and were less confined by social ideology and poetics. Fourth, motivated to gain a wider readership, most of the Western translators of Lu Xun's works in this stage adopted domestication as their main translation strategy. Fifth, strong reader interest in the publication of the Yangs' translations in China and overseas in this stage demonstrated the popularity of their translations.

Detailed analysis of the translation strategies used by the Yangs

The history of translations of Lu Xun's short stories into English reveals a clear pattern of growth and acceptability as the popularity of Lu Xun's works spread in the English-speaking world. Yang Xianyi and Gladys Yang made outstanding contributions to Lu Xun's worldwide recognition. They took the lead in translating all 33 short stories in three collections. Their faithful and smooth translation style won great popularity among English readers. The value of their translations was not just in providing reading material for their readers; their translations have also been used as a vital resource for future translators in retranslation. Lyell (1990, p. xlii) claimed that the Yangs' four volumes of *Selected Works of Lu Hsun* were "the first attempt at a systematic introduction to Lu Xun in English". Denton (1993, p. 175) commented that "their translation is both accurate and smooth." and Ge (1981, p. 29), the renowned Chinese translator, offered these words of praise: "When translating Lu Xun's works from English to the third language, most foreign translators use the Yangs' as the base version. From this perspective alone, they have made an exceptional contribution."

First employed by the Foreign Languages Press in 1952, Yang Xianyi and Gladys Yang started translating Lu Xun's works in 1953. Republications of published materials were used by the Yangs. In every translation they republished, they revised the preceding version – its wording, its tenses and its punctuation. For example, in translating "灰白色的沉重的晚云中间时时发出闪光，接着一声钝响，是送灶的爆竹；进出燃放的可就更强烈了，震耳的大音还没有息，空气里已经散满了幽微的火药香" (Lu, 2003), the translation in the 1972 version "From the pale, lowering evening clouds issue frequent flashes of lightning, followed by a rumbling sound of firecrackers celebrating the departure of the Hearth God; while nearer by, the fire crackers explode even more violently, and before the deafening report dies away the air is filled with a faint smell of powder" was revised to "Intermittent flashes from pallid, lowering evening clouds are followed by the rumbles of crackers bidding farewell to the Hearth God and, before the deafening reports of the bigger bangs close at hand have died away, the air is filled with faint whiffs of gunpowder" in the publication in 1980 – the later translation is more compact and flexible in structure and more accurate in wording. Their last revision was published in 1981. The remainder of this study uses the 1981 version of the Yangs' translations to illustrate their translation methods: literal translation, literal translation with footnotes, down-playing and omission.

Distinctive characteristics of the Yangs' translations

This section of the chapter examines three situations that define the characteristics of the Yangs' translations.

1. Literal translation as the main method

Working for the Foreign Languages Press as in-house translators, the Yangs were tasked with translating Lu Xun's collected stories for the purpose of "spreading Chinese culture." With a writing philosophy based on "faithfulness and fluency," the Yangs adopted literal translation as the main method to ensure that the meaning of the original writing would not be distorted. Examples are provided below. The use of bold text in the examples is my emphasis.

> Example: 但真所谓"塞翁失马焉知非福"罢，阿Q不幸而赢了一回，他倒几乎失败了。
>
> (Lu, 2018, p. 82)

However, the truth of the proverb "misfortune may prove a blessing in disguise" was shown when Ah Q was unfortunate enough to win and almost suffered defeat in the end. (Lu, 1981)

This extracted passage describes Ah Q, who seldom won in gambling and lost the money immediately. In the English language, "every cloud has its silver lining" is a saying that encourages people to remain hopeful even in hard times. However, the Yangs did not apply the English saying to translate "塞翁失马焉知非福" but used the phrase "misfortune may prove a blessing in disguise and vice versa," which refers to a Daoist Chinese saying: "Good fortune follows upon disaster; disaster lurks within good fortune." Because of their deep and rich knowledge of both Chinese and English languages and cultures, the Yangs were able to convey the nuances of Chinese philosophy to the readers in their translations.

> Example: 和尚动得，我动不得?
>
> (Lu, 2018, p. 87)

If the monk paws you, why can't I?

> (Lu, 1981, p. 79)

Ah Q, having been beaten soundly by the Bogus Foreign Devil, was consider-ing venting his anger on a third person, when a little nun from the Convent of Quiet Self-Improvement came walking towards him. He cursed the little nun for a while and pinched her bald head. When the nun fought back, Ah Q retorted "If the monk paws you, why can't I?" The Yangs' translation keeps the same rhetori-cal question and the same image of "monk" used in the source text to show Ah Q's justification of his acts. According to Buddhist teachings, monks were for-bidden to touch a woman's head. Ah Q assumed that even monks could touch a nun's head, so "why can't I?" The translation faithfully portrays Ah Q's vulgarity. The English proverb "Sauce for the goose, sauce for the gander" could basically convey Ah Q's self-justification, but it would not be as effective as the use of the questioning expression in showing Ah Q's psychological activity.

In addition, the word "monk" could express a Buddhist taboo in Chinese cul-ture. From the choice of diction and the use of rhetoric, the Yangs showed their preference for literal translation and their intention to remain loyal to the source text. Yang Xianyi (1998, pp. 83–84) was explicit about this: "the top principle as I insist, is to avoid any addition or omission on the source text. It is inappropriate to translate 'a flower' to 'a rose flower,' or to translate 'a red flower' to 'a flower.'" To him, faithfulness in translation was the primary and dominant principle.

Xin, Ma, & Wu (2018, p. 223) argued that

> it was out of their own admiration of Lu Xun and a close study of his works that Yang Xianyi and his wife translated Lu Xun. They had exquisite and accurate understanding of Lu Xun's thought and language features, and this ensured the accurateness in language use, means of rhetoric and cultural conversion.

2. Literal translation with footnotes as an alternative

When literal translation alone fails to convey the cultural meaning of the original text, the Yangs still employed foreignization as the translation strategy, and they would add footnotes so as to ensure proper conveyance of the Chinese culture.

Example: "过了二十年又是一个......"

(Lu, 2018, p. 118)

"In twenty years I shall be another ......"*

* "In twenty years I shall be another stout young fellow" was a phrase often used by criminals before execution to show their scorn of death. Believing in transmigration, they thought that after death, their souls would enter other living bodies. (Lu, 1981, p. 112)

"In twenty years I shall be another stout young fellow" was indeed an expres-sion often proclaimed by Chinese people to comfort themselves in the face of imminent death, reflecting "transmigration" in Chinese Buddhism. The Yangs made use of the idea of "transmigration" in the footnotes to help the English readers better understand Ah Q's mentality facing death.

Example: 未庄人都惊服，说这是柿油党的顶子，抵得一个翰林；

(Lu, 2018, p. 110)

All the Weizhuang villagers were overawed, and maintained that this was the badge of the Persimmon Oil Party,* equivalent to the rank of a Han Lin.

* The Freedom Party was called Zi You Dang. The villagers, not understanding the word "freedom," turned Zi You into Shi You, which means persimmon oil. (Lu, 1981, p. 103)

To represent the Weizhuang villagers, who were poorly educated and indifferent to their political rights, the Yangs translated *Shi You Dang* into Persimmon Oil Party literally. Considering that English readers might be unable to associate Persimmon Oil Party with a freedom party, the Yangs added a footnote to explain the relationship.

When interviewed by Qian Duoxiu and E.S-P. Almberg, Yang Xianyi expressed his dislike of the use of notes in translation and writing: "If the readers have to stop every now and then to read the notes, their flow of thought will be interrupted. That would be too bad" (Qian & Almberg, 2001, p. 20). As a result, one seldom sees the use of footnotes in Yang's translations and creative works (e.g. his autobiography and his short essays in Sinological studies). However, the Yangs did have to relinquish their personal translation and aesthetic preferences, and turn to footnotes to explain the true meanings of cultural differences to non-native readers in order to serve the greater purpose of "spreading Chinese culture."

3. Down-playing or omission of swearwords

Conforming to the general practice of the times, the Yangs adopted down-playing or omission of swear words that appeared in the source texts.

Example: 阿Q，你的妈妈的！你连赵家的用人都调戏起来，简直是造反

(Lu, 2018, p. 92)

"Curse you, Ah Q!" Said the bailiff. "So you can't even keep your hands off the Zhao family servants, you rebel!" (Lu, 1981, p. 84–85）

Amah Wu felt affronted knowing that Ah Q had designs on her. She cried, threatening to take her own life. The bailiff loathed Ah Q, cursed him with words. The more anger the bailiff vented, the more bitter the language was.

Example: 于是他未免有些"神往"了，况且未庄的一群鸟男女的慌张的神情，也使阿Q更快意。

(Lu, 2018, p. 104)

Ah Q could not help feeling rather fascinated, the terror of **all the villagers** only adding to his delight. （Lu, 1981, p. 97）

This example reflects Ah Q's psychological triumph or "spiritual victory." He addressed all the villagers with swear words to highlight his superiority.

Example: "这些东西忽然都学起小姐模样来了。这娼妇们......"
(Lu, 2018, p. 94)

"All of a sudden they're behaving like young ladies......"
(Lu, 1981, p. 86)

Since all the villagers knew Ah Q attempted to flirt with Amah Wu, all women including an 11-year-old girl avoided Ah Q. Ah Q felt aggrieved, and naturally had no good words for them.

In the above examples including the use of profanity, the swear words used by the figures in the story were important details reflecting the mentality of those from the lower class at that time and provided a mark of the realism embodied in Lu Xun's works. In translation, the Yangs down-played or even omitted the use of swear words, and this partially hindered an accurate representation of the thoughts and writing style contained in the original text.

There are at least two reasons for the down-playing or omission of swear words in the Yangs' translations. First, as an official organization, the Foreign Languages Press presented a national image to ensure that the accuracy and authenticity of language use in translations was strictly maintained. Second, Chinese society still held conservative values in the 1950s and 1960s, including that translations of Chinese works must project a positive image of Chinese culture. Hence, it was not uncommon for translators to downplay the use of profane or abusive words in translations.

However, in the three examples cited, the use of swear words conveying the vulgarity of the Chinese villagers and the social status of Chinese women was an important element in Lu Xun's critique of early modern Chinese society. A more faithful rendering of the profane words has been made by Lyell, as evidenced by his use of street-based four-letter words.

Findings and discussion

In the 1980s, Lefevere (1992, p. 7) introduced "rewriting theory" into the study of translation, bringing in key concepts like "ideology" and "poetics" to help scholars observe and analyze translation activities below the surface of the finished texts. This action was considered a breakthrough in Descriptive Translation Studies. Hermans (1999, p. 126) further explained its significance:

This literary system possesses a double control mechanism. One mechanism governs it largely from the outside, and secures the relations between literature and its environment. Here the key words are patronage and ideology. The other keeps order within the literary system, and here the operative terms are poetics and a somewhat less well defined group referred to variously as "expert," "specialists," "professionals" and also "rewriters."

That is to say, for the two most important extra-text elements, namely ideology and poetics, patronage governs the former, while professionals govern the latter.

The Yangs were translating Lu Xun's works under the patronage of the Foreign Languages Press, the official external translation publishing house affiliated with the China International Publishing Group, whose publications, as Zhang (2004, pp. 223–225) pointed out, are "of authority" and represent the national stance. Therefore, "translators are not given too much room for recreation, and are supposed to translate literally." That is to say, the ideological imperatives decreed by the patronage body set the translation standards for the Yangs. They needed to translate literally for the purpose of spreading Chinese culture and ideology, but they also had to clean up or omit any negative features of that image of Chinese culture (e.g. use of swear words).

It is accepted that translators' personal standards, competence, and aesthetic preferences matter in the process of translation. However, when translators' personal preferences violate the social norms, compromises may have to be made.

Considering translation norms, Toury (1995, p. 55) argues, "socio-cultural constraints have been described along a scale anchored between two extremes: general, relatively absolute *rules* on the one hand, and pure *idiosyncrasies* on the other. Between these two poles lies a vast middle-ground occupied by intersubjective factors commonly designated *norms*." His illustration of norms suggests that social and cultural constraints may not regulate translators' competence, but they do regulate their final decisions in translating. Hermans further explains (1999, p. 75) that "norms, that is, operate at the intermediate level between competence and performance, where competence stands for the set of options translators have at their disposal, and performance refers to the options actually selected." In other words, translators' competence interferes with the process of decision-making, whereas, social and cultural elements play a more important role when it comes to the final decisions of translators.

With these theories and examples in mind, we can summarize the major findings of the study as follows:

1   Translators' strategies and methods are determined by the ideology of patronage.

This was evidenced from the fact that the Yangs were employed by the Foreign Languages Press as in-house translators, and this supported their translation motive of "spreading Chinese culture." In this regard, the translation method known as "literal" translation was always primary.

2   Translators' strategy and methods are influenced by the poetics of the society.

Most of the Yangs' translations were done in the 1950s and 1960s when literal translation was preferred. During this period, translators were discouraged from adding or omitting any information related to the source text, and they were supposed to faithfully convey the original style and thought in the target text for faithfulness and authenticity.

3   If contradictory, translators' competence and aesthetic preferences should give way to translation norms determined by ideology and poetics.

A translator's personal experience and skills such as language capability and aesthetic value can exert a direct influence on a translation, The Yangs' exact understanding of Lu Xun's work, skillful use of languages, and profound knowledge of Chinese culture enabled them to produce formal, elegant, and faithful translations.

Though Yang Xianyi (1998, p. 83) believed "there should be no addition or omission on the source text," when his personal aesthetic preference or translation approach resulted in a conflict with the ideology of his patron or poetics, he had to give priority to the ideology and poetics.

Conclusion

From the first publication of Lu Xun's short stories in the English-speaking world till Yang Xianyi and Gladys Yang produced their translations, most of the translators took foreignization as their major translation strategy, in accordance with translation principles like "exactly representing Lu Xun's works out of admiration" (i.e. translators in the first stage) or "helping English readers learn more about Chinese writers" (i.e. translators in the second stage). Yang Xianyi and Gladys Yang's imperative was "spreading Chinese culture.". From 1990 to the present, English translators of Lu Xun's short stories have preferred to adopt domestication as the major translation strategy, with the idea of gaining more English readers and achieving commercial success in the publishing market. Lu Xun's short stories have been studied and translated in accordance with the changing requirements and conditions of the times, and translations have undergone a continuous improvement in quality.

Among the various translators discussed in this paper, Yang Xianyi and Gladys Yang have made the greatest contribution to the dissemination of Lu Xun's short stories in the English-speaking world. Take *Selected Stories of Lu Hsun* for example: this version has not only been re-edited and reprinted by Foreign Languages Press in China; it has also been reprinted by five American presses – Sentry Press (1972), China Books & Periodicals (1972), Norton (1977, 2003), Create Pace Independent Publishing Platform (2014), and Wildside Press (2016). In the U.S., at least 295 libraries hold English translations of Lu Xun's works published by Foreign Languages Press, and 795 libraries hold English translations of Lu Xun's works published by American and British presses. Through in-depth analysis of the Yangs' translations, this paper shows that translation strategies and methods can be greatly influenced by factors such as ideology, patronage and poetics.

References

Chan, M. (1975). Review: Chinese wasteland. *NOVEL: A Forum on Fiction, 8*(2), 268–271.
Denton, K. A. (1993). Review of diary of a Madman and other stories. *Chinese Literature: Essays, Articles, Reviews, 15*, 174–176.

Ge, B. Q. (1981). 阿Q正传在国外 [*The true story of Ah Q abroad*]. Beijing, China: People's Literature Publishing House.

Hermans, T. (1999). *Translation in systems: Descriptive and systemic approaches explained*. St. Jerome.

Lefevere, A. (1992). *Translation, rewriting and the manipulation of literary fame*. Routledge.

Lu, X. (1972). *Selected stories of Lu Hsun* (X. Y. Yang & G. Yang, Trans.). Beijing, China: Foreign Language Press.

Lu, X. (1981). *The complete stories of Lu Xun: Call to arms: Wandering* (X. Y. Yang & G. Yang, Trans.). Bloomington, IN: Indiana University Press.

Lu, X. (1990). *Diary of a Madman and other stories* (W. A. Lyell, Trans.). Honolulu, HI: University of Hawaii Press.

Lu, X. (2003). 祝福 [A new year sacrifice]. In 鲁迅精品文集 [*Selected collection of Lu Xun's works*]. Hohhot, China: Inner Mongolia Culture Press.

Lu, X. (2009). *The real story of Ah-Q and other tales of China: The complete fiction of Lu Xun* (J. Lovell, Trans.). Penguin.

Lu, X. (2014). *A Madman's Diary* (P. Meighan, Trans.). CreateSpace Independent Publishing Platform.

Lu, X. (2018). 呐喊 [*Call to arms*]. Nanjing, China: Yilin Press.

Lyell, William A. (1990). *Diary of a madman and other stories by Lu Xun*. Honolulu: University of Hawaii Press.

Qian, D. X., & Almberg, E. S.-P. (2001). Interview with Yang Xianyi. *Translation Review*, *62*, 17–25.

Toury, G. (1995). *Descriptive translation studies and beyond*. John Benjamins Publishing.

Wang, B. R. (2013). An overall view on the translation of Lu Xun's short stories: An interview with Julia Lovell. *Compilation and Translation Review*, *6*(1), 147–149.

Xiao, Q. (1983). Edgar Snow and China's new literary movement. In E. Snow (Ed.), *Living China* (J. R. Wen, Trans.). Hunan People's Publishing House.

Xin, H. J., Ma, X. X., & Wu, D. L. (2018). 杨宪益翻译研究 [*Translation studies of Yang Xianyi*]. Nanjing University Press.

Yang, X. Y. (1998). 略谈我从事翻译工作的经历与体会 [Some thoughts from my translation experiences]. In S. H. Jin & G. B Huang (Eds.), 因难见巧：名家翻译经验谈 [*Artistry in difficulty: Experiences of renowned translators*]. China Translation & Publishing.

Yang, X. Y. (2002). *White tiger: An autobiography of Yang Xianyi*. The Chinese University of Hong Kong.

Zhang, N. F. (2004). 中西译学批评 [*Criticism of translation studies in the east and west*]. Tsinghua University Press.

7 A study of contrasting translatorial methodologies in Ida Pruitt and Lao She's co-translation of *The Yellow Storm*[1]

Man Zhang

Introduction

The English translation of *The Yellow Storm* was completed in cooperation between the author Lao She and the translator Ida Pruitt, but the two translators each undertook different tasks in the specific translation practice. Lao She rewrote the original text and condensed the themes of the novel by abridging it, and Ida Pruitt translated Lao She's rewritten text into English. Prior to this collaboration, Lao She had co-translated his story *The Quest for Love of Lao Lee* (《离婚》) with Helena Kuo, who was a writer and translator in the United States. In the process of their productive collaboration, Lao She helped Helena Kuo understand the Chinese characters and sentences of the original text, and Kuo chose English words and made sentences with little interference from the writer. In contrast to this collaborative mode of Lao She and Helena Kuo's co-translation of *The Quest for Love of Lao Lee*, when Lao She (Lau Shaw) and Ida Pruitt co-translated *The Yellow Storm*, they could not actively interact because of their different tasks and purposes; hence it was a separate co-translation, a combination of Ida Pruitt's language constructions and Lao She's content constructions.

Prior to his visit to the United States, Lao She already had a rich experience in overseas travel and literary creation. George Kao (Gao), a Chinese-American scholar, had introduced Lao She to American literary culture through his criticism.[2] Additionally, the scholar Wang Chi-Chen translated and published several of his short stories.[3] However, after arriving in the United States, Lao She still faced the challenge of how to translate and introduce his own works.

Informed by these experiences, he gradually decided that the cultural stance suitable to the re-publication of *The Yellow Storm* in the United States should be acknowledging the bravery shown by the Chinese people in the War of Resistance against Japan. In Lao She's own words, the spirit of modern Chinese culture is a "strong culture," connoting its strength and resilience. Ida Pruitt sometimes had heated discussions with Lao She over the language choice or translation practices, but each stuck to their own views. Lao She was dissatisfied with the translation and suggested that the agent should ask a third party to improve the translated text. However, I argue that Ida Pruitt's unusual translation did not actually hinder Lao She's intention to spread the knowledge of Chinese culture, but enabled it.

Lao She's rewriting of *The Yellow Storm*: spreading strong culture

Lao She is one of the greatest writers in modern Chinese literary history. As a modern story teller, novelist, translator and dramatist, he is famous for his influential novel *Rickshaw Boy/Camel Xiangzi* (《骆驼祥子》, 1936) that describes the tragic life of a rickshaw puller in Beijing in the 1920s, which is considered to be a classic of modern Chinese literature. He is also known for *The Yellow Storm* (《四世同堂 》) which can be directly translated as *Four Generations under One Roof*, 1944–1950); *Cat Country* (《猫城记》 1932), a satire which is sometimes considered the first significant Chinese science fiction novel; *The Philosophy of Old Zhang* (《老张的哲学》 1926), his first published novel, written in London; and the play *Teahouse* (《茶馆》, 1957). Many of his works including these were translated into English. As a translator, Lao She translated many of his works himself, and sometimes he worked with co-translators

The Yellow Storm is the English translation of Lao She's novel *Si Shi Tong Tang* which is made up of three parts: "Huang Huo" (《惶惑》), "Tou Sheng" (《偷生》), and "Ji Huang" 《饥荒》). As one of Lao She's favorite works, the novel depicts Xiao Yang Juan Hutong (a famous alley) in Beijing during the Anti-Japanese War. The novel focuses on the Qi Family and follows their neighbors, the Qian Family, the Guan Family and other residents in the Hutong as well so that it introduces many ordinary people from all walks of life. It reflects the experiences of misery and humiliation and the complicated conflicts of Beijing citizens during the eight years of the war. The novel depicts their painful and difficult experiences when the country was ruined and the people were starving. Its themes include the cruelty of war, the destruction of human life and civilization, and the ups and downs of national destiny and national spirit. Through it Lao She appraises the ideal personality qualities for reviving the nation by comparing positive and negative cultural stereotypes, with the aim of strengthening the nation's vitality. When he conceived the novel, Lao She intended to write a masterpiece like the *Divine Comedy*, so in his English letter to Lloyd, he told his western agents that this novel was the best he ever wrote (Lao, 1993): "I like this novel very much myself, because it is the longest and probably the best book since I began writing" (p. 11). As anyone familiar with Lao She knows, the writer was a miser with words, and he was angry that editors and publishing houses had revised his manuscripts without permission. Regarding the English translation of this novel, Lao She said, "as for the English version, I think it is necessary to delete some parts, at least 200,000 words" (Lao, 1993, p. 11).

Lao She's creation of *The Yellow Storm* aimed not only to imitate the structure of the *Divine Comedy*, i.e. a trilogy of 100 chapters in all,[4] but also to share its motifs. But after 200,000 words were deleted, the outline and design[5] of the translated text changed. Lao's original work had 100 chapters, while the English translation has only 77 chapters; so the translation does not reproduce the creator's structure. Even so, Lao She believed that abridging was "very necessary" and explained that the original text had been too long.

But the situation was more complicated than that. During his visit to the United States, Lao She delivered public speeches on various occasions and engaged with American people from all walks of life, speaking solo or with the playwright Cao Yu. He was surprised to find that Americans' understanding of Chinese culture was limited to Chinese porcelain and the aesthetics of the poetry of the Tang and Song Dynasties (Lao, 1999a): "In the past, we introduced Chinese poetry of Song dynasty and antique vase of Kangxi Emperor's period to the United States, which made Americans aware only of our ancient achievements in literature and art" (p. 405), so Americans errantly believed that the characteristics of Chinese culture (and oriental culture more widely) were feminine in quality. Some Chinese immigrants also ridiculed and distorted their mother culture.[6]

What was more unacceptable for Lao She was that in 1948, Lao She and Helena Kuo co-translated *The Quest for Love of Lao Lee*, but it was superseded in circulation by Evan King's version. Lao's version sold only 18 books (Ma & Ren, 1997). This series of events forced Lao She to re-think the position of Chinese culture and literature in the arena of world culture and literature. "We are also people of the world, we are also part of the world, and we must enable American friends to really understand us . . . , and understand our culture" (Lao, 1999b, p. 406). He reflected that in a dual role of both writer and translator, he shouldered the responsibility and obligation to correct Americans' narrow understanding of his home culture.

Lao She even tried to translate into another genre, such as rewriting the novel "Breaking-Soul Spear" into an English play text *The Spear That Demolishes Five Tigers at Once*. Lao She gradually fostered his idea that modern Chinese "strong culture" should be disseminated in the United States. To explain what "strong culture" was, Lao She (1999b) gave the example of the character Zhao Xing Bang from "The Dragon and Snake of the Earth" and stated that "we fight for peace and get peace through fighting, I call this 'strong peace'! Only strong peace is true peace!" (p. 414). Subsequently, he stated that the concept of strong culture could be further defined as "the righteousness of the east, the straightness of the west, the kindness of peasants, and the discipline of soldiers" (p. 414).

Lao She's construction of the concept of strong cultural spirit in modern Chinese literature began in the early 1930s when he was creating the story "Two Boxers" (《二拳师》), though the work was later abandoned. Lao She's thought about the concept was present in other works such as "Breaking-Soul Spear" (《断魂枪》, 1935), "The Dragon and Snake of the Earth" (《大地龙蛇》, 1942), "Old Brand" (《老字号》, 1935), "New Mohammed" (《新穆罕穆德》, 1936), in addition to the masterpiece *The Yellow Storm*. For example, in *The Yellow Storm* Qi Rui Xuan and Qian Mo Yin are representatives of strong culture. Portraying Qian Mo Yin, Lao She put him through life-and-death trials in which he grew from a hermit into a real soldier. His hands once used for writing and painting finally took up weapons to confront the enemy. The novel describes how he changed after being weathered by all his experiences, which enriched his representation as a fighter.

As another example, Qi Rui Xuan is a round character, and a core part of his personality originates from the contradiction between duty to country and duty to family: to be a fighter or to be a filial son? These typical characters have been reproduced faithfully in the English novel. Since the strong cultural qualities conveyed through the core characters and the plot have been reflected in the translation, further descriptions of these key characters could then be abridged. For instance, the psychological states of Qi Rui Xuan include when he knew that students went to celebrate the fall of Baoding, and the sorrow of the Qi family when they mourned and buried Qi Tian You.

Some scholars have argued that this representative strategy has made "the confrontation between justice and speculation, the conflict between bravery and cowardice, and the struggle between fearless spirit and evil become more intense and dramatic" (Wei, 2011, p. 113). I agree with this claim. Readers should also note that being dramatic is one of the greatest features of Lao She's novels, and that is the case with the original text of *The Yellow Storm*. As a literary work, the rendering of details is an important factor of the success of the work, so maybe we can explain the aesthetic functions of Lao's representation in this way: Lao She advocates for the concept of karma and demonstrates the fairness, justice and bravery of strong culture in the struggle between good and evil by making the literary expression more "straightforward," which is matched by American society's value of directness in terms of content or form.

Other notable abridgements in the novel include customs, scenery and psychological activities. The abridged material also includes what Anthony Appiah named "thick translations" (1993) – voluminous background information to engender in the target text (TT) reader a deeper respect for the source culture and a greater appreciation for the way that people of other backgrounds have thought and expressed themselves. In this case he added details of the War of Resistance against Japan by the citizens of Peiping. Additionally, among other abridgements, he merged chapters 35 and 36 of the second part of the original text to form the first chapter of the translation.

Lao She, a writer and translator, made so many painstaking re-arrangements that the result was nothing less than a re-creation, which made the reading experience of the translation faster and more dramatic and went some way towards correcting the parochialism of Chinese culture that had spread in the West. At the same time, Lao She also hoped to identify and correct the distortions of the home culture in works of second-generation Chinese immigrants. Although he abridged some descriptions of customs in the translation, he also retained and even thick translated some of the customs such as the Mid-Autumn Festival, Fruit Day, and birthday celebrations for the elders. Prior to the translation of Lao She's novel, those customs had been most notably rendered by two Chinese-American writers: Pardee Lowe and Jade Snow Wong.[7] In these two Chinese writers' novels *Father and Glorious Son* and *The Fifth Chinese Daughter,* the authors had attempted to render China's cooking skills and unique ways of celebrating festivals. However, their descriptions may at times be read as sarcasm; those customs were interwoven with the cultural practices familiar to Americans and spoke to the phenomenon of the grandchildren hoping to abandon their national culture and looking forward to getting rid of the "yellow" people status, eager to become "white." They were problematic descriptions that taunted the Chinese home culture.

The translator Lao She, as a writer, combined detailed description of similar customs (Appiah's "thick translation") with depictions of the modern strong cultural spirit shown by the citizens of Peiping during the War of Resistance against Japan. His aesthetic methods including the use of the technique "thick translation" have undergone qualitative changes in his works, which in turn reflected the value of strong culture.

The translator Lao She was also a humorist. Even in the serious work *The Yellow Storm*, he did not omit his humor. The English title "The Yellow Storm" is an example; it was chosen by Lao She himself: "Miss Pruitt and I spent a weekend at her brother's home in Philadelphia. Walking with her in the woods, I got a rather good title for the four generations story – Yellow Storm" (Shu, 1993, p. 91).[8] Lao She's choosing "yellow" is informed by his creative talent as a writer: "yellow" in western culture can connote not only wealth, perfection, sun and light, but also timidity, betrayal, cunning, hypocrisy and jealousy.

In the mid-1940s, the popular use of its derogatory meanings was more common than its commendatory meanings. Lao She used this word to express many meanings: in the 1940s, representation of Chinese people in the "public opinion" of the United States included not only the images of justice, enthusiasm and kindness, but also the negative images of weakness, hypocrisy and cunning. Lao She used the English word "yellow" to express his agreement with the public opinion in the United States.

Lao She believed that Londoners (such as the British characters in "Mr. Ma and Son"), Romans and Americans had much in common with Chinese people. He portrayed the complexity of human nature that is shared by Chinese people and foreigners. Whether in Britain in the 1920s or in the United States in the 1940s, Lao She was hurt by the distortion of Chinese culture by Westerners. The combination of "yellow" and "storm" also implied that the one-sided understanding of Chinese culture formed in the United States and the West more widely could be swept away as by a storm.

One of the reasons for Lao She's thick translations of scenes depicting customs was to correct the ridicule of the mother culture by Chinese Americans. He added explanations and notes in the text to explain traditional Chinese customs. For example, Fruit Day is a local cultural custom in Beijing, so Lao She wrote in the original text only "the Fruit Day is coming." But in *The Yellow Storm*, he explained the origins of Fruit Day and then described what people would do during this day and its meaning. Because he wrote his translated text to perform this cultural reclamation, the irony of the word *yellow* includes satire and criticism of the self-belittling of Chinese Americans in the United States and the phenomenon of "built-in colonization"[9] among Chinese Americans.

Lao's use of the word also included eulogizing the War of Resistance against Japan. As is demonstrated in these multiple connotations, Lao She was critiquing the Chinese people as well as wider human nature, so his motive to disseminate modern Chinese culture contained a critique of the evil in the world culture, including the cultures of his own and the others.

The unusual translation of Ida Pruitt: opportunity to facilitate communication

If the aesthetic functions of the co-translated novel *The Quest for Love of Lao Lee* include cultural criticism, then the translation of *The Yellow Storm* not only continues that cultural critique, but also constructs a modern Chinese national image, and continues the representation of the spirit of strong modern Chinese culture that had become prominent since the 1930s. If the partners in translation of *The Quest for Love of Lao Lee* negotiated and compromised with each other, the cooperation between the two translators in the translation of *The Yellow Storm* was a form of separation and even resistance. According to the records, in the translation of the novel *The Yellow Storm*, and given Ida Pruitt's knowledge of and familiarity with Chinese languages, there was a division of labor between the two translators: Lao She read his novel to Ida Pruitt, and she immediately began translating it into English. But Lao She was not satisfied with Ida Pruitt's English, and he asked Miss Hertz, his first publishing agent, to take a look at it. Hertz was also dissatisfied with the translation: "When I showed Miss Hertz the first ten chapters of the translation, she told me it would be better to stop working with Miss Ida Pruitt at once" (Lao, 1993, p. 29). On April 22, 1948, Lao She wrote in his "Fifth Letter to Lloyd": "

> In order to maintain [the] Chinese flavor as much as possible, she often uses incoherent English . . . if I continue to co-work with Miss Ida Pruitt, it will be necessary to ask a third party to proofread the text. . . . I'm afraid that's why Mr. Renault thought it was too early to sign the contract.
>
> (Lao, 1993, p. 13)

Dissatisfied with Pruitt's translation, Lao She hoped to ask a third party to proofread the text. The author and the translator did not work together to discuss how to embellish, process and modify the translation as he had done with Helena Kuo when they had worked together on the translation of *The Quest for Love of Lao Lee*. Pearl S. Buck was the second publishing agent, and she rejected Lao She's request for a third party's intervention, whereupon Lao She asked Buck to read Pruitt's translation. After reading the first ten chapters, she praised the translation: "I asked for comments from Mrs. Walsh (Buck), who, after reading the first ten chapters, thought I could continue to work with Miss Ida Pruitt." At the same time Buck wrote to Lloyds: "I have read their translation. I think it is good. The book is supposed to have a favorable prospect" (Lao, 1993, p. 13).). In a letter to Wang Ying in the 1950s, Buck commented on Pruitt's translation: "[I] think that Ida Pruitt is the best option, because her translation of Lao She's *The Yellow Storm* is faithful to the original and beautifully presented" (Jiang, 2012).

Buck's role in supporting Pruitt's translation may be seen as an example of publishers manipulating the reception of a translation. Media institutions and publishers, including agents, often occupy positions of power at the center of the literary sphere, and they thus become mediators and controllers. As part of the publishing ecosystem, literary figures such as these can sometimes exert stronger influence on readers than language. "Different media telling the same story can have different rhetorical effects" (Wang, 2003, p. 9). Buck's affirmation of the translation enacts her power within publishing and using it, she also manipulated the publication and reception of the translation. Buck's further comment "Textual problems can be handled by competent editors" (Lao, 1993, p. 13) may be seen euphemistically to deny Lao She's criticism of Pruitt's translation. Therefore, despite being dissatisfied with Ida Pruitt's translation, Lao She had no choice but to relinquish his request. On July 21, 1948, he wrote critically in his "11th letter to Lauder": "My English is not so good and thus I am unable to comment on her style of writing, but it is now a bit risky to rely entirely on her" (Lao, 1993, p. 29).

What kind of language did Ida Pruitt use in translation that so dissatisfied Lao She? Before co-translating *The Yellow Storm*, Ida Pruitt had translated Wang Ying's autobiographical novel *Bao Gu* (1950s) and had written her own memoir *A China Childhood* (Pruitt, 1978). In the book, Pruitt often describes the utensils with national characteristics in transliterated Chinese characters, such as "k'ang" for "炕," "tou-fu nao" for "豆腐脑," "To nien ti tao lu tsou ch'eng ho; To nien ti hsi fu ao ch'eng p'o" for "多年的道路走成河，多年的媳妇熬成婆," and so on.

Transliteration is familiar to today's translators and researchers; it has become one of the commonly used methods for contemporary translators. But at that time it was regarded as a defamiliarizing and unacceptable "unusual translation."[10] In the English translation of *The Yellow Storm*, Ida Pruitt adopted a method that has also been considered a form of "unusual translation," that is, hard (literal) translation. For example, "carry the black cooking basin for her on your back" for "(为她)背黑锅"; "blow his mustache and glare" for "吹胡子瞪眼睛"; "a thousand-gold virgin" for "千金小姐"; "the sky was about to fall and the earth turn over" for "天翻地覆"; "blind cat hunting a dead mouse" for "瞎猫碰死耗子"; "scourge of soldiers and rampage of horses" for "兵荒马乱"; "the nail in one's eyes" for "眼中钉"; "writing with two pens" for "双管齐下"; and so on. Ida Pruitt's unusual translation cannot accurately be considered similar to Ezra Pound's borrowing from and imitating Chinese images informing the imagist movement in poetry, nor contemporary novelists Hughes's or Somerset Maugham's influential depictions of the Chinese cultural spirit nor even Chinese-American scholars George Kao's and Wang Chi-Chen's reluctance to incorporate Western literature due to their difficulties in promoting the modern Chinese writer Lao She in America. Pruitt's use of hard translation, which is more difficult than literal translation, comes from her love for objects and places in her past, and her attempting to reproduce the image of Chinese objects[11] in this way. It can be seen that Ida Pruitt adopted "unusual translation" to recall those special Chinese things such as Kang (bed), and latticed window that still lurked in her memory. In this way, literary representation may be seen as a site of what Jean Baudrillard claimed occurs with photographic representation: that it is "the place where the relationship between subject and object is reversed" (as cited in Liu, 2013，p. 88).

On the other hand, the translator also changed the reader's perception of Chinese culture through the medium of language itself, and the actual effect of "unusual translation" was to transfer the translation from politics and culture to the aesthetic of literature itself, thus constructing otherness of the translation, which was Lao She's expectation of the translation. Lao She was not entirely unfamiliar with Ida Pruitt's translation methodology; he had used this technique himself in translating Bernard Shaw's comedy *Apple Cart*.

Although Lao She and Ida Pruitt shared the general Chinese cultural context, there were also regional differences in terms of the situational contexts and the linguistic contexts, that is, the differences between Beijing culture and Shandong Penglai culture. For example, in Lao She's situational context the characters such as "窗户" and "床" in the original novel should correspond to "window" and "bed" in English, but for "bed" she chose "K'ang."

There were significant differences in their understandings of the purposes of translation. Lao She advocated for a form of traditional text translation theory because he prioritized acceptance by the target language culture, while Ida Pruitt used unusual translation techniques in order to serve the original culture instead of pandering to the target culture "The regularity and variation of novel language should serve the shaping of images, and the clarity and ambiguity of novel language should be based on consciousness and purpose" (as cited in Li, 2007, p. 73). Therefore, the combination of Ida Pruitt's persistence, the publisher's support for Pruitt's translation, and Lao She's final acquiescence successfully disseminated the strong version of Chinese culture and also constructed the identity of otherness in the United States.

The cultural nature of unusual translation

After the translation was published in 1951, *Saturday Literary Review* evaluated the translation as "not only one of the best novels published in China since the Second World War, but also one of the best novels published in the United States during the same period." According to the well-known critic Kornfield, "Lao She, the author of *The Yellow Storm*, seems to be closer to Tolstoy, Dickens, Dostoevsky, and Balzac's 'brilliant tradition' than any other western or European novelist" (Lao, 1993, p. 135).

Ida Pruitt's "unusual translation" contributed a lot to the success of *The Yellow Storm* in the United States. Her translation methodology may be understood to serve the readers. To do that, her translation brings out the differences between languages as much as possible. The relation between the target and the original texts may be seen as one of symbiosis instead of imitation. One major proponent of modern translation theory also holds that "'faithfulness' of individual words in translation cannot present exactly the same meaning as the original words, because compared with the poetics of the original text, they are not limited to the meaning referred to" (Benjamin, 1923, p. 78). The best way to reflect the difference between source and target language is literal translation or creative translation. Taking Ida Pruitt's translation of "招猫递狗儿" as an example, the English version of this idiom is "kiss the cat and play with the dog": "cat" and "dog" are terms of endearment in the western cultural context because they are beloved pets. In the context of the original novel, however, it carries a derogatory meaning in Chinese culture, which is "not doing serious things."[12] Mallarmé once said: "The multiplicity of language determines its imperfection. Because of the differences in idioms in various languages, everyone cannot speak out specifically like the truth" (Benjamin, 1923, p. 78). In order to avoid readers' mistakenly "materializing" or "semantic parochialism" Pruitt as translator did not attempt to replace the original text with existing expressions in the English cultural context, as well as avoiding increasing incongruous explanatory translation.

The relationship between language as a symbolic system and its meaning is unique, and the way of expression in each language is unique. The Chinese "猫" and "狗" and the English "cat" and "dog" correspond to the same ideographic objects (animal). However, due to the different ideographic methods, the cultural meaning of "猫" and "狗" in Chinese is not exactly the same as that of "cat" and "dog" in English. In many cases, the two cannot be exchanged for each other.

However, translation can sometimes fuse the components of different cultures together. A translation can expand the scope and field of the target language. "The translator makes the mother language richer by allowing the source language to infiltrate and revise it" (Benjamin, 1923, p. 79). Ida Pruitt imbued new cultural meanings into the English "cat" and "dog," which revived the usage of the words "cat" and "dog" and also potentially excited the readers' interest.

According to Itamar Even-Zohar, an Israeli scholar, only when translated literature occupies a central position in a poly-system of literature will translators choose foreignization strategies and participate in the process of creating a new and first-level model in the target language translation literature. Even if the translator needs to break the traditions of his own country, he will do whatever it takes to promote the development of his own literature (Even-Zohar, 2000, pp. 192–197) At the time of Ida Pruitt's translation of *The Yellow Storm*, China was often treated by Americans like a political tool for American interests. But Chinese poetics, it would later be claimed, "has to some extent become a way out for Westerners who have a sense of insecurity and anxiety" (Spence, 1997, p. 186). Ida Pruitt's translation of *The Yellow Storm* raised the novel to being a point of reference and exemplar for other translators For example the popularity of Evan King's translation of *Divorce* (《离婚》) may be seen to derive from his having rewritten the original text to end with "reunion."

For these reasons, it might be inferred that the failure of Lao She and Helena Kuo's translation of *The Quest for Love of Lao Lee* lies in the content. Although Lao She gives a detailed introduction and explanation of Chinese-style marriage in the preface of the translation, and compares the differences between Chinese and Western marriages, for American readers, there is a dissonance because there are heterogeneous values, ethics and morality ascribed to marriage which cannot be conveyed in an introduction or explanation alone. After the rewriting of Lao She, *The Yellow Storm* highlights the qualities of strong modern Chinese culture, such as justice, righteousness and courage, which are the same values as advocated in the United States. The unusual translation in language reflects only differences, but not estrangement.

Differences involve only "some of the characteristics of foreign culture, such as geography, customs, cooking, historical figures and historical events; while foreign places and persons' names, and some unusual foreign vocabulary are preserved" (Venuti, 2008, p. 160). Maintaining the "unusual foreign vocabulary" does not question or subvert the cultural values and beliefs of target languages; the estrangement the reader experiences originates from the conflict of values, ethics and morality.

As a translator, Lu Xun is a respected figure in the history of modern Chinese translated literature. In the *Collection of Foreign Novels*, Lu Xun and Zhou Zuo-ren adopted hard translation, which is similar to Ida Pruitt's unusual translation method. Lu Xun explained "almost 30 years ago I started using this 'new dress' ('新装' here refers to the hard translation method) to translate those poems of Poland poets." (Lu, 1981, pp. 355). It can be seen that Lu Xun adopted the method of hard translation because the content of the novel he chose to translate was in line with the values and outlook on life of the Chinese people. Pruitt's translation methods may be seen, then, as similar to those of Lu Xun, but also to the translation practices of contemporary western scholars. For example, in translating Derrida's "What is 'relevant' translation," Venuti (2001) wrote that he "tried to practice Derrida's proposition in the text" and "stayed as close as possible to his original French text, trying to create comparable text effects by duplicating his syntax, vocabulary and typesetting, although doing so distorts English into a new look."

This kind of "distortion into a new look" is bound to produce new cultural meanings. Although the words and syntax in various cultures and are different, the cultural intentions contained in these languages can complement each other, as they do in the Chinese "猫" and "狗" and the English "cat" and "dog" analyzed above.

Here's a vivid example: if Laozi's "Tao Te Ching 道德经" is translated into English, the first problem encountered is how to translate "Tao (道)." There are obviously no equivalent words in English. Translators generally translate "道" into "way," but the ideographic object of the English word "way" is very different from that of Laozi's "道," so the cultural meaning conveyed is also very different. Others translate "道" simply into "Tao." "What is "道"? If the reader consults the dictionary, all he can find in the dictionary is the interpretation of "道." For example, according to the Collins English Dictionary, "道" is "That in virtue of which all things happen or exist." The first sentence of "Tao Te Ching," "道可道，非常道," in vernacular words means that the way that can be told of is not an unvarying way. How does what "道" and "可道" mean correspond to Benjamin's "ideographic object" and "ideographic method"? What does "道" mean exactly? The cultural interpretations and explanations made with language can never cover the meaning of "道" in translation and can never be equivalent to the cultural connotations carried by "道."

In that phrase, Laozi pointed out the limitations of language more than 2000 years ago. But there are also gains in translation. The Chinese version of the Bible of the Hong Kong Biblical Association translates the first sentence of "The Gospel of John," "In the beginning was the Word, and the Word was with God, and the Word was God" into Chinese as "宇宙被造之前，道已经存在。道与上帝同在，道是上帝." In the sentence, "Word" is translated into "道." Regardless of the appropriateness, the Chinese "道" and the English "Word" complement each other in intention, and the translation gains vitality in the new cultural system.

Referring to disseminating Chinese culture abroad, Lao She (1999b) said in the 1940s, "the introduction to a small literary book and a script abroad is no less effective than a political paper" (404). This case study shows that dissemination of Chinese culture through literary translation can convey "cultural diversity" by adopting unusual translation as one of many ways. Unusual translation may arouse misunderstanding among readers as an exhibition to spread itself at a certain time, but its significance would come with the translator's persistence and the deep going of the communications among cultures.[13]

Notes

1 Part of this article was published in Chinese in the journal *Studies of Ethnic Literature*. I would like to express my thanks to Lei Yu who produced a first draft of this English translation.

2 In 1939, George Gao wrote an article "The Novels of Lao Sheh" and introduced Lao She and his major stories and novels for the first time to the United States.

3 In 1944, Wang Chi-Chen edited and published a collection of Chinese stories *Contemporary Chinese Stories,* including Lao She's 5 short stories "Black Li and White Li," "The Glasses," "Grande Takes Charge," "The Philanthropist," and "Liu's Court." This is the first time that Lao She's stories were translated into English and published in the United States. (Wang)

4 In fact, there were three volumes of the Chinese editions of *The Yellow Storm*, but there were not 100 chapters. For example, when *Famine* was published in the Novel Monthly in 1950, the author deleted the last thirteen chapters. However, this is beyond the scope of this paper, so it is not discussed here. The Chinese citations of *The Yellow Storm* in the paper are quoted from the 1979 edition by Bai Hua Literature and Art Publishing House, so only the page number is included for subsequent citations.

5 In 1951, Harcourt Brace Publishers again abridged the translation of Ida Pruitt when it was re-published: "The editors of Harcourt Brace Publishers have made some abridgements." (Hu and Shu, 1994, p. 808)

6 Although there is no published evidence to confirm that Lao She read Chinese-American novels, it can be inferred that he would have had some understanding of Chinese-American novels of the time from his visit to the Iowa Writers' Workshop; his long-term contact with Pearl S. Buck; his contact with George Kao, Lin Tai Yi, Lin Yu Tang's daughter, and the Renault Publishing Company; as well as his experiences of living with American artists in Yaddo, the artist's colony near Saratoga Springs, NY.

7 For example, such customs can be found in Pardee Lowe's novel *Father and Glorious Son* (1943) and Jade Snow Wong's novel *The Fifth Chinese Daughter* (1945).

8 Chinese translation: "一次, 我和蒲爱德小姐在费城她哥哥家里过周末, 我们一起在林中散步时, 我为这四代人的故事, 想到了一个相当不错的名字, 即黄色风暴。" The Chinese title 《黄色风暴》 from "Yellow Storm" was not translated by Lao She, but by his daughter Shu Yue. The Chinese translation of the 1951 edition of *The Yellow Storm* is 《风吹草动》, (English: *Wind Blows, Grass Moves*) and the translator is unknown.

9 The "built-in colonization" of Chinese people in the United States refers to the discrimination and exclusion faced by new immigrants from American-born ethnic Chinese. For representation of this phenomenon, see David Henry Hwang's 1979 play *F.O.B.* and Fae Myenne Ng's novel *Bone*.

10 In fact, Ida Pruitt's unusual translation is a combination of transliteration and hard translation. The English translation of *The Yellow Storm* mainly adopts hard translation.

11 The daughter of a missionary, Ida Pruitt recalls in her English memoir *A China Childhood*, that when she was a child, she was not satisfied with her parents' westernizing of the house decoration and her parents' attitude of superiority over the local Chinese people. She made no secret of her deep affinity for Chinese culture: "After moving into this ancient Chinese house, they removed the plaid window and replaced it with a powerful upright western window. The paper in the panes, originally used to inhale soft sunlight, remove heat and cold and prevent peeking, is now replaced by glass windows, hard and cold, and has to be blocked with curtains. It is more tasteful to decorate in the Chinese style." (Pruitt, 1996, p. 5)

12 Benjamin once said that what translators need to reproduce is something unfathomable, mysterious and poetic in literary works. Through "hard translation," Ida Pruitt attempted to reproduce something unique to Chinese culture, which was similar to Zhang Ailing's fifth translation of *The Golden Cangue* in the late 1960s. The author once wrote a paper entitled "Literary adherence – Translation from Word to Poetic Exploration" (*Journal of East China Normal University*, issue 5, 2011), devoted to the reasons behind the translator's use of this translation technique. Much of the discussion in that paper is also relevant to the analysis of Ida Pruitt's translation.

13 The same is true of the fact that in the 1970s, Bruce Lee's movies and the star himself – the male body – were very popular in the United States, and American audiences generally accepted the spirit of courage and justice transmitted in Chinese kung fu. Lao She's thoughts on modern Chinese strong culture included the spirit of Chinese traditional martial arts culture. For details, see Zhang Man's "Individualized Creation of Writers in Specific Cultural Field: Lao She and Folk Martial Arts Culture – centered on novel *Breaking-Soul Spear*" (*Journal of Zhejiang Normal University*, issue 5, 2011).

References

Benjamin, W. (1923). The task of translator. In R. Schulte & J. Biguenet (Eds.), *The theory of translation: Anthology of essays from Dryden to Derrida*. The University of Chicago Press.

Even-Zohar, I. (2000). The position of translated literature within the literary poly-system. In D. L. Venuti (Ed.), *The translation studies reader*. Routledge.

Gao, G. (1939). The novels of Lao Sheh. *China Institute Bulletin, 3*, 184–189.

Hu, J. Q., & Shu, Y. (1994). The loss of the end of The Yellow Storm and the retranslation of its abbreviation. In *Lao She's Research material* （老舍研究资料）(Vol. 2). October Literature and Art Press.

Jiang, Q. (2012, May 26). Pearl S. Buck and Wang Ying. *Yangzi Evening News*.

Lao, S. (1993). *Lao She's collection of English letters* (Y. Shu, Trans.). Qin Yuan Publishing House.

Lao, S. (1999a). The dragon and snake of the Earth. In *Complete works of Lao She* (Vol. 9). People's Literature Publishing House.

Lao, S. (1999b). The view of traveling to the United States. In *Complete works of Lao She* (Vol. 14). People's Literature Publishing House.

Li, Y. L. (2007). Study of the mutual carrier relationship between language, literature and culture and comparative literature. *Journal of Gansu Union University, 6*, 71–75.

Liu, X. (2013). Zero degree of photography: Jean Baudrillard's photographic works and his photographic ideology. *Literature and Art Research, 10,* 88–98.

Lowe, P. (1943). *Father and glorious descendant.* Boston: Little, Brown and Company.

Lu, X. (1981). *Complete works of Lu Xun* (Vol. 16). People's Literature Publishing House.

Ma, Z. Y., & Ren, R. Z. (1997). *A series of translation studies in China* (汉籍外译史). Hubei Education Press.

Pruitt, I. (1978). *A China Childhood.* Chinese Materials Center.

Pruitt, I. (1996). *A China Childhood.* Liaoning People's Publishing House.

Shu, Y. (1993). *Collection of letter written in English by Lao She.* Tianjin: Qin yuan chubanshe.

Spence, J. D. (1997). *Cultural similarities and cultural utilization.* Peking University Press.

Venuti, D. L. (2008). *Translator's invisibility: A history of translation.* Routledge.

Venuti, D. L. (2001). Introduction. *Critical Inquiry, 2.*

Wang, C.-C. (Ed.). (1944). *Contemporary Chinese stories.* Columbia University Press.

Wang, Y. C. (2003). *Literary theory.* Sichuan People's Publishing House.

Wei, S. H. (2011). English translation of *The Yellow Storm* and Lao She's consciousness of national image communication. *Literary Review, 4,* pp. 110–115.

Wong, J. S. (1945). *The fifth Chinese daughter.* New York: Harper and Row.

8 Strategizing Hong Kong literature in the world

Self-collaborative translation of Dung Kai Cheung's *Atlas*

Uganda Sze Pui Kwan

Introduction

In the environment of ever more rapid globalization, frequent migration, international travel and increasing transnational marriages – all of these resulting in an increase in bi- or multi-lingual speakers – self-translation has become a new phenomenon in cross-cultural communication. A decade ago, self-translation in translation studies was still a neglected form that was discussed only among translators. This situation has changed. Now, the act of self-translating enables authors to attempt to seize their own voices, to speak to new audiences, to present themselves afresh, and to amass direct responses through unmediated channels (Hokenson & Munson, 2007). The discussions have gone beyond the multilingual competence of authors and their adaptability to new cultures (Besemeres & Wierzbicka, 2007; Al-Omar, 2012, pp. 211–219).

With this new awareness, translation studies have been bursting with a tremendous amount of academic discussions. These discussions provide a refreshed perspective to unearth some previously neglected self-translatorial praxes by canonical writers. Some studies have anchored the analyses within postcolonial studies, demonstrating the attempts of the marginalized to articulate their voices, which refuse to be domesticated by normalized standards. Some studies have also provided a great juncture to diagnose how writers have redefined, reshaped or even discarded their previously cultural or national identities through self-translating in a new environment (Abdo, 2009, pp. 1–42; Besemeres, 2002, pp. 102–111). These astounding revisionist studies of the self-translatorial attempts of bilingual writers such as Rabindranath Tagore (1861–1941), Karen Blixen (1885–1962), Samuel Beckett (1906–1989), Milan Kundera (1929–), Nancy Huston (1953–) and many more in the Western literary scenes have unleashed new synergies in various fields of literary studies.[1]

Additionally, this new intellectual vigor has impacted the studies of Modern Chinese Literature. The self-translation praxes of cross-cultural writers like Lin Yutang (林語堂 1895–1976), Xiao Qian (蕭乾 1910–1999) and Eileen Chang (張愛玲1920–1995) have been widely re-examined within this new framework. Alongside the canonical writers from Modern China, the self-translated literary endeavors from non-mainstream Chinese literature deserve equal recognition, despite their small market. In this paper, I will examine a series of self-translation practices by a contemporary Hong Kong writer, Dung Kai-cheung (1965–), who has garnered a new wave of global attention through his translations.

Dung is one of the most accomplished writers in Hong Kong (Wang, 2011, pp. 80–85), and his works have captured the attention of Sinophone literary circles.[2] The long list of awards Dung has received also explains his canonicity in the literary scene.[3] His novel, *Ditu ji: Yige xiangxiang de chengshi de kaogu xue* (地圖集：一個想像的城市的考古學 *The atlas: The archeology of an imaginary city;* hereafter *The Atlas* for the original Chinese version)[4], is a cogent example that allows us to tease out the dynamics that affect self-translating minority literature such as that of Hong Kong. After the original work *The Atlas* was published in 1997, Dung Kai-cheung did not retreat to his literary shrine to let the text's literary value slowly ferment and quietly wait for it to be discovered by a broader literary readership. Instead he self-translated the work into English in 1998. As we shall see below, self-translation to him was a cultural practice as well as a form of artistic activism, finding a voice in the ever-shrinking publication arena and freedom of speech issues for Hong Kong literature in the face of the hegemonic power under the new imperialism, globalized capitalism and dominant national and international languages (Chow, 1992, pp. 151–170).

The most intriguing phenomenon, to him and to scholars who are fascinated by the cultural practice of self-translation, is that self-translation alone was not formidable enough for Dung to reach his goal (or *skopós*). He recanted his self-translation. Within a decade, he participated in another round of self-translation, this time collaborating with two widely acclaimed English-speaking translators, and Dung reached a prestigious international scholar, David Der-wei Wang, who advocates for Sinophone literature.[5] The collaborative effort finally led to the publication of the full English translation *Atlas: The archaeology of an imaginary city* (hereafter, *Atlas*) by Columbia University Press (hereafter, CUP) in 2012. More inspiring was that *Atlas* was awarded "Best Translated Work Award: Science Fiction and Fantasy Translation Awards" in 2013. The publication and the translation award rebutted the stereotypical perception of CUP's own initial reviewers that a colony could never produce literature, since it is presumably a cultural desert – the perception that by rights, there is no such thing as Hong Kong literature categorically.

Dung Kai-cheung's self-translations of *The Atlas* have not only generated two English versions (one full and one partial translation), but also provided him an opportunity to scrutinize his original creation. In the process of self-translation with the two celebrated translators, he touched up his original version with more poetic, aesthetic and idiomatic expressions[6] and published a new Chinese version a decade later. Through his rewriting of the original, our discussion of the work can move beyond the binary framework of source vs target text, and the single-dimensional or directional flow from one language to another language (Cordingley, 2013; Heydel, 2015; pp. 329–331). A close analysis of his act of self-translation within the context of collaborative translation, therefore, offers a new emulation to probe into the most entangling theoretical conundrum involved in modern translation theories: the epistemological question of the original, the authorial and hierarchical status of its copies, the ontological being of the first version and the historical propensities to create and procreate the progenies or its afterlife. Below we shall investigate the dynamics in this translation, retranslation, self-translation and team (collaborative) translation in which Dung took an active part over the last two decades.

The Atlas: the story and the structure

Before delving into respective versions of the translations, we shall briefly introduce the fictional story and its structure. *The Atlas* is a typical postmodern fiction, which invites readers to deconstruct, question, and refute the story the author weaves throughout the narration. The fictional text has no plot, no characters, no story, and no settings. One book review says that this text beckons the readers to wrestle with their brainpower (Hong, 2012, p. 69).

Indeed, *The Atlas: The archeology of an imaginary city* is a work that has piqued the interest of a broad array of audiences since its publication. The text's structure follows a reading of a series of maps, from the ancient to the contemporary. Together there are 50-odd very short analytical chapter-like essays, which are conglomerated into four sections: "Theory," "Cities," "Streets" and "Symbols," Each essay runs about one to two pages. The opening section, "Theory," excavates the name of "Hong Kong" as it appears on maps, from the ancient to the contemporary. "Cities" mainly deals with the history of the City of Victoria; at the time it was ceded to the British Empire in 1842 "Hong Kong" was only an island at the historical juncture of Empires as well as waters. And this is where the histories started. The third section, "Streets," contains episodes of legends, stories and myths, meticulously recounting the names of streets in Hong Kong and their relationship with the local people and their cultural memories. The last section, "Symbols," offers an abstract interpretation of the imagined city's past, present and future. The whole book literally ends at 1997 when map archaeologists discovered a book entitled *The 1997 Hong Kong Street Directory & Guide*. All these chapters are intricately related to each other while being standalone independent reflections of the place concerned and its contested histories.

The Atlas is more than an aerial capture of a locality reflected through a structured spatial representation of the landscape. It is also a compilation of an archeological journal about a city, now lost, which once existed, but which might also have never existed – a city that exists merely in the imagination. The title *"The archeology of an imaginary city"* recalls a host of antagonistic ideas, from real to unreal, which foretell its task to excavate the cultural memory of Hong Kong from oblivion. The paradoxical elements in the title testify to its ambition to capture the attention of trained readers.

The text is written in Chinese, published in Taiwan by choice, and hence is printed in traditional Chinese characters. The Chinese title of each chapter or section is equipped with its corresponding English title to present an air of foreignness. These Chinese and English titles contain an immense quantity of pseudo-academic jargon or sophisticated academese (Pinker, 2014, p. 84) to denote the scientific disposition of what should be presented in an academic treatise. The text is also filled with a great deal of specious translation to show that authoritative theory is referenced, coupled with a massive number of footnotes and citations to authenticate the scientific accuracy.

Beyond the academic display and an ostentatious objective scientific overtone are several excerpts narrated by a first personal "I." Furthermore, the text is embedded with different layers of narrations, one of which records the melancholic tone of a young lad who confesses to having an unsalvageable craving for the knowledge of this lost city, Hong Kong. The whole fiction can be seen as a reading and a recording of the archeological rediscovery of the past of historians and general citizens who try to reassemble from the stack of surviving scraps of historical maps the image of a city once named Hong Kong, until its demise in 1997.

When *The Atlas* was first published in 1997, it was widely agreed that the fiction was the author's response to the handover of Hong Kong to the People's Republic of China (PRC). The historical milieu at the time recorded an unprecedented soaring interest in the search for the cultural identity and history of the colonial city, which had come under British rule in 1842. Internationally, the world watched skeptically at how a highly capitalistic city was to be integrated into a socialist system. In the region, optimistic researchers from East Asia and working in Cross-Straits relations (i.e., Mainland-Taiwan relations) awaited the fruition of a "One Country Two Systems" with the hope of a possible implementation of a similar system in Macao and, particularly, Taiwan, Republic of China (ROC). Hong Kong, however, abounded with pessimism and apathy. Scholars professed the "disappearing of Hong Kong" (Abbas, 1997), while in 1995 *Fortune*, one of the world's largest economic magazines, forecast the "death of Hong Kong" (Kraar & McGowan, 1995).[7]

In a broader historical context, 1997 was situated at the closure of a century. The prevailing fin-de-siècle environment propelled a gloomy outlook: "the end of history." Historian Francis Fukuyama argued that the advent of Western liberal democracy might signal the endpoint of humanity's sociocultural evolution and the final form of human government (Fukuyama, 1992).

Despite appearing solemn, sentimental and heavy, *The Atlas* has a light-hearted side. The text alludes to and satirizes numerous celebrated literary works, creating a compelling inter-textual effect with many postmodernist writings across time and space. Brought to the minds of the readers of *The Atlas* are Marco Polo's city observation notes and the poetry of Charles Baudelaire's Flânuer, both of which allow the audience to reflect upon the authors' findings of the highly prosperous cities. *The Atlas* also pays tribute to postmodern literary giants Italo Calvino (1923–1985), Umberto Eco (1932–2016), and Jorge Luis Borges (1899–1986), just to name a few. Indeed, *The Atlas* straddles the genres of history, cartographical reading, archeological journal, fictional text and academic treatise.

The Atlas presented more than an ambitious writer demonstrating his literary skills. It was a political, cultural, and social manifesto of a local Hong Kong writer who presented his cultural identity at a specific historical perforation. The entire text is composed of authentic and imaginary historical evidence, claims and materials. The fabricated and made-up information has been built on the surviving historical accounts of Hong Kong. The purpose of posing this pseudo-historical inquiry is to pinpoint the arbitrariness between sign, signifier and meaning. It is designed to question the fixed national identities that the People's Republic of China's propaganda has claimed, that is that Hong Kong has historically been "a part of China" as evidenced by Chinese relics from as early as the Tang Dynasty that continue to be found in Hong Kong archeological sites. As any archeologist could avow, the relics only demonstrate that there had been human activity conducted in this particular geo-spatial location. Whether this proves Hong Kong has historically been "a part of China" or whether this human activity proves "the footprint left by a Hong Kong ancestor," which then can be wittily understood as "apart from China," were too far-fetched (Dung, 1998, pp. 45–47).

What *The Atlas* is trying to do is to highlight the political implications created out of historical materialities. Historical writing is simply an agency of pretension with which the bygone can be represented by language and words. *The Atlas* deploys a synthetic language that is predicated on the assumption that no truth could be found in the embedded historicity of the materials. In addition, the synthetic or hybrid language used throughout the text is a way to celebrate the cultural identity of Hong Kong, which has long been criticized as impure or hybrid, a concept that carried negative connotations in the city's early days, as Hong Kong people traversed between "pure" Chinese culture and "pure" British culture. It was only when postcolonialism arrived that this hybrid culture started to gain its cultural stature. Should purity come from ethnicity-race, nation-state, national identity, language, cultural literary status or lineage? Again, Dung leaves the reader to ponder.

The genealogical evolution of the original, multiple versions and translations

Before we delve into the complexities of the ontological question of the original, we should briefly provide a simple genealogical flow of the evolution of *The Atlas*, which helps to demonstrate the dynamics between the original and the translations, as when the former grew into multiple versions.

First published in Chinese by Taiwanese Unitas Publishing 台灣聯合文學 in June 1997, and so much in demand that it had its third print-run in July of that year, *The Atlas*, in the form of seven representative chapters, found its way into an anthology of Hong Kong fictional works via an English translation entitled *Hong Kong collage: Contemporary stories and writing* (hereafter *HKC*).[8] The collection was edited by translation studies scholar Martha Cheung in 1998 and showcased the writings of Hong Kong "when the city was steeped in anxiety about the future" (Cheung, 1998, p. v.).

The anthology was published by the Hong Kong Oxford University Press (the English department suspended in publishing). Chapters from the section "Streets," selected and translated by Dung, are included in the first section of "History" in *HKC*. These chapters are remarkable because they serve as an indicator of the author's choice from the perspectives of various international translators when the text is partially translated into Dutch, French and Macedonian languages. In the second section "Landmarks" of *HKC*, we find "A government house with a view" (Cheung, 1998, pp. 83–84). Another chapter, "The centaur of the East" (Cheung, 1998, pp. 202–204), is categorized in "Epilogue: 1997 and beyond," which are all translated by Dung. It is important to recognize these detailed facts of the anthologizing, because they present textual evidence to compare changes through various self-translations made by the author over time. We should begin with a sense of his debut translation:

> In the early days of the City of Victoria, the governors did not have a permanent residence and office, not until the erection of Government House on Government Hill in 1855. Yet in an 1856 map of the Central District, Government House was still only marked out in dotted lines, thus casting doubt on the exact date of its construction. "A government house with a view."
>
> (Cheung, 1998, pp. 83–84)

As we can see, Dung has taken up the double role as author and translator. This chapter title, originally marked as "總督府的景觀 A government house with a view" in the 1997 version, was transplanted into this 1998 English version. He made no changes. Dung simply faithfully translated himself. The editor also approved such direct transplantation. Here, the traditional cultural logic of translation prevails. The status of the original text as the source of meaning and authority remains unchallenged.

In 2006 another English translation emerged. In this translation, only one single chapter from *The Atlas* was selected. Bonnie S. McDougall, a highly experienced literary translator, initiated it. McDougall is an Australian sinologist and a veteran translator of Chinese texts into English from as early as her affiliation with the Communist Party's Central Compilation and Translation Bureau 中共中央編譯局 in the 1970s. She received a visiting appointment at the Chinese University of Hong Kong from 2006 to 2010 to teach translation and to take the editorship of the world-renowned literary translation magazine *Renditions*, published by the Chinese University of Hong Kong. During that time she translated the chapter "春園街 Spring Garden Lane," a chapter that Dung had not previously translated into English, and included it in the *Renditions* special issue of Hong Kong essays (*Renditions*, 2006, pp. 11–113). She produced the translation as a show of support for Hong Kong literature and an active engagement in the local culture. The later team/collaborative translation of *The Atlas* that would be published in 2012 originated in this earlier translation.

Later on, during the translation process of *The Atlas*, Bonnie McDougall frequently sought clarification from Dung as *The Atlas* is overloaded with local knowledge of Hong Kong and Cantonese colloquial expressions. Although bilingual in Chinese and English, Dung, like many Hong Kong writers, in his everyday life uses his mother tongue, Cantonese, which is a kind of topolect within the Sinitic language. The language he uses to express his creative mind is, however, the Standard Chinese language, on which the Mandarin Chinese syntax is based. Dung therefore deliberately used Cantonese in the writing to evoke a sense of belonging despite the fact that the original Chinese version was published in Taiwan. In the collaborative translation, Dung and McDougall relinquished Dung's 1998 English translation and invited Anders Hansson, an experienced and highly acclaimed literary translator, to join the team. It took about two or three years for them to finish the translation.

In the long preface written by the author and an introduction by the translators, co-translator Bonnie McDougall describes the content, background and the translation problems. She also unveils the author's intent, the translation *skopós*; and how the team conducted an unprecedented interaction between the author and translators at the "post-creation" and "post-translation" stages. These interactions traversed temporal spaces surpassing the original text, venturing into metatext, and uncovering the distribution of work, processes, and strategies of this translation:

> Each of us took responsibility for one or two parts, and each of us read and checked each other's drafts. It took about two years, partly because of the density of the writing, in particular the complex intertwining of fiction, fact and theory (or antitheory).
>
> (Bonnie McDougall, *The Atlas*, "Introduction," p. xxxii)

If a reader read *The Atlas* in 1997 and expected the version of 2012 by CUP to be its direct descendant, then in the first instance he would probably feel betrayed. But through a forensic study of the textual differences between the 1997 and 2012 versions he might come to know the abundant changes that have been made. We can sort the differences into 3 main groups.

(a) Language

Readers will notice that the English chapter titles in the original Chinese Source Text have been amended slightly in the English translation. As shown in Table 8.1, amendments in TT (underlined by me) have been made as a result of pragmatics, common usages or simply to improve consistency.

As we can see, changes are bound to be made in the translation because of the differences in grammatical structures and word choices between the source languages and the target languages, which are variants of Chinese and English respectively. There are plenty of examples in *The Atlas*. For instance, in 【S2】"Gordon's Gaol" has been amended to 【T2】"Gordon's Jail." We can thus safely conclude that this change is made for the American market as the term "gaol" is archaic and parochial. Whereas for the expression in 【S7】"the idea," now changes to 【T7】"idea," the determiner is removed to improve the function of

Table 8.1 Textual comparison between ST (1997) and TT (2012)

Source Text (ST) published in 1997, The atlas	Target Text (TT) in English translation in 2012, Atlas
Part Two: The City	
【S1】 ＜砵甸乍的顛倒視覺＞ Pottinger's reversed vision	【T2】 Pottinger's Inverted Vision
【S2】 戈登的監獄 Gordon's Gaol	【T2】 Gordon's Jail
【S3】 裙帶路的回歸 THE RETURN to KWAN TAI LOO	【T3】 THE RETURN of KWAN TAI LOO
【S4】 ＜維多利亞之虛構一八八九＞ 1889 Plan of Victoria 1889	【T4】 "Plan of the City of Victoria," 1889
【S5】 ＜四環九約＞four wans and nine yeuks	【T5】 The Four Wan and Nine Yeuk
【S6】 ＜總督府的景觀＞a government house with a view	【T6】 The View from Government House
【S7】 "指同一現實 **(the real)** 和理形 **(the idea)"**	【T7】 A Platonic relationship exists between counterplaces . . . . **"reality" or "idea"**

grammatical accuracy. It would be underestimating self-translating to describe it as a mechanical transfer, and collaborative translation is more than just a grammar check. Self-translating allows authors to slide between the axis of writing and rewriting between two languages and two cultures or to expose themselves to the respective readership. It sometimes forces the author to re-read, re-examine or re-assess their work from a reader's perspective. A prominent example was Milan Kundera's self-translation of his works from Czech to French after he moved to France in 1975, in which the content was also altered to a large extent (Woods, 2006). In Dung's case, he found the original title in his 1997 version in the section of "The city," "總督府的景觀 A government house with a view" problematic only when producing the collaborative translation. This title was later amended into "The view from Government House" in the English version of 2012. This implies that although Dung self-translated his work in 1998, self-translation did not necessarily propel him to reflect on the good and bad qualities of his original work.

(b) Historical content

Self-collaborative translation provided Dung a valuable opportunity to re-examine the text and to amend content that might not have been historically accurate. For instance, in the chapter titled "Mr. Smith's One-day Trip" (The atlas, 1997, p. 91), the source text indicates ". . . 雅加達等英國殖民地 . . . [British colonies including Jakarta . . .]" (my translation because *The Atlas* deleted this sentence). In the translation of 2012, it is replaced with "The ocean liner SS Sunrise sailed from England by way of [the] Mediterranean to the British colonies of India and Singapore . . . (Mr. Smith's one-day trip, *The Atlas*, p. 64)." Jakarta was obviously not a British colony; the error had to be dealt with, and this clause was hence deleted.

(c) Style

As said previously, *The Atlas* is a pseudo-academic treatise designed to satirize the pretensions of the objectiveness of science – the belief that scientific knowledge is immune from ideological manipulation. Post-structuralists have already reminded us about the entwined relationship of knowledge and power. Anyone engaged in knowledge production knows that one must use an immense amount of academic jargon and demonstrate extensive reading of scientific thought to attain the thoroughness required of an academic paper. Sometimes, papers are padded with extensive awkward translations to show that authoritative theory is referenced, and copious notes and citations of classics are included to show evidence. Such is the theoretical framework that has been set up by the "archaeology" in *The Atlas's* subtitle and the content of "Part 1: Theory." In this part of the text, there are footnotes that express the science of the text and the authoritativeness of the essay. However, In the English translation, the footnote appended to the chapter of "Extra territoriality" (The atlas, 1997, pp. 28–32) has been deleted. In the original the footnote was written in archaic Chinese prose, mimicking the historical Chinese style, which aggravated the historical value of the pseudo-finding of the archeological artifacts. For the Anglophone reader, this is not only irrelevant, but also indigestible.

Dung never explicitly divulged that he would rewrite the original version of 1997. Nor did he announce that he altered the original text. The change of the original remains an obscure fact. The metatextual transference among versions remained a solemn game. In 2011 an illustrated version of *The Atlas* was published by another press in Taiwan to promote the pictorial design of a young Hong Kong illustrator. Although this illustrated Chinese version was presented as a visually beautified version, it should be safe to surmise that Dung planned to use this version to incorporate all the changes made since the full-fledged English translation had been conceptualized.

Ever since this 聯經 (Linking Publishing) version was published, the genealogical development of the original and the subsequent translations was disturbed (Dung, 2011). As a result, the existence of the various translations into foreign languages since 2011 allows us to see that the ontological being of the original has been completely dismantled through the proliferation of versions including the Japanese full translation in 2012[9] and the two French partial translations in 2014 and 2016 (Dung, 2014, pp. 615–639; Dung, 2016, pp. 384–431). The partial translations respectively in Macedonian in 2013 (Dung, 2013, pp. 98–104) and Dutch in 2017 (Dung, 2012a), revealed that Dung replaced the original 1997 Chinese version and ensured that the global reception of *The Atlas* through translation would be based on his 2011 Chinese version. This can be summed up by the following two pictorial charts (Figure 8.1 and 8.2):

| 1997 | 1998 | 2006 | 2011 | 2012 | 2012 | 2013 | 2014 | 2016 | 2017 |
| Unitas | OUP | *Renditions* | Linking | Kawade | Columbia | *Kulturen zhivot* | *Critique* | *Jentayu* | *Terras* |

| Chinese (Original) | English (abridged) | English (abridged) | Chinese (revised from 1997) | Japanese (full) | English (full) | Macedonian (abridged) | French (abridged) | French (abridged) | Dutch (abridged) |

Figure 8.1 Translations of *The Atlas* in chronological order

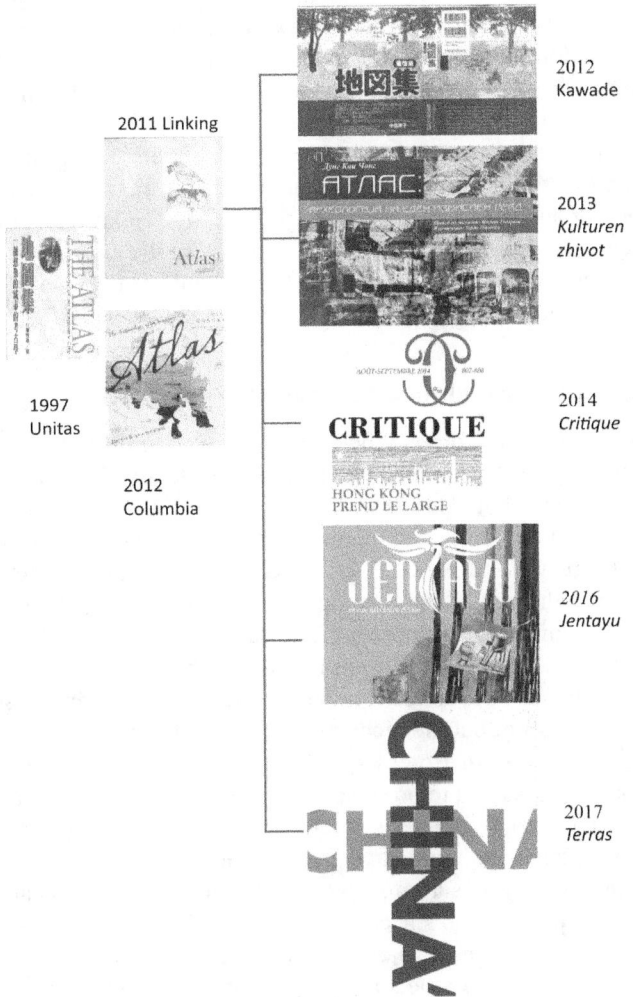

Figure 8.2 The rewritten version has replaced the original

After 2011, the translational flow or the synergies created by the translators and the author were no longer restricted to a one-way traffic flow: from the original to the translation, from the author to the translator. Instead, the translation sequence should be conceived as the following:

Another special feature of the English translation published in 2012 is that it comes with a long preface written by the author, titled "An archeology for the future." In this preface, he says, "I have learned many things from them [the two co-translators Bonnie McDougall and Anders Hansson] as a co-translator and have made revisions to the original Chinese text at various places that couldn't stand the close scrutiny of these two experienced teachers" (*The Atlas*, 2012b, p. xxxii). Here, Dung conferred a new authorial intent and bestowed his authority on his co-translators. Unlike Vladimir Nabokov, who always continued controlling everything as he self-translated his work with the co-translators (Beaujour, 1995, pp. 714–24), Dung used the analogy of teacher and student to describe the relationship between the translator and himself. He was a humble student and he was the receiver.

This has transformed the previous known power relations between the author and translators. *The Atlas* demonstrates a new model of self- and team-translations. Self-translation could preserve his sentiment and the textual form intact, but this collaborative translation enabled him to confront his limits and linguistic shortcoming and perfect the author's self-translation. More importantly, with the joint effort, the author and the translators made the invisible Hong Kong literature visible. This new visibility redressed Dung's criticism on the representation of Hong Kong in his translation *skopos*, "A large part of the reality of life here [Hong Kong] is unrepresented, unrevealed, and ignored," Dung lamented (*The Atlas*, 2012b, xii).

Self-collaborative translation as strategy

Self-collaborative translation may be a plausible way to deal with the marginalization of Hong Kong literature. The Hong Kong literary field has always been diverse and pluralistic but also scattered and contentious. An important initial fact that deserves our attention is that mainstream Hong Kong literature is written in the Chinese language, and although Hong Kong is a bilingual society and effective translation is the vehicle of governmental administration, Hong Kong literature written in English or literature translated into English is situated at the margin of society (Ho, 2003, pp. 5–25). There has always been a prosperous market for popular literature (such as romance, crime, thrillers, and non-fiction such as travelogues) in Hong Kong, but the niche market of highbrow literature is small. Yet the geopolitical position of Hong Kong has always been the centripetal point to publish dissident works and to produce translated works on politics and history.[10] The production and receiving mechanisms of Hong Kong publishing are directly related to Hong Kong's geopolitical cultural identity.

Hong Kong has served as a safe haven for Chinese intellectuals and dissidents to avoid political persecution since late imperial China. In the late 1930s, a huge number of Chinese mainlanders carrying immense capital migrated south to avoid political unrest in China after the long civil war between the Communist Party and the Nationalist Party (*Kuomintang*). The British Hong Kong government implemented liberal policies to avoid interfering – as long as neither *Kuomintang* nor the Communist Party instigated anti-British imperialist sentiments in the colony. The subsequent cold war that divided the world into ideological camps enabled Hong Kong to become a gateway of free trade in East Asia from the 1950s (Tay, 2000, pp. 31–38). Furthermore, copyright law implemented in the United Kingdom in 1956 was enacted on 12th December 1972 in Hong Kong, and The Berne Convention for the Protection of Literary and Artistic Works and the World Copyright Conventions have been implemented in Hong Kong since the 1970s. Understandably, Hong Kong became the spearhead of translating foreign literature with authorized copyrights in Greater China. During the 80s, Mainland China was still wretched from the Cultural Revolution (1967–1977) and it was not until 1987 that Taiwan's martial law came to an end; a political approach toward publication was dominating across the Straits. Situated in between the two Chinese ideological camps with their two distinct Chinese scriptal readerships (Simplified and Traditional Chinese characters), the colonial Hong Kong government's laissez-faire policy made Hong Kong a safe haven for knowledge circulation. Freedom of information, the rule of law and an independent judicial system that restrained the capitalist Hong Kong system made this place one of the most prosperous global publishing and book-trade hubs in the world (Ku & Ngai, 2004; Meyer, 2000).

Laissez-faire policy inevitably comes with a downside. The British Hong Kong government never proactively promoted Hong Kong literature. There was no state-sponsored patronage, and market forces alone shaped the publishing industry (Even-Zohar, 1990, pp. 47–48, 110). Citing Itamar Even-Zohar's polysystem theory, we would say that the literary vacuum was soon filled by capitalist power. The intertwining publishing strategy of printing popular books alongside much lower-selling "highbrow" literature, politically sensitive or profane, can be seen as an awkward business model to sustain. Some publishers when introducing foreign literature even highlight the popular texts that they have translated and introduced into the local Hong Kong market to enlarge their market share. The strategies used to promote the works of Seichō Matsumoto 松本清張 (1909–1992) and Murakami Haruki 村上春樹 (1949–), such as suppressing the philosophical quest in the latter's works, demonstrate the unconventional tactics used in promoting translated Japanese literature in Hong Kong in the 1970s and 80s.[11] Many local Hong Kong bookstores need to sell an extraordinary amount of stationery and fancy tie-in products, such as those of Disneyland, to pay the skyrocketing rents in order to stay in business; and many local literary writers need to live double lives: anonymous columnists or writers of popular fiction by day while pursuing their literary endeavors by night.

Like many widely acclaimed highbrow literary writers in Hong Kong, such as Xixi (西西 or張彥, 1938 –), Dung strategically chose Taiwan to launch his literary debut in the mid-1990s, highlighted the large literary and cultural backdrop of Hong Kong. Taiwan's sturdy literary market, full-fledged literary mechanisms, and robust reading community in the Chinese language have made it an ideal publication outlet for highbrow literary works to gather broader readerships. Dung chose to publish in traditional Chinese characters in Taiwan as an effort to preserve the literary taste, and he retranslated his previously self-translated works into more lyrical English with other prominent translators for a wider international audience. His choice can be seen as one way for a local writer to avoid compromising literary quality in the highly commercialized and ever-politicized local market in order to survive the severity of the environment and preserve his critical voice.

Conclusion

Translating is one means to secure the prosperity and vitality of Hong Kong literature in the world. After being published in the Chinese language to satisfy the demands of the Chinese market (Sinophone circles that go beyond mainland China and Taiwan), these literary works from Hong Kong enter the international arena and world market of literature through translation. Self-collaborative translation would also be a viable strategy in the post-colonialist era because it allows the author to actively present himself with someone with whom he is willing to share the author's authority in the process of translation. Indeed, the translated text can also be published with the author's approval or after discussion with the author even if the author herself does not participate in the translation process. But when considering the content of the text, it is important for the author and the translators to work together to reflect the author's voice and opinions and keep them authentic. In any event, if an author chooses to translate his work himself, he needs to examine his work critically and skeptically, taking the viewpoint of the reader, sentence by sentence, carefully thinking about the elements within each word. Even if the author and the translator happen to be the same person, the roles, responsibilities, and voices are different, and scholarly work in this area continues to illuminate the consequences and significance of those differences.

Acknowledgments

The author wishes to thank the following editors, designers, translators and publishers for granting copyright and their provision of high-quality images.

Audrey Heijns (Terras, Dutch translation); Alena Chow (Research Center for translation Hong Kong); Jerome Bouchaud (Jentayu, French translation); Zoran Poposki and Marija Todorova (Kulturen zhivot; Macedonian translation).

Notes

1 As of now, the research on the self-translation (or auto-translation) endeavor of Samuel Beckett and Milan Kundera are the most prominent.
2 For the definition of Sinophone literature, see Shih, Tsai, and Bernards (2013), Jing and Wang (2010).
3 To name just a few awards he has received over the years: Unitas Fiction Writing Award for New Writers in Taiwan (1994), the United Daily News Literary Award in Taiwan (1995), Hong Kong Arts Development Council Rookie Award (1997), Best Artist of the Year (Literature) (2008), Hong Kong Book Fair Author of the Year (2014).

4 For easy reference, publications in the Chinese and Japanese languages will be trans-literated according to *Hanyu pinyin* (Mandarin) and the Hepburn system, followed by their respective original title and then an English gloss.

5 See the interview with David Der-wei Wang, Professor of Chinese at Harvard University, in which he unveiled how the translation was dismissed by Columbia University Press in the first round of reviews with the criticism: "there is no such category as Hong Kong literature" (as cited in Chan, 2014).

6 Self-translation offers a valuable opportunity for the author to confront their writing self. See Nikolayev (1999, pp. 37–41), Perry (1981, pp. 181–192).

7 *Fortune Magazine* proclaimed the "death of Hong Kong" in their featured story published on June 26, 1995.

8 These chapters are: "Possession street" (Cheung, 1998, pp. 40–41); "Scandal point and the military cantonment," (Cheung, 1998, pp. 42–44); "Aldrich Street," (Cheung, 1998, pp. 44–45); "Ice House Street" (Cheung, 1998, pp. 46–47); "Sugar Street (Cheung, 1998, pp. 47–49); "Sycamore Street" (Cheung, 1998, pp. 49–51); "Tsat Tsz Mui Road" (Cheung, 1998, pp. 51–52).

9 *Chizushū* 地图集 (*Atlas*) has been translated into Japanese by two professional and experienced academic translators Fuji Shōzō 藤井省三 and Kyōko Nakajima 中島京子.

10 The best example would be the strategic choice of Hong Kong to be the publishing site of the full Chinese translations of the majestic works by two Harvard professors and historians, Ezra F. Vogel and Roderick MacFarquhar (Vogel, 2011; MacFarquhar, 1974a, 1974b, 1987). Both world-acclaimed Chinese experts saw Hong Kong as a beacon of hope in upholding publication and academic freedom on Chinese soil and hence chose presses in Hong Kong (Chinese University of Hong Kong Press and New Century Press respectively) to arrange the translation, distribution and publication of the full Chinese translated versions of their books. Their mainland Chinese versions have been censored (Jacobs, 2013; Bury, 2013; Bao, 2019). I owe many thanks to these two historians who shared with me their deep conviction that Hong Kong was where they would publish their full Chinese versions during my visiting appointments at the Fairbank Center for Chinese Studies at Harvard University in 2014. The validity of Vogel and MacFarquhar's statements of course arguably expired in 2015 when the Causeway Bay Bookstore incident erupted.

11 Hong Kong was the first Chinese reading community in Greater China to translate the two Japanese literary giants through a proper copyright liaison and the global distribution rights of the Chinese versions in the 70s and 80s (Kwan, 2009, pp. 205–265; Kwan, 2013, pp. 100–124).

References

Abbas, A. (1997). *Hong Kong: Culture and the politics of disappearance*. University of Minnesota Press.

Abdo, D. M. (2009). Textual migration: Self-translation and translation of the self in Leila Abouzeid's *return to childhood: The memoir of a modern Moroccan woman and Ruju 'Ila Al-Tufulah*. *Frontiers: A Journal of Women Studies, 30*(2), 1–42.

Al-Omar, N. A. M. (2012). The self-translator as cultural mediator: In memory of Jabra Ibrahim Jabra. *Asian Social Science, 8*(13), 211–219.

Bao, P. (2019, February 16). Roderick MacFarquhar: A remembrance. *China File*. Retrieved from www.chinafile.com/reporting-opinion/viewpoint/roderick-macfarquhar-remembrance

Beaujour, E. K. (1995). Translation and self-translation. In V. E. Alexandrov (Ed.), *The Garland companion to Vladimir Nabokov* (pp. 714–24). Garland.

Besemeres, M. (2002). Immigrant embarrassment and self-translation in Andrew Riemer's "The Habsburg Café". In R. Dalziell (Ed.), *Selves crossing cultures: Autobiography and globalization* (pp. 102–111). Australian Scholarly.

Besemeres, M., & Wierzbicka, A. (Eds.). (2007). *Translating lives: Living with two languages and cultures*. St. University of Queensland Press.

Bury, L. (2013, October 22). Author bows to Chinese censorship of his Deng Xiaoping biography. *The Guardian*. Retrieved from www.theguardian.com/books/2013/oct/22/author-chinese-censorship-den-xiaoping-biography

Chan, E. (Director). (2014, October 5). The rose of the name: The map of Dung Kai-cheung (Part 1). [Television series episode] In Lo, C. W. (Producer), *Outstanding Chinese Writers Series II*. Radio Television Hong Kong.

Cheung, M. P. Y. (1998). Acknowledgments. In M. P. Y. Cheung (Ed.), *Hong Kong collage: Contemporary stories and writing* (p. v). Oxford University Press.

Chow, R. (1992). Between colonizers: Hong Kong's postcolonial self-writing in the 1990s. *Diaspora: A Journal of Transnational Studies, 2*(2), 151–170.

Cordingley, A. (2013). *Self-translation: Brokering originality in hybrid culture*. Continuum.

Dung, K.-C. (1997). *The Atlas: The archeology of an imaginary city*. Unitas Publishing.

Dung, K.-C. (1998). *Tongdairen* 同代人 *Contemporaneities* (pp. 46–47). Sanren Chuban.

Dung, K.-C. (2006). Atlas (B. S. McDougall, Trans.). *Renditions: Hong Kong Essays, 66*(Autumn), 11–113. (Original work published 1997)

Dung, K.-C. (2011). *The Atlas: The archeology of an imaginary city*. Linking Press. (Original work published 1997)

Dung, K.-C. (2012a). *Atlas* (A. Heijns, Trans.). *Terras, 13*. (Original work published 1997). Retrieved from https://tijdschriftterras.nl/fragmenten-uit-atlas/

Dung, K.-C. (2012b). *Atlas* (K.-C. Dung, A. Hansson, & B. S. McDougall, Trans.). Columbia University Press. (Original work published 1997)

Dung, K.-C. (2013). *Atlas* (M. Todorova Trans.). *Kulturen zhivot Cultural Life*, 98–104. (Original work published 1997)

Dung, K.-C. (2014). *Atlas* (S. Veg, Trans.). *Revue Critique, 8*, 615–639, 807–808. (Original work published 1997)

Dung, K.-C. (2016). *Atlas* (G. Gaffric, Trans.). *Jentayu: Cartes et Territoires, 4*, 384–431. (Original work published 1997)

Even-Zohar, I. (1990). Polysystem studies. *Poetics Today: International Journal for Theory and Analysis of Literature and Communication, 11*(1), 47–48, 110.

Fukuyama, F. (1992). *The end of history and the last man*. Maxwell Macmillan.

Heydel, M. (2015). Self-translation: Brokering originality in hybrid culture. *Perspectives Studies in Translatology, 23*(2), 329–331.

Ho, E. (2003). Connecting cultures: Hong Kong literature in English, the 1950s. *New Zealand Journal of Asian Studies, 5*(2), 5–25.

Hokenson, J. W., & Munson, M. (2007). *The bilingual text, history and theory of literary self-translation*. St. Jerome.

Hong, T. (2012). Book review of *Atlas: The archaeology of an imaginary city*, by K. Dung. *Library Journal, 137*(11), 69.

Jacobs, A. (2013, October 19). Authors accept censors' rules to sell in China. *The New York Times*. Retrieved from https://nyti.ms/17VD8Ch

Jing, T., & Wang, D. (Eds.). (2010). *Global Chinese literature: Critical essays*. Brill.

Kraar, L., & McGowan, J. (1995, June 26). The death of Hong Kong. *Fortune Magazine*. Retrieved from https://archive.fortune.com/magazines/fortune/fortune_archive/1995/06/26/203948/index.htm

Ku, A. S., & Ngai, P. (Eds.). (2004). *Remaking citizenship in Hong Kong: Community, nation and the global city*. Curzon.

Kwan, U. (2009). Honkon ni okeru chishiki seisan no ryōiki to murakami haruki no fukyū 香港における知識生産の領域と村上春樹の普及 The field of cultural production and the dissemination of Haruki Murakami in the 80–90s. In Fuji Shōzō (Ed.), *Murakami Haruki Sutadīzu* 村上春樹スタディーズ *Haruki Murakami studies* (pp. 205–265). Wakakusa Shobo.

Kwan, U. (2013). Honkon 1980-nendai ni okeru Seichō Matsumoto hon'yaku būmu 香港 1980 年代における松本清張翻訳ブーム The reception of Seichō Matsumoto in 1980s Hong Kong. *The Studies of Seichō Matsumoto* 松本清張研究 *Seichō Matsumoto Kenkyu, 14,* 100–124.

MacFarquhar, R. (1974a). *The origins of the cultural revolution: Contradictions among the people, 1956–1957.* Columbia University Press.

MacFarquhar, R. (1974b). *The origins of the cultural revolution: The great leap forward 1958–1960.* Columbia University Press.

MacFarquhar, R. (1987). *The origins of the cultural revolution: The coming of the cataclysm, 1961–1966.* Columbia University Press.

Meyer, D. R. (2000). *Hong Kong as a global metropolis.* Cambridge: Cambridge University Press.

Nikolayev, S. G. (1999). Autotranslation as a specific variety of poetical transversion. *Rostovskaya Elektronnaya Gazeta, 28*(4), 37–41.

Perry, M. (1981). "Thematic and structural shifts" in autotranslations by bilingual Hebrew-Yiddish writers: The case of Mendele Mokher Sforim. *Poetics Today, 2*(4), 181–192.

Pinker, S. (2014). *The sense of style: The thinking person's guide to writing in the 21st century.* Penguin.

Shih, S. M., Tsai, C. H., & Bernards, B. (Eds.). (2013). *Sinophone studies: A critical reader.* Columbia University Press.

Tay, W. (2000). Colonialism, the cold war era, and marginal Space: The existential conditions of four decades of Hong Kong literature. In P. Chi & D. Wang (Eds.), *Chinese literature in the second half of a modern century* (pp. 31–38). Indiana University Press.

Vogel, E. F. (2011). *Deng Xiaoping and the transformation of China.* The Belknap Press of Harvard University Press.

Wang, D. (2011). A Hong Kong miracle of a different kind. *China Perspectives, 1,* 80–85.

Woods, M. (2006). *Translating Milan Kundera.* Multilingual Matters.

9 English translation of Mo Yan's *Life and Death Are Wearing Me Out*

A cognitive narratology perspective[1]

Lu Shao

Cognitive narratology: origin and development

Cognitive narratology is one of the three most influential branches[2] of postclassical narratology.[3] While the term "cognitive narratology" was initially proposed by Manfred Jahn (1997), this strand of narratology was built upon Fludernik's influential work *Towards a "Natural" Narratology* (1996).[4] As an emerging interdisciplinary approach, cognitive narratology provides a cognitive basis for narrative analysis by integrating the concepts from classical narratology with those of other disciplines,[5] cognitive sciences in particular. Cognitive narratology explores the relationship between narrative and mind by unraveling the role of cognition processes in narrative comprehension, and the ways in which recipients (including readers and audiences) reconstruct the "storyworlds" (Herman, 2002) in their minds. It analyzes how narratives stimulate thinking – especially how the recipients can be prompted by textual cues to understand narratives through certain cognitive strategies. Also, it discusses the ways in which characters' perception and experience of the events, as well as their states of mind, can be represented in narratives and be inferred and interpreted through textual cues by the recipients. As an important branch of postclassical narratology, cognitive narratology reveals the interaction among "textual cues," "narrative (generic) conventions" and "(conventional) cognitive frames" (Shen, 2005, p. 156; Shen & Wang, 2010, p. 244).

Considered "one of the most prominent and fast growing strands of postclassical narratology" (Shen, 2004, p. 8), cognitive narratology has contributed its special part to the analysis of narrative works and to the revitalization of narrative studies in the West (Shen & Wang, 2010, p. 245). Through textual cues, it studies the cognitive and psychological processes in readers' interpretation of stories. This approach thus prioritizes interpretation and reception of narrative works, shifting the analytical focus from "texts" in classical narratology to "reader-text relationships."

While scholarship on cognitive narratology has proliferated in the West (Bortolussi & Dixon, 2003; Fludernik, 1996, 2003; Herman, 2002; Jahn, 1997, 2005; Ryan, 2003), research in this area is a fairly new endeavor in China, with only limited discussions found in Shen (2004), Shen and Wang (2010), Zhang (2011),

Tang (2013) and Shang (2013). There is a lack of more focused theoretical exploration, let alone empirical studies that apply cognitive narratology to specific cases. Currently, cognitive narratology is still at a rudimentary stage of development in China. Existing studies in this regard mostly offer general introductions to the theory but have not yet initiated systematic and in-depth examinations. Application of cognitive narratology to translation studies is even more rare, and no attempt so far has been made at developing this strand of narratological approach to the contrastive analysis of original and translated literary texts.

Drawing upon cognitive narratology, this chapter studies the English translation of Mo Yan's *Life and Death Are Wearing Me Out* with an eye to revealing the dynamics among "textual cues," "narrative (generic) conventions" and "(conventional) cognitive frames." Hopefully, this context-based, scientific research stance can counterbalance the trend of translation criticism, which has been dominated by cultural studies since the 1980s (Shen & Wang, 2010, p. 245).

Cognitive narrative levels in Goldblatt's English translation

With regard to the position of the narrator on cognitive narrative levels, narrative can be divided into first-diegetic narrative and second-diegetic narrative (or meta-diegetic narrative; hypodiegetic narrative). In the first-diegetic narrative, the enunciating subject is extradiegetic, i.e., located outside the story, while in the second-diegetic narrative, the narrating subject, which coincides with the given character(s), is intradiegetic, i.e., located inside the story (Herman, Jahn, & Ryan, 2005, pp. 107–108).

Comparing the source text (ST) and the target text (TT), one finds that the original modes of narration are altered in the English translation. The alterations are manifest in three aspects and can be described accordingly in terms of three types of narrative "transgressions," i.e., metalepsis; paralipsis; and pseudo-diegetic, or reduced metadiegetic (Genette, 1980, pp. 195–196, 234–237; Prince, 1987, p. 78).

Metalepsis

Metalepsis refers to the situation in which the boundaries between narrative levels are violated when, for instance, an extradiegetic narrator intrudes into the narrated scene and event. Genette (1980, pp. 234–235) summarizes metalepsis as

> any intrusion by the extradiegetic narrator or narratee into the diegetic universe (or by diegetic characters into a metadiegetic universe, etc.), or the inverse, . . . [which] produces an effect of strangeness that is either comical . . . or fantastic.

Principally, one narrative level can be transited to another through the act of narrating. Even if other ways of transit do exist, they are deemed "transgressive" (Genette, 1980, p. 234; Phelan & Rabinowitz, 2005, pp. 547–548). The term, metalepsis, is thus expanded by Genette to describe any forms of transgressions that occur between narrative levels. Such a process of transgressions, or specifi-cally, metalepsis, has been observed in Goldblatt's English translation of *Life And Death Are Wearing Me Out*, which can be illustrated through three examples as below:

Example 2.1–1

ST: 均分土地，历朝都有先例，但均分土地前也用不着把我枪毙啊！

(Mo Yan, 2006, p. 7)

[Back translation: Equal division of land had its precedents in previous dynasties, but before the equal division of land [they] needn't have to shoot me!]

TT: Parceling out land has its historical precedents, I thought, so why did they have to shoot me before dividing up mine?

(Goldblatt, 2008, p. 7)

In the ST context (Mo Yan, 2006, pp. 6–7) from which the above example is taken, the narrator reflects on China's land reforms in an amusingly satirical tone, implying that compared to the land reforms in feudal China, the one during the 1950s was nothing new – both were about land re-allocation; what was worse than the previous reforms was that the one in the 1950s involved eradicating land owners. The translator explicates this message by rendering the ST into: "Parcel-ing out land has its historical precedents, I thought, so why did they have to shoot me before dividing up mine?" (Goldblatt, 2008, p. 7). This rendition indicates that the landlords were shot dead in order to divide up their lands. As a result, the original self-mockery is replaced by critical judgment loaded with western read-ers' values and stereotypes – China's land reform in the 1950s was so brutal that not only would the land owners' property be confiscated, but their lives would also be taken away. By criticizing China's politics and deriding the land reform in particular, Goldblatt's translation seems to cater to the expectations of west-ern readers. Moreover, "I," as in the reporting clause "I thought . . .," originally pointing to the narrator at the extra-diegetic level, now seems to intrude into the intra-diegetic level and function as a character in the TT. Such intrusion creates a comical and absurd effect, resulting in metalepsis.

Example 2.1–2

ST: 我西门闹堂堂正正、豁达大度、人人敬仰。接手家业时虽逢乱世，既要应付游击队，又要应付黄皮子,...

(Mo Yan, 2006, p. 10)

[Back translation: I Ximen Nao was dignified, generous and respected. When taking over family business, though in times of chaos, not only had to deal with the guerrilla forces, but also had to deal with the puppet soldiers . . .

TT: I, Ximen Nao, a man of dignity, open-minded and magnanimous, was respected by all. I had taken over the family business during chaotic times. I had to cope with the guerrillas and the puppet soldiers, . . .

(Goldblatt, 2008, p. 11)

In Chapter 2, where the historical background is described, when mentioning the guerrillas and the puppet soldiers,[6] the ST narrator adopts a sarcastic tone by treating the guerrilla forces and the puppet army on an equal footing, implying that in the eyes of the landlords, the guerrilla forces were not different from the puppet army – they were both responsible for the domestic turmoil, and both were enemies of the landlords. Translating this episode, the translator adopts the first-person point of view to turn the original mixture of homodiegetic and heterodiegetic narrative into a homodiegetic one. Consequently, the omniscient third-person point of view observed in the source narrative is altered into a first-person point of view in the target narrative, relaying the landlord's faintly rebellious and reactionary remarks. Under the impact of the translator, the original multiple narrative levels are thus conflated into a singular, homodiegetic one. This change bears resemblance to the so-called "thin translation,"

Example 2.1–3

ST: 好了，西门闹，知道你是冤枉的。...

(Mo Yan, 2006, p. 4)

[Back translation: All right, Ximen Nao, know that you were unfairly treated . . . .]

TT: All right, Ximen Nao, *we* accept your claim of innocence . . .

(Goldblatt, 2008, p. 5)

In the example above, the narrator, "we," at the extra-diegetic level, suddenly enters the narrated scene and event, thus resulting in metalepsis.

Through the analysis of the three examples above, it can be seen that the metalepsis that occurs in the translation is similar to what is known as "transgression" in classical rhetoric – it is commonly seen with minimal impacts on the overall narrative effects. Also, by making use of the dual temporality as manifest in story (second-diegetic narrative) and narration (first-diegetic narrative), the translation seems to render these two levels of narratives in a contemporaneous manner; the time gap that exists between the story and the narration is thus consequently filled up. The metalepsis as shown above can be understood in terms of "oblique translation" (Vinay & Darbelnet, 1995), a type of translation method posited as opposed to "direct translation" (Vinay & Darbelnet, 1995). Given the potential structural and conceptual differences between the ST and the TT, it would sometimes be highly difficult to bring about the original stylistic effects without re-ordering the syntactical and lexical sequences through oblique translation. On the contrary, if the TT units substitute for the ST units through direct translation, this would only result in a translated text that is unacceptable in both meaning and style.

Paralipsis

In narratives which are told by altering narrative levels, "metalepsis forms a system with prolepsis, analepsis, syllepsis, and paralepsis" (Genette, 1980, p. 235). Our study finds that along with metalepsis, the devices of analepsis and paralipsis can also be observed in the translated narrative.

Analepsis is referred to by Genette (1980, p. 40) as "any evocation after the fact of an event that took place earlier than the point in the story where we are at any given moment." The ST is comprised of five books, and each of the first four books features respectively a kind of animal, i.e., Donkey, Ox, Pig and Dog (Book Five concerns the Big-headed Lan Qiansui[7]). Through such an order, the animals go through transmigration one after another. This can be taken as the sequence of events. When it comes to Book Five, the story comes back to the beginning point of Book One, leading to analepsis in terms of temporal sequence. Our analysis finds that analepsis remains unchanged in the TT.[8]

Paralipsis, together with paralepsis (not applicable in this study), are terms used by Genette (1980, p. 195) when "infraction of focalization" is discussed. Paralipsis can be broadly understood as the situation where certain necessary information is deliberately hidden by the narrator from readers. Specifically, there can be "omission of some important action or thought of the focal hero, which neither the hero nor the narrator can be ignorant of but which the narrator chooses to conceal from the reader" (Genette, 1980, pp. 195–196). The occurrence of paralipsis in the TT is linked to the "point of view transgressions" (Shen, 2001, p. 164), and can be regarded as a form of fuzzy translation which stands between literary and literal translation, or can be interpreted in a way similar to the changes in the narrative levels. Paralipsis can be confused with point of view transgressions (Shen, 2001 p. 197), since the two are not easily distinguishable from each other. Nevertheless, different from paralipsis, the transgressions in the sense above mean that one mode of focalization goes beyond its own boundary as if it intrudes into another mode. For instance, the diegetic narrator perceives beyond its restricted scope of vision as if it becomes an omniscient narrator, who can focalize the inner thoughts of other characters or events that it does not witness by itself. Basically, there are two types of "transgressions of modes of focalization" (Shen, 2001, p. 159) in Goldblatt's English translation: overt and covert. They are coupled with paralipsis and pseudo-diegetic narrative – the two forms of narration concerned with not only the narrative voice but also the narrative perspective.

In the TT, the important action or thought of the focal characters tends to be frequently omitted. Of the main characters (Donkey, Ox, Pig, Dog, Big-headed Lan Qiansui, or Lan Jiefang), or the narrator, "I" (the ghost of Ximen Nao), none is likely oblivious of certain actions or thoughts; however, the narrator in the TT decides to conceal such information from the readers. Accordingly, the narrative discourse does not reflect wholly the narrator's understandings of the events concerned. In other words, what is conveyed through the TT narrator is less than what is actually known by itself. This change, caused by offering less information than what is expected, can be considered as paralipsis in terms of overt focalization transgressions. Notably, except for the translation of personal names, no notes of any form (including intratextual gloss, endnotes and footnotes) are supplied in the TT, when the proper names of certain socio-historical backgrounds are rendered into English. For example, the term "Huanxiang Tuan" (还乡团, literally: Returning-to-Homeland Group) (Mo, 2006, p. 27, 168) appears twice in the ST. The translator renders the first instance as "the Landlord's Restitution Corps" (Goldblatt, 2008, p. 33), whereas the entire two paragraphs (1,031 Chinese characters) (Mo, 2006, pp. 168–169) containing the second instance are completely omitted (Goldblatt, 2008, p. 199), along with one of the paragraphs (195 words) that precedes this term (Mo, 2006, p. 167). In the Chinese historical and cultural context, Huanxiang Tuan refers to the Kuomintang (KMT) regime's armed force composed mainly of landlords during the Chinese Civil War (or the Third Revolutionary War) between KMT and the Chinese Communist Party. Here, the translator does not adopt the method of "thick translation" (Appiah, 1993, 2012; Herman, 2003), thus diluting the historical and cultural specificity that should have been implied through the term.

Pseudo-diegetic

Pseudo-diegetic refers to the case "when a second degree narrative is brought up to the level of the primary narrative" or "when a metadiegetic narrative functions as if it were a diegetic one" (Prince, 1987, p. 20). That is to say, pseudo-diegetic concerns narrative levels – when the secondary narrative that is embedded in the primary narrative somehow takes the shape of the primary narrative (for instance readers may forget such embeddedness), there occurs pseudo-diegetic – a term that by no means refers to "fictional" events as in a novel.

In the ST, Mo Yan speaks through the eponymous narrator "Mo Yan," by saying:

(1) 莫言在他的小说《苦胆记》里写过这座小石桥，写过这些吃死人吃疯了的狗。他还写了一个孝顺的儿子，从刚被枪毙的人身上挖出苦胆，拿回家去给母亲治疗眼睛。 . . . (Mo Yan, 2006, pp. 7–8)
   [Back translation: Mo Yan has written in his novel *Kudan Ji* (The Story of Bitter Gallbladder) about this stone bridge, about these dogs feeding on the dead man. He has also written about a filial son, who cut the gallbladder out of an executed person and brought it home to his mother to cure her eye diseases . . . .]
(2) 莫言那小子在他的小说《太岁》中写道：
   . . .马智伯的儿子马聪明紧张地说： . . .
   这小子，真是能忽悠啊。 (Mo Yan, 2006, pp. 13–14)
   [Back translation: That young fellow, Mo Yan, wrote in his novel *Tai Sui*:[9]
   . . . Ma Congming, the son of Ma Zhibo, said nervously . . .

That young fellow, how deceptive he is!]

(3) 这件事被你那个怪诞朋友莫言写到他的小说《人死屌不死》里了。 . . .
(Mo Yan, 2006, pp. 10–11)

[Back translation: This incident was written by your weird friend, Mo Yan, in his novel *Ren Si Diao Bu Si* (The Man Dies while His Dick Does Not) . . .]

(4) 就像莫言那厮在他的新编吕剧《黑驴记》中的一段唱词 . . . (Mo Yan, 2006, p. 25)

[Back translation: Just like the song written by the guy Mo Yan in his new play *Heilü Ji* (The Story of Black Donkey) . . .]

(5) 一九五四年十月一日，既是国庆日，又是高密东北乡第一家农业合作社成立的日子。那天，也是莫言那小子出生的日子。 . . . (Mo Yan, 2006, p. 26)

蓝脸家那头驴会飞的传说，至今还被西门屯里那些老人们提起。当然，在莫言那厮的小说里，更被描写得神乎其神。(Mo   Yan, 2006, p. 43)

[Back translation: On the first of October, 1954, the National Day, also the day that marked the founding of the first agricultural cooperative in Gaomi, Northeastern County, on that day, Mo Yan, that little boy, was born . . .

The legend about the flying donkey in Lan Lian (Blue Face)'s family was still told by the old people in Ximen Village. Of course, that legend was even described as something miraculous in the story by the guy Mo Yan.]

In the ST narrator's accounts quoted above, old-time works such as *Heilü Ji* (The Story of Black Donkey), *Kudan Ji* (The Story of Bitter Gallbladder), and *Tai Sui* mentioned above bear no links to the flesh-and-blood author Mo Yan; in fact, Mo Yan in real life has not written any books under those titles.

In an interview (Mo Yan, 2009) Mo Yan clarified that *Kudan Ji* does not exist. It is in fact a fictional account he fabricated when writing *Shengsi Pilao* (2006), and could be thus considered a pseudo-intertextual element. However, Goldblatt renders the title of this work into *The Cure*, a published translation by Goldblatt based on one of Mo Yan's works. As a result, *The Cure* in the TT (Goldblatt, 2008, p. 8) is intertextually related to the article that is included in Goldblatt's translation volume (1995, pp. 172–181), giving a real identity to the text that is non-existent and fictional in the eyes of the flesh-and-blood ST author, Mo Yan.

Example 2.3–1

Throughout the ST there are only two occurrences of the personal name Ma Congming, one of which could be found in excerpt (2) quoted above, where Mo Yan amusingly writes through an embedded narrative: "That young fellow Mo Yan . . ." and towards the end, he summarizes through the third-person omniscient perspective and comments on the character-narrator Mo Yan: "That young fellow, how deceptive he is!" (Mo Yan, 2006, p. 14). Here, the primary narrative as focalized through the third-person omniscient narrator is at the extradiegetic level. Overall, this episode involves double changes in narrative perspectives: the omniscient point of view is initially adopted to introduce the character named Mo Yan and *Tai Sui*, the story told by him; this is then altered into the first-person point of view, before the narrative slides further back to the third-person omniscient point of view at the end.

In the same quoted episode above, Ma Congming's father, Ma Zhibo, makes his appearance. He is one of the characters as well as the narrator in the embedded narrative. In the primary narrative (as opposed to the embedded narrative), the ST says "村里一个惯于装神弄鬼的风水先生马智伯跑到牲口圈边 . . ." (Mo Yan, 2006, p. 13) [Back translation: In the village, a feng shui master, Ma Zhibo, (who) was good at practicing mysterious rituals, ran towards the pen . . .]. In the TT, this sentence is translated into "Ma Zhibo, a feng shui master who was given to putting on mystical airs, came running up to the pen . . ." (Goldblatt, 2008, pp. 14–15). The translation omits the prepositional phrase "in the village"; also, the culture-specific reference "feng shui" is directly rendered into Pinyin through zero translation, without being italicized to signal the use of a loan word. The translation, by introducing this foreign term to the English readers, works to legitimize such usage, seemingly echoing Lu Xun's proposal "to introduce the language of a new culture to the general public."[10]

Qualitative and quantitative foregrounding from a cognitive narratological perspective

Foregrounding is regarded as a distinctive feature of literary texts. This notion originated from Russian Formalism which holds that "literary works are special by virtue of the fact that they foreground their own linguistic status, thus drawing attention to how they say something rather than to what they say" (Baldick, 2015, p. 144). Foregrounding refers to "stylistic variations" that "hypothetically prompt defamiliarisation, evoke feelings, and prolong reading time" (Miall & Kuiken, 1994, p. 389). According to Leech and Short (1981, p. 48), foregrounding can be qualitative, i.e., "deviation from the language code itself," or it can be quantitative, i.e., "deviance from some expected frequency."

Both qualitative and quantitative foregrounding are manifest in Goldblatt's English translation. The reasons for such foregrounding are two-fold: on the one hand, Goldblatt faithfully renders the linguistic and narrating style of the author, Mo Yan, making such individualistic style salient and defamiliarizing in the target culture; on the other hand, the differences between Chinese and English linguistic systems also set the stage for creating salience. The TT which closely adheres to the ST could in fact deviate from the ST, leading to "rebellious" translation. Whether or not the original author's idiosyncrasies should be retained in the translation depends on two factors: first, the importance of the foregrounded expressions; second, the degree of the acceptability of the marked features in the target language. If the TT retains the linguistic markedness of the original author so much so that they run counter to English conventions, the TT would read awkwardly and would be prone to reception failure. Given that, the translation is supposed to conform to the target language conventions and surrender the less important linguistic and narrating style of the original author so as to downplay the salient features.

Findings and discussions

By comparing Mo Yan's original text and Goldblatt's English translation from the perspective of cognitive narratology, the current study arrives at the following findings: First, the narrative levels as seen in the TT narrator's focalization and its voice have been reduced compared to the original text. This has increased the fuzziness of the translated text, producing a sense of fuzzy beauty. For instance, in the TT, the first-person narrator "I" is of multiple identities: it equates with both the narrating self – Big-headed Lan Qiansui, and the experiencing self – the animal(s) which undergoes transmigration. Second, metalepsis, paralipsis and pseudo-diegetic devices are observed in the translated narrative. These changes in the modes of narration are accompanied by the transgressions of the boundaries between intradiegetic and extradiegetic levels as well as those between homodiegetic and heterodiegetic levels. Also, frequent transgressions of modes of focalization, both of overt and covert types, are observed in the TT. Third, the modes of focalization adopted in the TT are multi-layered and of a complicated nature, lending the TT an aura of mystery. In other words, the plots are constantly concealed when one mode of focalization switches to another. For instance, the inner life of a given character is presented from an external point of view, while a focal character could perceive other characters' thoughts or even observe a given scene from which the character is absent. Fourth, the translated narrative shows continuous shifts in both "vision" and "voice." It is alternately focalized through the narrating self (with a retrospective perspective) and through the experiencing self. Such alternations are observed between the omniscient point of view and the internal point of view as well. In addition, the events are occasionally presented according to the story time, and occasionally, the (pseudo-) time of the narrative through analepsis or analeptic narration. These oscillations have enhanced the overall narrativity of the translated discourse. Last and most important, by abridging the original content and substantially removing quotation marks and reporting verbs, the translation has altered the dialogues in the ST into free indirect discourse (FID) in the TT, thus weakening the cohesive role of English verbs. This special treatment, however, does not necessarily mean that the translation is tainted with value judgement. On the one hand, this translation method, by withholding certain information, could create a beauty of literary fuzziness and bring forth enigmatically enjoyable reading experiences; on the other hand, the translation may pose a greater challenge for general readers who usually favor light-hearted readings for entertainment. For critics and translation scholars, though, such an approach to translation merits our further study.

Based on this analyses, it is believed that when exploring common patterns as shared by target readers' cognition processes in understanding the narrative structures of a novel, it is the "generic readers" – regardless of their genders, races, classes, experiences and spatial-temporal locations – that should be taken into account. However, when analyzing the characters' thoughts or psychological states, the specific identities of a given character and his/her spatial-temporal locations should be considered as variables that may influence the readers' comprehension. Meanwhile, by comparing the thematic differences between the ST and the TT, the specific contexts for the production of the ST and those for the interpretation of the TT should be scrutinized. The issue of how the varied perspectives adopted by two different groups of readers – those of monolingual texts and those of bilingual texts – can converge with each other also merits our further investigation. In general, the successful reception of Goldblatt's English translation by the target readership can be attributed to the alterations of cognitive narrative levels as well as to changes in stylistic features.

Conclusion

This chapter has made an attempt to bridge the gap between cognitive narratology and translation studies. By taking Mo Yan's most popular novel *Shengsi Pilao* and its English translation *Life and Death Are Wearing Me Out* by Howard Goldblatt as a case study, the chapter has closely examined the differences between the ST and the TT from the perspective of cognitive narratology. By analyzing the narrator's position on the narrative levels and his position relative to the story, the chapter finds that the original modes of narration have undergone changes in the translation, which are explained in terms of metalepsis, paralipsis and pseudo-diegetic narration. Along with the changes, there are also transgressions of boundaries between both homo/hetero-diegetic levels and intra/extra-diegetic levels. The successful reception of the translation can be attributed to these altered modes of narration and point-of-view transgressions. By adopting translating and narrating techniques that diverge from previous practice, the translator has experimented with some new modes of narration, revealing to the target readers the beauty of fuzziness and bringing them refreshingly delightful reading experiences.

This study may provide theoretical implications and analytical models for future research which aims to study literary translation within the framework of post-classical narratology. It is believed that cognitive narratology is instrumental for the analysis of literary translation – it helps reveal how the narrator and the characters in the TT may differ from their counterparts in the ST in terms of their varied experiences, or more specifically, their diverging cognitive frameworks, patterns and features. This study may contribute to demonstrating how the emerging disciplines of cognitive narratology and translation studies can be integrated and they can be made mutually beneficial through a rigorous, interdisciplinary approach.

Acknowledgements

The author wishes to acknowledge the support in the writing up of this article from two sources. One was the China National Social Sciences Young Researchers Fund Project: "A Cognitive Stylistic Study of the Geographical Features of Alai's Fictions and the Contrasts Between Their Parallel Chinese-English Texts" (14CYY002), and the other was the Sun Yat-sen University Special Incubation Project for Major Achievements in Liberal Arts: "A Study of the Dissemination and Reception of Contemporary Chinese Literature in 'the Belt and Road Initiative' Countries and Regions".

Notes

1 This chapter is a modified English version of the Chinese article "认知叙事学视域下的莫言《生死疲劳》葛浩文英译本研究" which originally appeared in Luo, X. (Ed.). (2016).《亚太跨学科翻译研究·第2辑》(pp. 132–142). Tsinghua University Press.

2 Cognitive narratology, rhetorical narratology and feminist narratology are considered to be the three most influential branches of postclassical narratology.

3 The term "postclassical narratology" was devised by Herman (1999), and it was used to distinguish the narratological approach from classical narratology – the French narratological tradition represented by such figures as Barthe, Todorov, and Genette.

4 *Towards a "Natural" Narratology* is considered by Herman (2003, p. 22) as one of the seminal texts for the development of cognitive narratology. Fludernik's (1996) book laid important groundwork for cognitive narratology by formulating a theoretical model based on conversational or "natural" narrative and drawing on a number of tools (the idea of schemata, prototype theory, and so on) from the cognitive sciences.

5 These other disciplines include artificial intelligence, cognitive psychology, discourse analysis, etc.

6 The narration was set against the historical background of the War of Resistance against Japan in the 1930s, more commonly known as the Second Sino-Japanese War. After the Japanese invasion of Northeast China, Manchukuo was established as a puppet state of the Japanese Empire. The Chinese Communist Party mobilized guerrillas to fight against both the Japanese army and the Chinese puppet army of the Manchukuo. (The Chinese phrase "黄皮子" [literally: yellow skin] is a colloquial slang expression referring to weasels; it is used satirically in this context to refer to the puppet army in yellow uniforms.) The puppet army, acting in the interest of the Japanese empire, plundered resources and properties from landlords. Almost in the same period, during the Chinese Civil War, the Chinese Communist Party launched land reform campaigns to abolish the feudal land tenure system.

7 Although Book Five (An End and a Beginning) is not solely dedicated to Big-headed Lan Qiansui, it does mention his transmigration.

8 However, paralipsis, originally absent in the ST, finds its way into the translated narrative.

9 Tai Sui is the God of the Year in the Chinese culture. The ancient Chinese believed that each year was dictated by a god based on the zodiac stars opposing the planet Jupiter during its 12-year orbital cycle. It is believed that a person whose birth sign clashes with the Tai Sui of the year will face misfortunes or disturbances for the whole year.

10 "Translation – in addition to introducing the original content to the Chinese readers – carries a very important function: (it) helps us to create China's new modern language . . . it means to introduce the language of a new culture to the general public." (Lu Xun, 2009, p. 336)

References

Appiah, K. A. (1993). Thick translation. *Callaloo, 16*(4), 808–819.

Appiah, K. A. (2012). Thick translation. In L. Venuti (Ed.), *The translation studies reader* (pp. 331–343). Routledge.

Baldick, C. (2015). *The Oxford dictionary of literary terms* (4th ed.). Oxford University Press.

Bortolussi, M., & Dixon, P. (2003). *Psychonarratology: Foundations for the empirical study of literary response*. Cambridge: Cambridge University Press.

Fludernik, M. (1996). *Towards a "natural" narratology*. Routledge.

Fludernik, M. (2003). Natural narratology and cognitive parameters. In D. Herman (Ed.), *Narrative theory and the cognitive sciences* (pp. 243–267). CSLI Publications.

Genette, G. (1980). *Narrative discourse: An essay in method* (J. E. Lewin, Trans.). Cornell University Press. (Original work published 1972)

Goldblatt, H. (Trans.). (1995). The cure. In H. Goldblatt (Ed.), *Chairman Mao would not be amused: Fiction from today's China* (pp. 172–181). Grove Press.

Herman, D. (1999). Introduction: Narratologies. In D. Herman (Ed.), *Narratologies* (pp. 1–30). Ohio State University Press.

Herman, D. (2002). *Story logic: Problems and possibilities of narrative*. University of Nebraska Press.

Herman, D. (2003). Introduction. In D. Herman (Ed.), *Narrative theory and the cognitive sciences* (pp. 1–30). CSLI Publications.

Herman, D., Jahn, M., & Ryan, M. L. (Eds.). (2005). *Routledge encyclopedia of narrative theory*. Routledge.

Hermans, T. (2003). Cross-cultural translations studies as thick translation. *Bulletin of the School of Oriental and African Studies, 3*, 380–389.

Jahn, M. (1997). Frames, preferences, and the reading of third-person narratives: Toward a cognitive narratology. *Poetics Today, 18*, 441–468.

Jahn, M. (2005). Cognitive narratology. In D. Herman, et al. (Eds.), *Routledge encyclopedia of narrative theory* (pp. 67–71). Routledge.

Leech, G. N., & Short, M. H. (1981). *Style in fiction: A linguistic introduction to English fictional prose*. Longman.

Lu Xun. (2009). Lu Xun he Qu Qiubai guanyu fanyi de tongxin [The correspondence between Lu Xun and Qu Qiubai about translation]. In X. Luo & Y. Chen (Eds.), *Fanyi lunji* (xiuding ben) [*An anthology of essays on translation*] (Rev. ed., pp. 335–343). The Commercial Press.

Miall, D. S., & Kuiken, D. (1994). Foregrounding, defamiliarization, and affect response to literary stories. *Poetics, 22*(5), 389–407.

Mo Yan. (2006). *Shengsi pilao* [*Life and death are wearing me out*]. The Writers Publishing House.

Mo Yan. (2008). *Life and death are wearing me out: A novel* (H. Goldblatt, Trans.). Arcade Publishing. (Original work published 2006)

Mo Yan. (2009, January 8). Mo Yan responded to questions on *Life and death are wearing me out*. *China Writer*. Retrieved from www.chinawriter.com.cn/2009/2009-01-08/42088.html

Phelan, J., & P. J. Rabinowitz (Eds.). (2005). *A companion to narrative theory*. Blackwell Publishing.

Prince, G. (1987). *A dictionary of narratology*. University of Nebraska Press.

Ryan, M.-L. (2003). Cognitive maps and the construction of narrative space. In D. Herman (Ed.), *Narrative theory and the cognitive sciences* (pp. 214–242). CSLI Publications.

Shang, B. (2013). *Dangdai xifang houjingdian xushixue yanjiu* [*Contemporary western narratology: Post-classical perspectives*]. People's Literature Publishing House.

Shen, D. (2001). Breaking conventional barriers: Transgressions of modes of focalization. In W. V. Peer & S. Chatman (Eds.), *New perspectives on narrative perspective* (pp. 159–172). State University of New York Press.

Shen, D. (2004). Xushi jiegou yu renzhi guocheng – Renzhi xushixue pingxi [Narrative structure and cognition process: On cognitive narratology]. *Waiyu Yu Waiyu Jiaoxue* [*Foreign Languages and Their Teaching*], *9*, 1–8.

Shen, D. (2005). Why contextual and formal narratologies need each other. *Journal of Narrative Theory*, *35*(2), 141–171.

Shen, D., & Wang, L. (2010). *Xifang xushixue: Jingdian yu houjingdian* [*Western narratology: Classical and postclassical*]. Peking University Press.

Tang, W. (2013). *Wenben, yujing, duzhe: Dangdai Meiguo xushi lilun yanjiu* [*Text, context, reader: A study on contemporary American narrative theory*]. Shanghai World Publishing Company.

Vinay, J.-P., & Darbelnet, J. (1995). *Comparative stylistics of French and English: A methodology for translation* (J. C. Sager & M.-J. Hamel, Trans. & Eds.). John Benjamins Publishing Company. (Original work published 1958)

Zhang, W. (2011). Renzhi xushixue de yinjin yu wenxue yanjiu de xin tuozhan [The introduction of cognitive narratology and new areas of literary studies]. *Sixiang Zhanxian* [*The Ideological Front*], *3*, 137–138.

10 Transferring the self-reflexive function

Translation of Chinese metafictions

Will Gatherer

Introduction

Within a rapidly liberalizing economic and social landscape during the 1980s under Deng Xiaoping, Chinese literature experienced one of its most diverse, challenging and creative movements within its recent history. A wide range of authors such as Ma Yuan (马原), Yu Hua (余华) and Ge Fei (格非) led a drastic reinvigoration of post-Mao literature as part of the Chinese "Avant-garde" (先锋派 *xianfengpai*) movement. Coming after a period of tightly controlled literary practice, determined according to rigidly applied tenets of socialist realism, this group of authors produced a radically new literature that critics would subsequently identify as being part of a nascent postmodernism within China. A key component of this postmodernist literature was the appearance of self-reflexive "metafiction"[1] which subverted, transcended and corrupted the conventions of literary "realism."

Although many of the most famous works of fiction from this era have been translated into English, the process of translating the self-reflexive function within literature can be incredibly complex and has arguably been significantly overlooked within translation studies. At the heart of this complexity is the fact that the defamiliarization function[2] of self-reflexivity is inherently intertextually linked to established literary conventions: a "traditional" realist fiction which is being acted upon. Metafictions often do not follow a straight path towards an act of representation but rather can often plot an ontologically destabilized course that is highly context- and culture-specific. Metafictions are often problematic as they often overtly expose their own architecture or constructedness through the use of metanarrative or other self-reflexive devices. In addition, metafiction can often require a reader within a particular linguistic and cultural context to engage in a form of "refracted" reading whereby the text is interpreted intertextually against the expectations of how a conventional text *should* function.

These dynamics can be understood through Derridian *différance* and deconstruction in that the "deferred" text against which the actual text creates meaning is the sum total of the cultural, linguistic and aesthetic conventions and expectations held within the act of communication between the author and the reader.

Applying this approach to translation exposes the inherent weakness of simple theories of "equivalence" and "faithfulness"[3] given that all texts operate in relation to other texts as "intertexts" so that "a text cannot stand in a clear relation of priority to any other, and a text and its translation cannot therefore stand in a clear opposition to each other" (Littau, 1997, p. 82). Metafictions can be doubly challenging in this regard in that they often render this implicit intertextual dynamic *explicitly* within the texts themselves. The challenge for the translator of metafictions therefore is how can a text's self-reflexive fictionality (its constructed "deconstructedness") and its self-reflexive intertextuality (the "deferred" other texts which they function in relation to) be explicitly transferred given that these dynamics operate within a fragile and unstable framework of cultural and linguistic conventions? Furthermore, if this self-reflexivity is not transferred or is untranslatable then what are the consequences given that self-reflexivity can radically alter how a text is read?

This chapter therefore aims to analyze the dynamics of self-reflexivity and the extent to which it is transferred from Chinese to English. The texts chosen for this study include various forms of the self-reflexive function and are broadly representative of the different types of metafiction which featured in the literature of the Chinese avant-garde:

It is important to note that although the source texts of the above were all written within a few years of one another in the mid to late 1980s, the translations themselves span nearly 20 years and are all by different translators. One text by Ma Yuan has been translated by two different translators, the first as *A Fiction* and the other as *Fabrication*, and therefore, with this text the comparative differences in the translation strategies for the same text can be analyzed.

Text 1) Ge Fei Flock of Brown Birds

In the Author's Preface to *Flock of Brown Birds*, Ge Fei refers to this work as a piece of 'pioneer' literature (a literal translation of 'avant-garde') and states that

Table 10.1 A selection of Avant-garde texts

	Author	*Title*	*Chinese Title*	*Translator*	*Date published*
Text 1	格非 **Ge Fei**	*Flock of Brown Birds*	褐色鸟群	Poppy Toland	2016
Text 2	余华 **Yu Hua**	*One Kind of Reality*	现实一种	Helen Wang	1993
Text 3	余华 **Yu Hua**	*The Past and the Punishments*	往事与刑罚	Andrew Jones	1996
Text 4	马原 **Ma Yuan**	*A Fiction*	虚构	Herbert Batt	2011
Text 5	马原 **Ma Yuan**	*Fabrication*	虚构	J.Q. Sun	1993
Text 6	马原 **Ma Yuan**	*Under the Spell of the Gangdisi Mountains*	冈底斯的诱惑	Herbert Batt	2011

"as one of the pioneer works which is regarded as having revolutionised style and form, I can say that *Flock of Brown Birds* aspires to use language in a completely new way and by doing so, to express an awareness of its own existence" (Ge Fei, 2016, p. 8). In this, Ge Fei is highlighting the obvious self-reflexivity of this challenging, obscure and "dream like" novel to the reader. *Flock of Brown Birds* is a highly surreal novel which in many ways resembles a "self-begetting novel," an early prototype of metafiction formulated by Stephen Kellman which he describes as "an account, usually first-person, of the development of a character to the point at which he is able to take up his pen and compose the novel we have just finished reading" (Kellman, 1980, p. 3). The narrative contains an "author" figure named Ge Fei who is attempting to write a novel "in the style of The Revelations of St John" to dedicate to his deceased lover and who in the process also engages in a dialogue with a female companion:

ST: "我发觉你的故事有些特别。棋说。
怎么？
你的故事始 终是一个圆圈，它在展开情节的同时，也意味着重复。只要你
    高兴，你就可以永远讲下去。不过，你还是接着讲下去吧。
我呷了一口咖啡，继续对棋描述以后发生的事。"

TT: "I've discovered something unusual about your stories, Qi said.
What's that?
Your stories are circular. The plot development is basically repetition. As long as
    you're enjoying yourself, you could just keep going ad infinitum. But carry
    on telling it anyway.
I took a sip of coffee, and went on to tell Qi what happened next."

(Ge, 2016, p. 48)

There are several instances like the passage above in which the "author" is discussing the "telling of stories" or where this author figure refers to the "novel" he is writing. The intertextuality which is present through the reference to "The Revelations of St John" is only relevant to the hypothetical "novel" that the author is writing in the narrative and not to the narrative itself; such a metafictional structure, however. in which an "author" is writing a novel and also narrating a "story" draws attention to the fictitiousness and constructedness of the narrative itself. This self-reflexive function is transferred in the narrative and strengthened paratextually through the author's preface. However, the apparent ambiguity of the text is linked to a deeper intertextual dynamic which is highly dependent on the reader's contextual knowledge: Under the prescriptive framework of socialist realism in China, which had only recently been dismantled when *Flock of Brown Birds* was written, ambiguity (both in the sense of structural ambiguity and of moral ambiguity – through not clearly delineating between "good" and "bad" characters, for example) had been effectively prohibited. Therefore, within the liberalized cultural environment in which the "avant-garde" authors were writing, ambiguity had deep political and philosophical implications and was a common feature of many forms of literary and cultural output during the mid-to-late 1980s in China. But this dynamic has not been transferred along with the self-reflexivity in the translated text, so in spite of the clear presence of the self-reflexive devices in the translated text, their function nevertheless is still diminished.

2) Yu Hua "One Kind of Reality"

In contrast to *Flock of Brown Birds*, the self-reflexivity within Yu Hua's 1988 novella "One Kind of Reality" is much more subtly constructed and presents a significant challenge to the translator. The text is a complex and surreal narrative of violence, exploitation and opportunism in which a husband is murdered and his body is sold by his wife. The text, however, breaks realist conventions in a highly absurd and comic manner because the husband remains sentient throughout the instances of violence and injustice enacted upon him:

ST: "我被释放了。"山岗说。
他的声音嗡嗡的，于是她就问："你感冒了？"
"也许是吧。"他回答。
她想起抽
屉里有速效感冒胶囊，她就问他是否需要。
他摇摇头，说他没有感冒，他身体很好，只是半个脑袋没有了。她问他那
    半个脑袋是不是让一颗子弹打掉的。他回答说记不起来了。"

TT: "I've been released," he said.
His voice sounded hoarse, and she asked, "Have you got a cold?"
"Maybe," he answered.
She remembered that there were some fast-acting cold capsules in the drawer and
    asked him if he wanted one.
He shook his head and said he didn't have a cold. He was all right, it was just that
    he didn't know where the other half of his head was.
She asked if the other half of his head hadn't been blown off by a bullet. He said
    he couldn't remember."

(Zhao, 1993, p. 178)

The surrealism here has a clear comic effect but also suggests a different form of reference through which violence is not interpreted literally but metaphorically. The husband's continued consciousness after a violent death heightens the ironic tension between the cold brutality of violence and the banality of its consequences by removing the mechanism through which the experience of violence is articulated through pain, suffering and grief. Despite this text "malfunctioning" according to the principles of realism, this alternate mode of reference is left somewhat stranded due to the fact that "One Kind of Reality" is a parody of "Family admonition" (*jiaxun*家训) literature, a very broad term referring to a long lineage of Confucian texts which revolved around admonishing inappropriate and unfilial behaviour. The intertextual self-reflexivity of this text is therefore facilitated through a subversion of familiarized literary and cultural conventions, which are entirely lost within an English speaking context. The parodic function of literature is often heavily reliant upon intertextuality and a specific set of expectations and contextual knowledge on the part of the reader, which creates a refracted interpretation whereby the text is read as if it is *against* what it is not; the translation of "One Kind of Reality" arguably only translates the first half of that dynamic. This perfectly demonstrates the complexity of transferring the self-reflexive function within the translation process. Even perfectly "acceptable" textual translations can fail due to implicit extratextual factors which have to be made explicit in the translated text.

3) *Yu Hua*, The Past and the Punishments

The Past and the Punishments is one of Yu Hua's most famous novellas from his early literary output in the 1980s. It revolves around two themes, which would become core components of the author's writing sensibility: violence and history. This text is metafictional in a similar way to "One Kind of Reality" in that it includes parodic intertextual self-reflexivity through which Yu Hua recalibrates the violence of history as a dialogue between a Beckettian[4] pseudo-couple of "the punishment expert" and "the stranger." In the following passage, for example, history itself is being anthropomorphized and given bodies which suffer the trauma of human flesh:

ST: 对一九六七年十二月一日，他施予宫刑，他割下了一九六七年十二月一日的两只沉甸甸的睾丸，因此一九六七年十二月一日没有点滴阳光，但是那天夜晚的月光却像杂草丛生一般。而一九六〇年八月七日同样在劫难逃，他用一把锈迹斑斑的钢锯，锯断了一九六〇年八月七日的腰。最为难忘的是一九七一年九月二十日，他在地上挖出一个大坑，将一九七一年九月二十日埋入土中，只露出脑袋，由于泥土的压迫，血液在体内蜂拥而上。然后刑罚专家敲破脑袋，一根血柱顷刻出现。一九七一年九月二十日的喷泉辉煌无比。

TT: He had drawn and quartered January 9, 1958, tearing it into so many pieces that it had drifted through the air like a flurry of snowflakes. He had castrated December 1, 1967, cutting off its ponderous testicles so that there hadn't been a drop of sunshine on December 1, 1967 while moonlight that evening had been as dense as overgrown weeds. Nor had August 7, 1960, been able to escape its fate, for he had used a rust-dappled saw blade to cut through its waist. But the most unforgettable had been September 20, 1971. He had dug a trench in the ground, in which he had buried September 20, 1971, so that only its head was still exposed. Owing to the pressure exerted on the body by the surrounding earth, September 20, 1971's blood had surged up into the head.

The punishment expert had proceeded to crack open its skull, from which a column of blood had immediately spurted forth. The fountain of September 20, 1971, had been extraordinarily brilliant.

(Yu, 1996, pp. 120–121)

The passage above has been translated very literally, with no apparent interventions, which opens up potential issues in terms of the transfer of self-reflexivity. It is clear that the text is not functioning along realist lines, and indeed the inclusion of the pronoun "it"[5] when referring to historic dates suggests a type of metaphoric reference creating a direct link between the concept of historical events and the violence contained within them. In translation, however, this becomes problematic for two reasons: first, readers may not be aware of the parodic qualities of this text in terms of how it subverts classical forms of historical writing in Chinese. Second, these dates only function within a Chinese historical context. While readers are expected to have sufficient contextual knowledge of Chinese history to resolve the second issue, the first issue requires some form of intervention, which can be found within the translator's postscript:

The 'labyrinth" that Yu Hua constructs in *The Past and the Punishments* is reminiscent of Borges' metaphysical narratives of time and space, necessity and coincidence. Through-out the volume, finally, Yu Hua's attention to the description of surface detail – at the expense of the inner life of the character – may well remind us of Robbe-Grillet's revolt against the tenets of realist fiction . . . While other stories are not as directly predicated on past literary models, they infuse contemporary settings with echoes of traditional beliefs and practices, to unsettling effect . . . Both *1986* and *The Past and the Punishments*, finally, are predicated on yet another sort of textual tradition – ancient historical records that detail the punishments meted out to those who had run afoul of the social order."

(Yu, 1996, p. 265)

Whereas within "One Kind of Reality" the surrealism pushed the reader away from realist readings of the text into a position where the parodic self-reflexive functions of the text were unclear, here the reader is given the information to be able to traverse this gap of intertextuality. Transferring the self-reflexivity of texts such as *The Past and the Punishments* highlights the ideological and epistemological divergences of the intended reader in comparison to the original and requires a form of transculturation. But this process is incredibly problematic and requires a form of hermeneutic translation that may require the translator to commit to a particular interpretation of the original text. The translator's postscript quoted above also refers to other texts by Yu Hua which are structurally very similar to "One Kind of Reality" and suggests that they should be interpreted as a "pastiche of traditional story types" with their "moral imperative" (Yu, 1996, p. 265) removed. Through rendering explicit that which is implicit in the original, the translator has established a framework of reading through which the text's self-reflexivity can become apparent and successfully transferred paratextually.

4) Ma Yuan "The Spell of the Gangdise Mountains"

"The Spell of the Gangdise Mountains" (冈底斯的诱惑 *Gangdisi de youhuo*), one of Ma Yuan's most famous texts, is a fascinatingly complex and highly self-reflexive "polyvocal" text with various different narratives about exploration, expeditions and hunting set in Tibet. The text's "kaleidoscopic" structure means that the three main narratives, each narrated by a different and at times unknown narrator, are all intertwined to the extent that it is often very hard for the reader to discern who in the narrative is "speaking" and to whom. Of all the texts analyzed within this chapter, Ma Yuan's by far contains the largest number of self-reflexive devices. This following passage alone, for example, contains a dazzling array of different forms of intertextuality and self-reflexivity:

ST: "可我一直闹不清楚，姚亮为什么要说 –
《海边也是一个世界》
呢？我不明白这个也字是什么意思。莫非姚亮早知道陆高将来要上大学？知
　　道你大学毕业要到西藏？知道注定还有一个关于陆高的故事：
《西部是一个世界》
？　不然为什么姚亮要说：海边(东部)也是个世界呢？　姚亮肯定知道一切。
　　天呐，姚亮是谁？

TT: I've never understood why Yao Liang said:
The Seaside is also Another World
I don't understand what the word "also" means here. Could Yao Liang have
　　known that there would be a story about Lu Gao called:
The West of China is Another World
Otherwise why would Yao Liang say the seaside (the East of China) is also
　　another world? Yao Liang knows everything it seems. Who on earth is Yao
　　Liang anyway?"[6]

(Ma, 1993, p. 2)

The passage above contains two intertextual references, one of which is a real text *The Seaside is also Another World*,[7] written by Ma Yuan, which in this passage is being presented as having been written by a character within the text. The other text, *The West of China is Another World*, is a fictional text about another character within this text. The two characters referred here, Lu Gao and Yao Liang, are a recurring "pseudocouple" which appeared throughout many of the author's early works. Sometimes they act as "stable" characters, while in other texts by the author they act as narrators, authors, or even "argue back" with "Ma Yuan" within the text itself. To add to the complexity of this intertextuality, here the unknown narrator is suggesting that the real text is somehow a response to the fictional text, which explains the usage of the word "also" (也 *ye*) in the title. If translated directly without any form of intervention[8], the full intertextual and referential meanings of the source text can be appreciated only if the reader has read *The Seaside is also Another World* and therefore can decode the overtly fictional self-reflexive intertextuality employed here. Given that that novel by Ma Yuan has not been translated into English this would only apply to readers who have previously read Ma Yuan's work in Chinese, a seemingly unlikely target reader of the author's works in English translation. In the translation of "The Spell of the Gangdise Mountains," however, this passage has been omitted in its entirety, and that is but one of many examples of interventions that omit highly self-reflexive elements of the original.

In addition to widespread omissions, there are also significant translation interventions of a structural nature. Within the original text the narrative shifts imperceptibly between different narratives and narrators creating a kaleidoscopic "polyvocal" narrative. The translated text, however, has been radically restructured so that the various separate narratives with different narrators are clustered together. The chapter sequence is re-ordered as follows:

TT chapter order:

1, 2, 3, **5, 6, 7, 4, 8, 10, 9**, 11, 12, 13, 14, 15

Additionally, the separate narratives are divided up into three separate parts and labelled as follows:

1   "The Hunt" – Parts I, II, III, IV, V, VI
2   "The Sky Burial" – Parts I, II, III
3   "The Singer of the Epic" – Parts I, II, III, IV, V, VI

Elsewhere there are also interventions in the form of textual additions that are entirely absent in the original, such as in the passage below:

> It's time to end this story. You've been to the mountains to stalk the wildman, you've been to a sky burial, you've heard Lu Gao's tale of the two brothers Dhonyo and Dhonsup [sic].[9]
>
> (Ma, 2011, p. 254)

These and similar interventions, which are employed throughout the translation, have a cumulative effect of removing overtly fictional and metafictional elements of the text, reducing structural ambiguity, strengthening the delineation between different narratives and narrators and reinforcing a more conventional narrator/reader dynamic. This is not to say, of course, that these interventions are invalid or deficient per se, the creative turn in translation of course allows for translation to become an act of rewriting rather than rigidly pursuing the highly problematic concept of equivalence. But the self-reflexivity has not been transferred within the translation process, and the translation reads much less like a metafiction than the original. This is somewhat curious given the fact that the introduction to *Ballad of the Himalayas: Stories of Tibet*, written by one of the most prominent scholars on Chinese postmodernism, Yang Xiaobin, alerts the reader to the fragmentary, polyvocal and self-reflexive nature of Ma Yuan's texts:

Ma Yuan's narrative heterogeneity dissipates the illusion of an intact subject, fragmenting the narrative persona that projects signification . . . These sections, pieced together without explanation, construct a multifarious structure. The unified narrative voice that predominates in modern Chinese fiction is disintegrated. Ma Yuan leaves inexplicable gaps among these voices and, therefore, presents a void in the narrative subject.

(Ma, 2011, p. ix)

There is a clear contradiction therefore between the contextual framing of this text and the specific strategies employed within its translation, which suggests that a more realist "rewriting" may not align with the intended reader expectations of this postmodern text.

5) Ma Yuan "A Fiction" & 6) "Fabrication"

"Fabrication" or "A Fiction," according to the two different translation titles, is undoubtedly still Ma Yuan's most famous text to this day. "Xugou" (虚构),[10] as it is titled in Chinese, is a highly self-reflexive narrative which features a narrator figure called "Ma Yuan" infiltrating a Tibetan leper colony and ultimately engaging on an absurd epistemological quest within this environment. "Xugou" is a highly challenging novel which features graphic depictions of sex with a leper woman and acts of bestiality and violence. "Xugou" has many of the same self-reflexive devices as "The Spell of the Gangdise Mountains" such as shifts between different narrators, an "author" narrator within the text engaging in a "dialogue" with his readers, and the destabilization of such traditional framing devices as the rupturing of diegetic levels within the narrative.

Given that there are two different translations of "Xugou," it is evident that there are significant divergences between the two versions. Fundamentally, "A Fiction" engages in the same strategy of widespread interventions, particularly in the form of omissions, all of which have the effect of reducing the self-reflexivity of the text. In fact, in the translation the text is re-organized and structured so that it no longer imperceptibly shifts between different narrators:

Chapter sequence in TT – 1, 4, 5, 6, 7, 2, 3, 8, 9, 10, 11, 12, 13, 14, 15, 16, 17, **18, 20, 21, 22, 19**

Furthermore, various other self-reflexive devices include intertextual references to *Le Baiser au lépreux* by François Mauriac (1922) and *A Burnt-Out Case* by Graham Greene (1960), which the narrator states as being the sources of his inspiration for writing this narrative. In addition, significant passages of self-reflexivity have also been omitted such as the entire passage below:

ST: 细心的读者不会不发现我用了一个模棱两可的汉语词汇，可能。我想这一部分读者也许不会发现我为什么没有用另外一个汉语动词，发生。我在别人用发生的位置上，用了一个单音汉语词，有。

我不讲语言学教程，这个课题到此为止。
我写了一个阴性的神祇，拉
萨河女神。我没有说明我在选择神祇性别时的良苦用心。

Careful readers will invariably have noticed that I have used an ambiguous Chinese word, "possible". I think that this group of readers perhaps won't be able to work out why I didn't use a different verb, "happen." Where other people use the word "happen" I use another monosyllabic word – 'exist."
I am not going to give a linguistics class though so let's end this topic here.
I've written about a goddess in *The Goddess of Lhasa River*. I haven't explained how I agonised over choosing the gender of that god."[11]

This passage above is a crucial component of the original text's self-reflexivity in that it solidifies the verisimilitude of the narrator and the "reader" in the text, creates intertextual references to other works by Ma Yuan, and enables a form of textual self-reflexivity by creating a metanarrative about the specific words being utilized in the narrative itself. This last dynamic is also particularly problematic for the translator, in that the text's status as a translation would become more pronounced if this linguistic self-analysis were transferred without any form of intervention: A literal translation of *danyin hanyuci* (单音汉语词) in the passage above, for example, which means "monosyllabic," would create an absurd situation in which a narrator in English refers to the Chinese word choices in the text as it appears (in two syllables) in English. This ironically would make the text even more self-reflexive and overtly fictional and, in a sense, even more postmodern and metafictional. However, it would also drastically increase the visibility of the translation process and in turn the translator, which according to Venuti (2018, p. X) is rarely considered to be an effective strategy for producing a "readable" translation.

The implementation of such widespread omissions results in dramatically lower levels of self-reflexivity in the translated text and also in a significantly more "stable" narratorial figure who is less visible, less overtly fictional and less in conflict with the effective narration of the represented world. In contrast, almost none of the omissions and subjective interventions that reorganize the text's structure are present within the version of the story translated by J.Q. Sun and named "Fabrication." In the passage above, for example, the translation of the textual self-reflexivity has been transferred as follows:

Careful readers will invariably have noticed that I have used an ambiguous word, "possible." I think that this group of readers perhaps won't be able to work out why I didn't use a different verb, "happen." Where other people use the word "happen" I use another word – "exist."

(Ma, 1993, p. 365)

Here the text has been recalibrated so that the narrator is referring to the word choices within the text without overtly referring to the language in which the words were written. Elsewhere, though, the following passage, which was omitted from "A Fiction," has also been retained, a choice that again foregrounds this tension within the text:

ST: 用汉字汉语。我到西藏好像有许多时间了。我不会讲一句那里的话

TT: I write in Chinese. I've been in Tibet now for quite some time, I can't speak a word of the language though.

(Ma, 1993, p. 365)

There is an odd logic at play here that risks increasing the visibility of the translation process or at least compromising the verisimilitude of the translated narrator. Nevertheless, "Fabrication" does not transfer the full self-reflexive function of the original in its entirety: the one instance in which it fails to do so demonstrates how the self-reflexive function can often be incredibly subtly constructed and therefore easily diminished within the translation process:

ST: 我不是个满足于"想一想不是也很好吗"海明威式的可以宽解愁肠的男人。我想了就一定得干，我干了。海明威是个美国佬。
我不敢夸口我是唯一敢这么干的人。因为我进玛曲村认识的第一个人就是另一个这么干的。他说他也不是第一个。
（二）
你看我有多大年龄。说你第一眼时的直观判断。不要怜悯我。不要说那些想使我高兴一点的话。不不。我说了别这样。"

TT: I am not the sort of person who, like Hemingway, is content with "Isn't it nice just to imagine?" Whatever I imagine, I do. That's why I did it. That Hemingway was an American.
I cannot boast that I was the only man fit for such adventures. The first person I met when I entered the village of Maqu was another such person, and he told me that he had not been the first.
2
"TELL ME HOW OLD I LOOK. Give me your immediate impression based on a first glance. Don't go easy on me. Don't say anything just to make me feel better, please don't."

(Zhao, 1993, p. 103)

The translated passage above contains a minor intervention which nevertheless ruptures a key self-reflexive device: In the transition from chapter 1 to chapter 2 within the original text, it is not possible to detect that the narrative focalizer has changed from the text's protagonist figure to its antagonist. It is only in the transition into chapter 3 when the narrator shifts back again that the reader is able to decipher after the fact that this narrative shift has occurred. This is a crucial self-reflexive device within the narrative because it transfers the intimacy established in the author/reader dynamic onto a specific character in the text. By merely including an inverted comma at the start of chapter 2, the translation here does not retain this self-reflexive structure, and as minor and insignificant as this may seem, even subtle framing devices such as this can dramatically alter the way the text can be read. Overwhelmingly, however, these two translations represent very different translation approaches in terms of the degree to which they transfer self-reflexivity.

Conclusion

Self-reflexivity is a highly complex dynamic within literature that influences how the text functions in various different ways. This self-reflexive function can be established either within the text in the form of overtly fictional metanarrative, or outside the text through structural and intertextual dynamics which the narratologist Monica Fludernik differentiates as "narrational self-reflexivity" and "non-narrational self-reflexivity" respectively (Fludernik, 2003, p. 19). Both of these dynamics ultimately become problematic because they place pressure on the ability of the translator to remain "invisible." Venuti, of course, argues that the "invisible" translator has become firmly established as the natural signifier of a "readable" and "fluent" translation given the "general tendency to read translations mainly for meaning, to reduce the stylistic features of the translation to the foreign text or writer, and to question any language use that might interfere with the seemingly untroubled communication of the foreign writer's intention" (Venuti, 2018, p. 1).

However, the issue with translating metafictions is that they often place pressure on the ability of the translator to maintain this acceptable level of readable invisibility: When a metafictional narrator in Chinese discusses their choices of specific Chinese words used in the text, the overt fictionality of the narrator actually is amplified when it is translated into English, thereby adding an overtly fictional and highly visible translated narrator on top of the shadow of the metafictional narrator underneath. Such instances of narrational self-reflexivity within the texts analyzed here have been transferred with varying degrees of success: In some cases, this self-reflexivity is omitted, and in others it is partially diminished. There are no examples in these texts, however, in which this function is somehow strengthened or reinforced. Likewise, similar difficulties with the transfer of self-reflexivity can be found in the examples analyzed here in which the text's non-narrational self-reflexivity requires an intervention to make explicit the implicit contextual and intertextual information which cannot be transferred solely through a translation of the text itself. To transfer this kind of self-reflexivity therefore, "the translator's dual activities of reading and writing" become foregrounded in that paratextual elements are required to frame a particular type of reading of the text (Godard, 1990, p. 91). This not only exposes the translator's visibility but also forces the translator to commit to a certain interpretation of the text, neither of which are necessarily safe territory given that, as Derrida states, a gloss or a translator's note "even in the best of cases, the case of the greatest relevance, confesses the impotence or failure of the translation" (Derrida & Venuti, 2000, p. 181).

Translating metafictions, therefore, may require translators to break many of the accepted norms of "readable" translations. But it could be argued that these conventions actually contradict the logic of metafictions anyway, given that metafictions often deliberately destroy their own readability through logical impasses, broken narrative structures and overtly fictional and therefore *visible* narrators. In this way, transferring self-reflexivity in the translation process actually exposes the core concern of poststructuralist approaches to translation as a whole:

> Translation, as well as any other form of writing, is always manipulation for some purpose. No discourse is free from ideology. There is no such thing as objective truth, and thus the most dangerous manipulator is not the one who does it openly but the one who claims to be objective. The danger then lies in the invisibility of the translator, not in the act of translation itself.
>
> (Koskinen, 1994, p. 451)

As metafictions often actively embrace the concept that "there is no such thing as objective truth" within their destabilizations of conventional realist framing devices, the translation of self-reflexive texts therefore may be the best test cases for visible or even overtly fictional translations in which the translator is free to engage in what Venuti refers to as self-presentations (Venuti, 2018). Within the examples of Chinese metafiction analyzed in this study, therefore, the most successful transfers of self-reflexivity are located in the translations that are the most willing to expose their own "translatedness,": translating metafictions appears to require the translator to "come out from under the cover and openly show her/his manipulation" (Koskinen, 1994, p. 451).

Notes

1 One of the earliest critics to identify Chinese avant-garde literature as being metafictional was Henry Zhao who attributed this phenomenon to a "crisis of codes" within the post-socialist-realist landscape. (Zhao, 1992, pp. 90–99)
2 I refer to this in the sense that it is brilliantly explored by Brian McHale in *Constructing Postmodernism (1992)*.
3 As Kaisa Koskinen has argued, "fidelity" in translation itself is an ideological concept that is inherently unstable so that "what kind of translation is regarded as a faithful reproduction of the original depends on which of the characteristics of the original are seen as meaningful and essential to reproduce. There does not necessarily exist any unanimity over these essential qualities." (Koskinen, 1994, pp. 446–452)
4 I use this term deliberately as a reference to analysis on Samuel Beckett's frequent usage of coupled characters, for example, Mercier and Camier within *Mercier and Camier* and Vladimir and Estragon in *Waiting for Godot*. Yao Liang and Lu Gao have been understood by many critics in China as a symbolised "ego" and "id" duality, representing two sides of the author's conscience. However, I believe Yao Liang and Lu Gao are best understood as a pseudocouple as they are often employed highly self-reflexively and are often engaged within the text in a complex relationship with the "author."
5 This pronoun is not present in the original since it is not grammatically necessary in Chinese in this passage. When translated into English a pronoun is required here; this

necessary intervention, however, strengthens the overt fictionality and self-reflexivity of the text.

6 In this instance, the English translation here is my own.
7 This short story was Ma Yuan's first published work in China. Published in 1982, this text is relatively obscure even for readers with a knowledge of Ma Yuan's early literary works and has not been translated into English.
8 By "intervention" here I am referring to Bastin's definition of "subjective interventions": "Subjective interventions are dependent on the translator's context and will for multiple reasons: historical, ideological, political or belonging to a particular sociocultural community. Those are the interventions that I call deliberate. Indeed, objectively, nothing obliges the translator to act that way." (Bastin, 2014, p. 76).
9 This is an individual misspelling of the name "Dhondhop" which is used elsewhere throughout the translation.
10 In terms of the different translation of this term, "Fabrication" is arguably more accurate given that it is a literal and more direct translation of the abstract noun *xugou* (虚构) whilst "a fiction" would more directly correlate to *yi pian xiaoshuo* (一篇小说).
11 The English translation here is my own.

References

Bastin, G. L. (2014). Adaptation, the paramount communication Strategy. *Linguaculture*, *1*, 76.

Derrida, J. & Venuti, L. (2000). What is a "relevant" translation? *Critical Inquiry*, 174–200.

Fludernik, M. (2003). Metanarrative and metafictional commentary: From metadiscursivity to metanarration and metafiction. *Poetica*, *35*(1/2), 1–39.

Ge Fei. (2016). *Flock of brown birds*. Penguin.

Godard, B. (1990). Theorizing feminist theory/translation. In S. Bassnett & A. Lefevere (Eds.), *Translation: History and culture* (pp. 87–96). Frances Pinter.

Kellman, S. G. (1980). *The self-begetting novel*. Columbia University Press.

Koskinen, K. (1994). (Mis)translating the untranslatable: The impact of deconstruction and post-structuralism on translation theory. *Meta: Journal des Traducteurs/Translators Journal*, *39*(3), 446–452.

Littau, K. (1997). Translation in the age of postmodern production: From text to intertext to hypertext. *Forum for Modern Language Studies*, *33*(1), 81–96.

Ma, Y. (1993). Fabrication. In H. Zhao (Ed.), *The lost boat: Avant-garde fiction from China*. Wellsweep.

Ma, Y. (2011). Ballad of the Himalayas: Stories of Tibet (H. J. Batt, Trans.). MerwinAsia.

McHale, B. (2012). *Constructing postmodernism*. Taylor & Francis.

Venuti, L. (2018). *The translator's invisibility: A history of translation* (3rd ed.). Routledge.

Zhao, H. (1993). *The lost boat: Avant-garde fiction from China*. Wellsweep.

Yu, H. (1996). *The past and the punishments*. University of Hawai'i Press.

Zhao, H. (1993). The rise of metafiction in China. *Bulletin of the School of Oriental and African Studies*, *1*, 90–99.

Part III
Voice of translators

11 Translating between languages

Carlos Rojas

In a short essay first published in 1953 and subsequently included as the afterword to the English translation of *The Magic Mountain*, Thomas Mann remarks that his novel

> is a very German book, and that might be the reason foreign critics very much underestimated its universal appeal. A Swedish critic, member of the Swedish Academy, with a decisive voice in the Nobel Prize awards, told me in public, and very decidedly, that nobody would dare to venture a translation of this book in a foreign language, as it was absolutely unsuited to such a purpose. That was a false prophecy. *The Magic Mountain* has been translated into all the European languages, and, so far as I can judge, no other of my books has had an equal success – I may say with pride that this is especially the case in America.
>
> (Mann, 1953/1999, p. 724)

Although it is unclear when precisely this discussion with the Swedish critic took place, it should be noted that Mann's multi-hundred-page novel first appeared in English translation in 1927, only three years after the publication of the German original. Moreover, the author's characterization of his novel as "a very German book" is rather ironic, given that the content of the work is emphatically international.

Set in a sanatorium in the Swiss Alps, the work describes how the protagonist, the German Hans Castorp, goes to the sanatorium to visit his cousin Joachim, who is being treated for tuberculosis. What had originally been scheduled as a brief visit, however, is extended after Castorp is himself diagnosed with tuberculosis and is admitted to the sanatorium as a patient. During his subsequent seven-year stay, Castorp interacts with an international cast of patients and visitors, including Ludovico Settembrini, who is from Italy, and his intellectual antagonist Leo Naphta, who is from Spain but with a Jewish-Polish background. The characters converse mostly in German but also periodically employ other languages, and Mann often reproduces the foreign-language utterances in the original. For instance, shortly after Castorp arrives at the sanatorium, he is greeted by the director, who immediately addresses him in several different languages in quick succession:

> "Well, young'un, *on me dit, que vous avez pris froid. Wy, kaschetsja, prostudilisj, Lei è raffreddato.* I hear you have caught a cold. What language do you speak? Oh, I see, you are young Ziemssen's guest. I am due in the operating-room. Somebody there to be chloroformed, and he has just been eating bean salad. I have to have my eyes everywhere. Well, young 'un, so you have a cold?"
>
> (Mann, 1953/1999, p. 164)

This practice of representing foreign-language dialogue in the original languages continues throughout the novel. Although in some cases the foreign-language text is parsed in German (such as in the preceding passage), in others readers are expected either to be able to read the foreign-language portions in the original or to infer their meaning from context.

In fact, to the extent that Mann's novel presents a challenge for the translator, this is arguably not so much because the work is too provincial (as Mann suggests in his afterword), but rather precisely because it is so heteroglossic. That is to say, while it is often assumed that a translator's main task is to find equivalencies between the languages of the source and target texts, a bigger challenge is to negotiate the relationship between different linguistic modalities present within the source text itself. Indeed, as Jacques Derrida once observed in a discussion of Paul Celan, "everything seems, in principle, *de jure*, translatable, except of the mark of the difference among the languages within the same poetic event" (Derrida, 2005, p. 209).

Although many of the non-German portions of *The Magic Mountain* are quite short and their meaning can often be extrapolated from the context (as is the case in the discussion between Castorp and the sanatorium director), the work does contain one quite lengthy foreign-language passage. At the end of the first half of the novel, in a chapter titled "Walpurgis Night," Castorp enters into an extended conversation with the Russian Clavdia Chauchat, with whom he had been enchanted ever since she first arrived at the sanatorium. As Mann observes in his afterword, in the context of a discussion of the fact that he has been asked to discuss his novel in English, the conversation between Castorp and Chauchat unfolds mostly in French, which is a second language for both speakers:

> Oddly enough, it is not a difficulty for me, but rather the reverse, that I have to discuss *The Magic Mountain* in English. I am reminded of the hero of my novel, the young engineer Hans Castorp. At the end of the first volume, he makes an extraordinary declaration of love to Madame Chauchat, the Kirghiz-eyed heroine, veiling its strangeness in the garment of a foreign tongue. It eases his embarrassment and helps him to say things he could never have dared say in his own language. "*Parler français,*" he says, "*c'est parler sans parler, en quelque manière.*" In short, it helps him over his inhibitions – and

an author who feels embarrassed at having to talk about his own works is in the same way relieved at being able to talk about them in another language.

(Mann, 1953/1999, p. 719)

Mann suggests that – both for his characters and for himself – the foreignness of speaking or writing in a second language can potentially be liberating, permitting a discussion of intimate matters that otherwise have been considered too intimate. In Freudian terms, Mann is describing a quality that could be described as uncanny – which is to say, something that appears unfamiliar and, at the same time, deeply familiar (Freud, 1919/1974, pp. 217–256). For Mann and his characters, the relative unfamiliarity of speaking in a language that is not their own paradoxically makes it easier to discuss topics that are intensely personal, and hence otherwise might appear all-too-familiar.

Of course, the Walpurgis Night dialogue works – both in the original German and in many of the other European languages into which the work was subsequently translated – because it can be assumed that most educated European readers of the novel would either already know French, or at least would have had enough exposure to the language to be able to understand this sort of relatively simple dialogue. Therefore, by leaving the French portions of the dialogue in the original, without providing a translation, the author permits readers to directly experience the sort of "strangeness" of a "foreign tongue" that characterizes the way in which Castorp and Chauchat themselves experience the language.

However, when the novel is translated into non-European languages – and particularly languages from outside the French empire – the chances increase that the French portions of the Walpurgis Night dialogue would be inaccessible to readers if left untranslated. In fact, the novel itself alludes to this possibility that non-Europeans cannot be presumed to have the same familiarity with major European languages, and it later describes that possibility in an interaction between Castorp and the Dutchman Mynheer Peeperkom, who arrives at the Sanatorium with Chauchat. After a debate, in German, between Castorp and Peeperkom, the narrative notes that there was "a young Chinaman at the other end of the table, who possessed too little of the language to understand what had been said, but had yet assiduously listened and looked, clapped his hands and called out: *Très bien, très bien*" (Mann, 1953/1999, p. 551).

Conversely, although all of the foreign-language elements that Mann incorporates into the work are from other European languages, he does include a suggestive allusion to Chinese in a passage in which Castorp is debating Naphta over the status and significance of literature. The narrator notes that Naphta cited China as model, apparently in a positive manner, though Castorp feels that the emphasis on memorization within the Chinese literary and cultural setting is at odds with what feels to be real literature. The narrator explains how

it disturbed [Castorp] not a whit that Naphta referred him to China, where such a witless idolatry of the alphabet obtained as had never been the case in any other land, and where one might become a field-marshal if one could draw the forty thousand word-symbols of the language – a standard, one would think, directly after a humanistic heart! – Ah, Naphta well knew – pitiable scoffer though he was! – that it was a matter not of drawing symbols but of literature as a human impulse, of its spirit, which was Spirit itself, the miraculous conjunction of analysis and form

(Mann, 1953/1999, p. 524).

Although the novel, in this particular passage, does not reproduce Naphta's comments about Chinese directly, it does permit readers to extrapolate what he might have been referring to. In particular, the reference here is to an impromptu debate between Naphta and Settembrini that begins with a disagreement over the status of Virgil and quickly expands to cover a broader question of the status of "the Mediterranean, classic, humanistic tradition," which Settembrini is attempting to defend but which Naphta is questioning on the grounds that it is "but the intellectual garb and appurtenance of a bourgeois liberal age" (Mann, 1953/1999, p. 521). In the uncited remark in question, Naphta evidently offers China as an instructive counter-example of a culture that values humanistic ideals but which is outside of the Western cultural tradition. Moreover, not only does the narrator not cite Naphta's remark directly, in referring to it indirectly via Castorp's negative reaction, the emphasis is instead on Castorp's assertion that Chinese is characterized by a "witless idolatry of the alphabet" that is deeply at odds with Western humanist ideals.

Moreover, the visions of China, Chinese literature, and the Chinese language cited in these two passages were themselves undergoing a dramatic transformation during precisely the same historical period that Thomas Mann was writing his novel. As Mann notes in his afterword, the original inspiration for the work came during a three-week trip that he made to a sanatorium in Davos in 1912, to visit his wife, who was recuperating from a "wet spot" in her lung. Mann worked on the novel for the next twelve years, until it was finally completed and published in 1924. Coincidentally, 1912 was also the first year of China's first republic, and it was also during the 1910s that China's overlapping New Culture and May Fourth movements began advocating a whole-scale reassessment of China's cultural values, its social institutions and even its language. In particular, reformers recommended that the formal written version of the language ("classical Chinese," or *wenyan wen* 文言文) – which was used for most types of writings, but which differed markedly from the oral form of the language that people used in their everyday lives – be replaced with a written language based instead on the modern vernacular (*baihua wen* 白話文).

The switch from *wenyan wen* to *baihua wen* was literally a process of translation. To be more precise, it was a process of double translation – translating an oral version of the language into a written one, so as then to be able to translate a traditional written form of the language into a new oral-based one. During the early years of the language reform movement, readers presumably would have viewed texts written in *baihua* as deeply uncanny, in the Freudian sense of being simultaneously familiar and unfamiliar. That is to say, these texts would have struck readers as deeply familiar, given that they were written in a language that was modelled more closely on the oral language than was the classical Chinese that they were used to, but at the same time a language with which they presumably would have also appeared deeply unfamiliar (at least initially), given that it was composed in a Chinese language that had not previously existed in written form.

The uncanny status of this new *baihua wen* was particularly evident in one of the earliest texts to be composed in the modern vernacular: Lu Xun's (魯迅 1918) short story "Diary of a Madman" ("*Kuangren riji*" 狂人日記). A major figure in the May Fourth movement, Lu Xun played an important role in helping to develop a vernacular form of the Chinese written language that quickly became the standard for most types of writings. Lu Xun's story famously opens with a one-paragraph preface written in a formal version of *wenyan wen*, and then immediately switches to a very colloquial version of *baihua wen* for the diary proper. For many readers today – and even more so for Lu Xun's contemporaries – the story's abrupt shift of linguistic register is startling, and is an important structural element of the work itself. At the same time, however, this shift in linguistic modality presents an interesting challenge for the work's translators. Among English-language translators, for instance, William Lyell attempted to preserve the original story's shift in linguistic modalities by translating the *wenyan* preface into a form of formal, antiquated English, while rendering the diary proper into a very colloquial form of contemporary American English (Lu Xun, 1990, pp. 29–41).

Although Lyell's version is not perfect (the translation contains a number of errors and unexplained omissions), it does nevertheless make a good-faith effort to reproduce the original work's shift in linguistic register. Curiously, the most influential English-language translations of the story make no discernible effort to have the translation convey the shift from the *wenyan wen* of the preface to the *baihua wen* of the diary proper. For years, the most widely read English version of the work was the one produced by the husband-wife team Gladys Yang and Yang Xianyi, which renders both the preface and the diary into the same workman-like English prose (Lu Xun, 1973, pp. 3–13). More recently, when Julia Lovell retranslated the story for the new Penguin Classics edition of Lu Xun's selected works, she similarly left invisible the transition from the preface to the diary portion of the story, translating both sections into essentially the same register of English (Lu Xun, 2009, pp. 21–22).

A similar point could be made in reverse about Chinese translations of Xiaolu Guo's English-language novel *A Concise Chinese-English Dictionary for Lovers* (Guo, 2007). Originally from the city of Wenling, in Zhejiang province, Guo is an author and a director who wrote her first two novels in Chinese (published in 2000 and 2003, respectively). After emigrating to Britain in 2002, however, Guo decided to begin writing fiction in English, so as to be able to connect more effectively to a Western readership. Her first English-language novel, *A Concise Chinese-English Dictionary for Lovers*, is structured as a first-person journal written by a young Chinese woman who has just arrived in London for the first time. The protagonist arrives in London with a rather rudimentary knowledge of English, and the work's premise is that each diary entry is preserved and reprinted exactly as the fictional protagonist wrote it at the time, errors and all. Over the course of the year that the protagonist spends in London, her English improves dramatically, and this improvement is clearly visible in the sophistication of the language found in the diaries. By the end of the protagonist's year-long stay in London, which is also the end of the novel, the diary entries are quite eloquent and reflect an impressive mastery of the language.

Clearly, the *form* of Guo's novel (and specifically the gradual transformation of the language in which the diary is written) is as important as the work's content. Curiously, however, although there are currently two complete Chinese-language translations of the novel (published in China and Taiwan, respectively), neither of them makes any attempt to preserve the original work's linguistic transformation. Instead, from the very first diary entry, they translate the protagonist's imperfect English into perfectly correct – and even eloquent – written Chinese (Guo, 2008, 2009). It should be noted, however, that both of these Chinese translations were published in bilingual editions, such that readers could see, on the same page, the English and Chinese versions of each diary entry. It could be argued, accordingly, that the Chinese versions of the entries are not intended to stand in for the original, as is the case with many translations, but rather merely to supplement it – the same way that film subtitles supplement the film' original dialogue without replacing it (thereby allowing film viewers to hear the intonation and inflections of the original dialogue, while at the same time ensuring that they are also able to have ready access to the dialogue's basic meaning).

Although provocative at the time, the type of vernacular writing promoted by the *baihua* movement has now become the default in China and throughout Greater China. Standard Mandarin (also known as *Putonghu* 普通話 or *Guoyu* 國語) is now routinely used for most types of writing, both formal and informal. Although this modern form of written Chinese evolved out of the May Fourth *baihua* movement, its contemporary significance is not so much that it is a direct transcription of oral speech (which was the premise of the *baihua* movement), but rather that it is a standardized form of the language that functions as a sort of written lingua franca for Chinese speakers – even if in practice, for many Chinese, this standard Mandarin diverges sharply from the dialect of Chinese that they speak on a daily basis.

Even before the early 20th-century *baihua* movement, there had been many examples of literary works written in a language that attempted to approximate more closely the language as it was spoken in the day. For instance, late-imperial vernacular novels were composed in a language that was significantly more informal than the *wenyan wen* of the time, even if this form of the vernacular also differed significantly from the *baihua* that would be developed in the early 20th century. Some of these late imperial vernacular novels made an explicit attempt to replicate regional dialects. Perhaps most famously, the dialogue of Han Bangqing's 1892 novel *Haishang hua liezhuan* 海上花列傳 [*Biographies of Shanghai Flowers*] is composed in the Wu dialect of the Shanghai region, and the language presented enough of a challenge that the novel was not widely read until Eileen Chang 張愛玲 published a *baihua* translation of the work several decades later. Chang was so enamored of the work that she subsequently translated it yet again, this time into English; the English translation was complete but unpolished at the time of her death in 1995, and after the manuscript was discovered among her effects, Eva

Hung spent several years editing it, and ultimately published the revised version in 2007 (Han, 1983, 1991, 2007).

Many contemporary works also incorporate elements of the local dialect, as seen, for instance, in the work of Yan Lianke 閻連科. Originally from a rural region of the central Chinese province of Henan, Yan often incorporates local dialect into his novels. Although Chinese readers with no prior experience with the dialect might find some of this local vocabulary unfamiliar, linguistically speaking they probably will not have a major problem understanding his work. Moreover, given that most of Yan's works do not go out of their way to underscore the foreignness of this local vocabulary, or contrast it with more standard Mandarin, a translator could therefore simply treat Yan's Henan-inflected Chinese as the work's source language, and translate it into the target language the same way that she would translate any other text.

Although most of Yan's fiction does draw attention to its use of local dialect, one significant exception is his 2004 novel, *Shouhuo* 受活 (translated as "Lenin's Kisses"; Yan, 2004). Not only is the novel's title a dialectal term not found in standard Mandarin, the main body of the work repeatedly signals that it is using specialized vocabulary with which it does not expect average readers to be familiar. It does this by repeatedly including endnotes in which the author defines and explains words and phrases that are either associated with the local dialect, or else have a specific historical significance with which the novel's readers are not expected to be familiar. At the same time, however, it is also clear that these endnotes are not intended to serve merely as a supplement for those readers who happen to be unfamiliar with the dialect, but rather they are an essential element of the work itself. This is because, in addition to containing explanations of the vocabulary in question, many of the endnotes also include lengthy discussions of the novel's historical backdrop, collectively accounting for approximately half the length of the overall novel. If a reader were to skip over the endnotes because she was already familiar with the vocabulary in question, she would also end up skipping over key portions of the work's narrative development.

When I translated Yan's novel into English, accordingly, I felt it was important to preserve the novel's shifts between standard written Chinese, on one hand, and the local vocabulary. If I were to translate these dialectal terms into the same standard English as the rest of the novel, the novel's premise that the terms in question needed to be defined and explained would not make very much sense. The late Chinese-French translator Sylvie Gentil, in her prize-winning translation of the novel, cleverly solved this problem by translating the dialectal terms into corresponding French dialectal terms (Yan, 2004, 2009). For the English translation, however, I felt that it would be difficult to find existing dialectal terms that did not also carry strong (and potentially distracting) regional connotations, and therefore I settled for coining English terms that I hoped would carry the same mix of familiarity and unfamiliarity with which typical Chinese readers would have viewed the dialectal terms in the original. For instance, the term used in the Chinese title of the novel, *Shouhuo* 受活, is an example of precisely this sort of local dialect, and when the same term appears in the very first sentence of the work, it is accompanied by an endnote that offers a dictionary-type definition:

Dial. (Used mostly in Western Henan and Eastern Henan's Balou mountains). The term means enjoyment, happiness, and passion, and also carries connotations of finding pleasure in discomfort, or making pleasure out of discomfort.
(Yan, 2004, p. 1, 2012, p. 1)

In translating the corresponding term into English, I decided not to use an existing term such as "to enjoy" and instead I coined the term "to liven." This coinage resonates with the English verb "to live" the same way that the Chinese term *shouhuo* 受活 resonates with the verb *huozhe* 活著 ("to live"), while at the same time conveying a sense of unfamiliarity and strangeness that is hopefully comparable to what Chinese readers would associate with the original.

I encountered a similar challenge when asked to translate some excerpts from Hong Kong author Dung Kai-Cheung's 董啟章 novel *Shijian fanshi* 時間繁史 ("Histories of Time"; Dung, 2007). A native Cantonese speaker, Dung frequently includes Cantonese elements in the dialogue portions of his fictional works. This practice is particularly prominent in *Histories of Time*, which contains lengthy sections that are written almost entirely in colloquial Cantonese – featuring syntactical structures, phrases, words, and even individual characters that are rarely found in standard Mandarin. In fact, the novel contains so much colloquial Cantonese that it even includes a multi-page glossary offering definitions of many common Cantonese words and phrases. Readers find themselves repeatedly switching back and both between these sections written in colloquial Cantonese, and other sections written in what resembles standard Mandarin or *Putonghua*, but which Dung Kai-Cheung actually prefers to view as the standard written form (*shumianyu* 書面語) of Cantonese.

In translating some excerpts from Dung's novel for a recent edited volume on contemporary Chinese science fiction (Dung, 2007, 2018), I debated how to render the Cantonese sections of the novel. One possible solution that I briefly entertained was to render the colloquial Cantonese sections of the novel into another Asian variant of English (for instance, Singaporean English, or Singlish). In the end, however, I decided to translate the colloquial Cantonese portions into the same register of English as the narrative portions of the work, but presented them in a different type face in order to register visually the shifts back and forth between the two different linguistic registers in the original text (I also included an explanation of this strategy in my preface to the translation).

Finally, similar issues also came up in my translation of a book-length collection of short stories by the ethnically Chinese Malaysian-born author Ng Kim Chew 黃錦樹 (Ng, 2001, 2016). Ng – who was born and grew up in Malaysia, but then came to Taiwan for college and graduate school, where he now lives and works as a university professor – writes fiction exclusively in Chinese, but in a very hybrid Chinese. His fiction frequently includes not only multiple different Chinese dialects, but also words and phrases from other languages, such as English, Japanese, and Malay. At various points throughout his works, Ng incorporates hand-drawn versions of ancient oracle bone script – which is one of the earliest extant forms of the written Chinese, but which is virtually unintelligible to contemporary readers without specialized training. Conversely, some works go in the other direction, incorporating non-linguistic symbols that contain no discernible linguistic meaning. In my English translations of his stories included in *Slow Boat to China*, I generally preserved the original stories' foreign-language elements (including non-Chinese words or phrases). My sense is that Ng's stories do not necessarily assume that the typical Chinese-language reader will be familiar with most of the foreign-language elements in question, and in some cases the stories include short explanations of the foreign-language vocabulary, while in other cases the stories leave it to the reader to infer from context the meaning of the foreign-language terms.

While most of the non-Mandarin elements of Ng's stories are words or phrases from other Chinese dialects or other languages, in some cases Ng departs even further from Chinese, and even from language itself. In "Monkey Butts, Fire, and Dangerous Things" (猴屁股、火與危險事物) for instance, the story revolves around an ethnic Chinese man from Singapore who, on account of his early affiliation with the Malayan Communist Party, has been exiled to a remote island where he is the only human inhabitant. The protagonist has kept a document titled "Secret Files from Malaya's Communist Period," listing a number of former communist activists – but the list, as reproduced in Ng's story, becomes increasingly incoherent as it progresses, and by the end it consists entirely of seemingly meaningless graphic elements such as ↖↑ *c/o* and # & * ♀(needless to say, each of these symbols has an identifiable meaning in its own right, but in the novel they are used in a way that bears no discernible relationship with their accepted meanings).

In two other stories included in the *Slow Boat to China* volume – both of which originally appeared in Ng's third collection of stories: *Youdao zhi dao* 由島至島 (*From Island to Island*), published in Taiwan in 2001 – this practice of incorporating non-lexical elements into his works is taken to an extreme. One story, which is listed under the title "Supplication" (訴求) in the 2001 volume's table of contents, consists of a single paragraph of meaningless symbols, while another, "Untouchable" (不可觸的), consists of five pages of completely blank paper. Both texts function as purely perlocutionary utterances, in that they do not attempt to transmit meaning directly but rather, through their very existence, effectively interrogate the limits of language as a communicative practice.

References

Derrida, J. (2005). *Sovereignties in question: The poetics of Paul Celan*. Fordham University Press.

Dung, K.-C. 董启章. (2007). *Shijian fanshi: Yaci zhiguang* 時間繁史. 啞瓷之光 [*Histories of time: The lustre of mute porcelain*]. Rye Field Publishing.

Dung, K.-C. (2018). Histories of time (excerpt). In C. Rojas (Trans.), M. Song & T. Huters (Eds.), *The reincarnated giant: Chinese science fiction in the twenty-first century: Taiwan, Hong Kong, and the PRC*. Columbia University Press. (Original work published 2007)

Freud, S. (1974). The "uncanny". In *The standard edition of the complete psychological works of Sigmund Freud, Vol. XVII (1917–1919): An infantile neurosis and other works* (pp. 217–256). (Original work published 1919)

Guo, X. (2007). *A concise Chinese-English dictionary for lovers*. Vintage Books.

Guo, X. 郭小櫓. (2008). *Lianren ban zhongying cidian* 戀人版中英詞典 (P. Guo 郭品潔, Trans.). Dakuai wenhua.

Guo, X. 郭小櫓. (2009). *Lianrenban zhongying cidian* 恋人版中英词典 (Y. Mou 缪莹, Trans.). Xinxing chubanshe.

Han, B. (1983). Haishang hua [Shanghai Flowers] (E. Chang, Trans.). In *Zhang Ailing quanji* 張愛玲全集 [*The complete works of Zhang Ailing*] (Vol. 10, 11). Huangguan congshu.

Han, B. 韓邦慶. (1991). *Haishang hua liezhuan* 海上花列傳 [*Biographies of Shanghai Flowers*], *Zhongguo jindai wenxue daxi* (Vol. 3). Shanghai shudian.

Han, B. (2007). *The singsong girls of Shanghai* (E. Chang & E. Hung, Trans.). Columbia University Press.

Lu Xun. (1973). A Madman's Diary. In G. Yang & X. Yang (Trans. & Eds.), *Silent China: Selected writings of Lu Xun* (pp. 3–13). Oxford University Press.

Lu Xun. (1990). Diary of a Madman. In W. Lyell (Trans.), *Diary of a Madman and other stories* (pp. 29–41). University of Hawaii Press.

Lu Xun. (2009). *The real story of Ah-Q and other tales of China: The complete fiction of Lu Xun* (J. Lovell, Trans., pp. 21–22). Penguin.

Mann, T. (1999). The making of the Magic Mountain. In H. T. Lowe-Porter (Trans.), *The Magic Mountain*. (Original work published January 1953). Vintage.

Ng, K. C. 黃錦樹. (2001). *Youdao zhidao* 由島至島 [*From Island to Island*]. Rye Field Publishing.

Ng, K. C. (2016). *Slow boat to China and other stories* (C. Rojas, Trans. & Ed.). Columbia University Press.

Yan, L. 閻連科. (2004). *Shouhuo* 受活. Chunfeng wenyi chubanshe.

Yan, L. (2009). *Bons baisers de Lénine* (S. Gentil, Trans.). Picquier.

Yan, L. (2012). *Lenin's Kisses* (C. Rojas, Trans.). Grove Atlantic. (Original work published 2004)

12 Translating Yu Hua

Allan H. Barr

If 20 years ago you had told me that by now I would have translated five books by a major contemporary Chinese author, I might have been rather taken aback. At that time, I saw myself almost exclusively a scholar of Ming and Qing literature, and I had no great ambition to become a translator.

But in retrospect it makes sense to me that translation came to figure more prominently in my life. When I was young, translation played a significant part in my study of foreign languages. I grew up in Britain, where in the 1960s and 1970s translation was a standard classroom activity if you were learning a classical language, like Latin or Greek, or even a modern language, like French. The first volume of David Hawkes' translation of *Shitou ji* 石头记 (*Story of the Stone*) was published the same year that I began the formal study of Chinese, reminding me how powerful and eloquent literary translation can be. In my Chinese classes at university, translating texts into English was again a standard procedure, and my undergraduate thesis took the form of an annotated translation of several Judge Bao stories from a Qing collection, *Longtu gong'an* 龙图公案 (*Longtu's Court Cases*). When I moved on to an academic career, my research focused on classical fiction, but I always kept an eye on developments in contemporary literature, and as the literary scene in China became more vibrant in the late 1980s and early 1990s, I became all the more interested in what was happening.

Although Yu Hua had made a name for himself in China as early as 1987, it was not until the mid-1990s that his work really gained my attention. Visiting Guangzhou in 1996, I bought a copy of his third novel, *Xu Sanguan maixue ji* 许三观卖血记 (*Chronicle of a Blood Merchant*), which I thoroughly enjoyed, and on a trip to Beijing in January 1997 I happened to pick up – at one of the roadside news kiosks still common in those days – the latest issue of the magazine *Zuojia* 作家 (*Writer*), which carried Yu Hua's story "Huanghun li de nanhai" ("Boy in the Twilight"). Vivid and poignant, it made a deep impression on me. Two years later, a collection of Yu Hua's short stories was published in China, with "Huanghun li de nanhai" as its title story. Thus began my first foray into literary translation.

Boy in the Twilight

Initially I was unsure how much time and energy I wanted to devote to translation, and *Huanghun li de nanhai* attracted me in part for its compact size. It was a slim volume of twelve short stories; the whole text came to only a hundred thousand characters. If I was to have a first stab at literary translation, this seemed like a good place to start. At the time, a large proportion of published translations were of works set against the backdrop of the Cultural Revolution, and I felt that these stories of Yu Hua's, which avoided any overt reference to politics, offered a refreshing new take on the Chinese experience. I also enjoyed the book's humor – often rather dark humor, admittedly, but humor all the same, and humor was something missing in a lot of contemporary Chinese literature that I had read.

Most of all, I felt that Yu Hua's narrative language lent itself well to translation into English. In China, some critics suspect that Western readers like Yu Hua's books because of their implicit critique of Chinese society. There may be some truth to this, but I think that what is actually more important is that Yu Hua writes in a fashion highly compatible with Western tastes. I am struck, for example, by how closely Yu Hua's writing practice corresponds to the celebrated "rules of writing" that Elmore Leonard, the American crime author, once enumerated. Consider, for example, the following rules on Leonard's list:

5   Keep your exclamation points under control.
7   Use regional dialect sparingly.
8   Avoid detailed descriptions of characters.
9   Don't go into great details describing places and things.
10 Try to leave out the part that readers tend to skip. (Leonard, 2001)

Although Yu Hua is no crime writer and may well never have read these rules, his writing seems to be guided by just such principles, with the result that readers of Yu Hua often find it as difficult to put his books down as Leonard's readers do his crime novels.

I met Yu Hua for the first time during a visit to Beijing in April 2001. At that point, he told me, the only foreign translators he had met focused exclusively on modern China, and he was rather tickled that a Ming-Qing scholar had also developed an interest in his books. Over dinner, he gave his blessing to my proposed translation of *Boy in the Twilight*, and within days I had begun work.

It took much longer than I had imagined, however, for the translation to reach its intended audience. By the time I had completed the manuscript, in early 2003, Yu Hua's American editor was busy preparing for the release of the English editions of *To Live* and *Chronicle of a Blood Merchant*, and she was not immediately ready to commit to a third book. Once these two novels were published, sales were not so encouraging as to warrant, in her view, the immediate publication of this rather bleak set of short stories, and so *Boy in the Twilight* was put on the back burner. There it stayed for more than ten years, until the book's ultimate release in 2014. By then, of course, the stories were no longer as up-to-the-minute as they once had seemed. The long delay did bring some advantages, however, in that it gave me the chance to revise the manuscript multiple times, and it gave a variety of readers the chance to pick the stories over and make some helpful suggestions.

The language of *Boy in the Twilight* is simple. But this simplicity, I found, presents challenges to the translator. Yu Hua touched on this issue in a recently published essay, in connection with his best-selling novel, *Huozhe* 活着 (translated into English as *To Live*):

> I always used to think that *Huozhe* would be easy to translate, since its narrative language is written in very simple Chinese, but later my Japanese translator, Iizuka Yutori, told me that the book is actually very difficult to translate. "The language is indeed simple," he said, "but it's full of flavor, and it's hard to convey that flavor in translation."
>
> (Yu, 2018a, p. 190)

To convey the flavor of Yu Hua's writing, I found, it is important to give each word no more and no less than its proper weight. Precisely because Yu Hua uses rather few and rather simple words, it is vital that the translation communicates the full meaning that they have in the context in which they appear. Otherwise, the language can sometimes seem flat and limp. So, for example, when translating the last sentence in "Their Son," I elected to render it as follows:

> Maybe the future would bring more and more difficulties, but this did not distress them unduly, for they could see their son was now his own man.
>
> (Yu, 2014, p. 149)

> 以后的日子也许会越来越艰难，他们并不为此忧心忡忡，他们看到自己的儿子已经长大了。
>
> (Yu, 1999, p. 133)

Although the conventional translation of *zhangdale* 长大了 is "grown up," in this case "his own man" seemed to better capture Yu Hua's meaning. And in the book's lighter moments, as in "Why Do I Have to Get Married?," it seemed particularly important to measure my words well, so as to bring out the wry humor in the situation:

> When Pingping opened the door, I found that she had changed. She had put on some weight, it seemed, or maybe she had lost some.
>
> (Yu, 2014, p. 160)

> 当萍萍为我打开他们的房门时，我发现萍萍的样子变了一些，她好像是胖了，要不就是瘦了。
>
> (Yu, 1999, p. 150)

A second issue that came up when translating *Huanghunli de nanhai* – and, later, Yu Hua's other books – was how to handle repetition. For example, in the brief title story, "Boy in the Twilight," the word *kan* 看 ("look") appears no less that forty-five times, often in such phrases as 看到 or 看着, supplemented occasionally by similar expressions such as *wangqu* 望去 ("looked into the distance") or *zhushizhe*注视着 ("watching fixedly"). English seems generally less tolerant of repetition than Chinese, and I often found that reducing or eliminating repetition heightened the impact of Yu Hua's narrative in English translation, in a "less is more" dynamic.[1] When translating the following passage from "Boy in the Twilight," for example, I consciously avoided translating *kandao* 看到 in the second sentence, since I had both "could see" in the preceding sentence and "look" in the following one:

> 男孩的嘴张了开来，孙福看到了他嘴里已经咬碎的苹果，就让卡住他脖子的手使了使劲。孙福看到他的眼睛瞪圆了。有一个人对孙福说：
>
> "孙福，你看他的眼珠子都快瞪出来了，你会把他卡死的。"
>
> (Yu, 1999, p. 26–27)

> As the boy's mouth opened, Sun Fu could see chewed-up bits of apple inside. He tightened his vise-like grip on the boy's throat, until his eyes began to bulge.
>
> "Sun Fu," somebody said, "look, his eyeballs are practically popping out of his head. You're going to strangle him."
>
> (Yu, 2014, p. 25)

Alas, despite my efforts to hone the leanness of Yu Hua's prose, at least one reviewer has suggested I have sometimes not gone far enough.[2]

A third issue that I became aware of when translating *Boy in the Twilight* is the importance of tempo – how to adequately replicate the pace of Yu Hua's writing. Yu Hua often uses long sentences with a series of independent clauses held together simply by commas. In the absence of grammatical structures that create links between the clauses, the translator is often tempted to divide this kind of sentence into multiple shorter sentences. But this runs the risk of slowing the tempo and losing some of the smooth fluidity that makes Yu Hua so readable. While recognizing that it's not practical to replicate completely the form of Yu Hua's sentences, I made an effort to capture the flavor of his writing by using open punctuation that would allow a sentence to flow as freely as possible.

Here, for example, is a rather characteristic long sentence, taken from Yu Hua's story, "Pengyou" 朋友 (Friends):

> 我不知道昆山姓什么，这个镇上很多人都不知道她的姓，但是我们都知道昆山是谁，昆山就是那个向别人借了钱可以不还的人，他没有香烟的时候他会在街上拦住别人，笑呵呵地伸出两只宽大的手掌拍着他们的口袋，当拍到一盒香烟时，他就会将自己的手伸进别人的口袋，将香烟摸出来，抽出一根递过去，剩下的就放进自己的口袋。
>
> (Yu, 1999, p. 169)

In translation, it did not seem feasible to keep this passage intact as a single sentence – I found it worked best to divide it into three sentences. To compensate, I reduced the number of commas, so that there is no more punctuation in the translation than there is in the original:

> I didn't know Kunshan's last name – nor did many of the locals – but we all knew perfectly well who he was. He was the man who would borrow money from people and not bother to pay them back. When he ran out of smokes, he would stop passersby in the street and cheerfully pat their pockets with his broad palms, and once he had located a pack of cigarettes he would slip an a hand into the pocket and extract the cigarettes, offering one to their owner and depositing the remainder in his own pocket.
>
> (Yu, 2014, p. 184)

Here is a second example of a long Yu Hua sentence, punctuated this time with eight commas:

> 那 时 候 已 经 是 下 午 了， 阳 光 的 移 动 使 昆 山 他 们 站 着 的 地 方 成 为 一 片 阴 影， 他 们 看 到 了 走 出 来 的 石 刚， 石 刚 站 在 了 阳 光 下， 他 的 左 手 胳 膊 上 像 是 套 着 一 只 篮 球 似 的 缠 着 那 件 帆 布 工 作 服， 他 的 右 手 提 着 那 条 水 淋 淋 的 手 巾， 毛 巾 垂 在 那 里， 像 是 没 有 关 紧 的 水 龙 头 一 样 滴 着 水， 使 地 上 出 现 了 一 滩 水 迹。
>
> (Yu, 1999, p. 176)

Once again, I found it impossible to cram all this content into a single English sentence: I opted to divide into four sentences, instead. At the same time, through sparing use of commas, I tried to ensure that the corresponding passage in translation is not noticeably slower in tempo than the original Chinese text:

> It was afternoon by this time, and the shadows had begun to lengthen, so now the spot where Kunshan and the others stood was in the shade. They watched as Shi Gang emerged into the bright sunlight. With the rolled-up boiler suit wrapped around his elbow it looked almost as though he had a basketball tucked under his arm. His right hand gripped the sodden towel, which dripped water like a leaky tap and made a damp patch on the ground.
>
> (Yu, 2014, p. 190)

Ever since André Lefevere published his *Translation, Rewriting, and the Manipulation of Literary Fame*, we have been conscious of mechanisms deployed by editors and critics that may shape a book's reception. In this connection, it is worth noting that as *Boy in the Twilight* moved closer toward publication, Yu Hua's American editor proposed that the book be given a subtitle: "Stories of the Hidden China." Yu Hua voiced no objection, and I went along with the suggestion also, for it actually mirrored my own view about these stories. Although not all readers reacted favorably to the subtitle, at least one reviewer responded sympathetically, noting:

> The subtitle of Yu Hua's newly translated collection of short stories, *Boy in the Twilight: Stories of the Hidden China*, may seem like a marketing ploy to give the book an exotic appeal. It may also seem redundant: isn't it standard for writers of fiction to explore life's obscure realms? Natural as these reactions are, it helps to consider the biases of today's global audience. As contemporary Chinese literature has become more widely read, more often translated, and more hotly debated, the default response has been to view it through the lens of modern politics. The English-language market tends to encourage this attitude. [. . .] Hua's "hidden" China, in contrast, is one of regular people: not allegorical caricatures or media archetypes, but men and women struggling to sort out their lives in the early years of reform.
>
> (Calvert, 2014)

Cries in the Drizzle

In the years following our dinner in Beijing, Yu Hua and I saw each other quite regularly. We spent several days together during his American book tour in November 2003, and when I visited him in China the following summer, he had a question for me: Would I be interested in translating his first novel, *Zai xiyu zhong huhan* (*Cries in the Drizzle*)?

Cries in the Drizzle occupies a rather unusual position in Yu Hua's oeuvre. Although it is seen by some in China as his finest novel, it failed to create much of a stir when first published there, and it remains much less popular than his other two novels of the 1990s. A British editor who declined to make an offer for the UK rights to my English translation may have put her finger on the reason for the novel's limited appeal when she wrote of *Cries in the Drizzle*:

> I thought it gave a very interesting, intimate insight into village life in China and the relationships between both members of the community and within families – most of which seem fraught with violence and high drama! However, I think the disjointed structure Yu Hua has chosen to employ makes for less than compelling reading, and makes it hard to engage fully with the characters' fates. I can envisage this novel earning admiring reviews, but not appealing widely to readers.
>
> (Wang, 2006)

I myself was conscious that *Cries in the Drizzle* was not the easiest book to like, but I was loath to decline Yu Hua's invitation, and to my relief his American editor proved willing to publish my translation, despite her own reservations about the book's marketability.

Zai xiyu zhong huhan is written in a polished, writerly style that differs from the more everyday language of Yu Hua's later novels. Its sentences often have a firm grammatical structure and a rich lexicon, studded with four-character phrases. The elegantly phrased narrative is punctuated with snatches of vivid, often earthy, direct speech. My goal was to tell Yu Hua's story in equally polished English and to present the dialogue in equally colorful English idiom.

Some portions of *Cries in the Drizzle* are particularly reliant on *telling*, as opposed to *showing*, and in them dialogue plays a rather small role. In the opening section of Chapter 3, for example, there are only a dozen or so lines of direct speech in well over twenty pages of narrative. The dialogue being so limited, I felt that when it did appear it was all the more important to exploit the opportunities offered to bring characters to life, and this led me sometimes to slightly intensify the effects, as in this rendering of a typically blunt statement by Sun Kwangtsai, the narrator's father:

> He would sit on the doorsill and ramble on like an old biddy, muttering to himself mournfully, "People are so much more trouble than sheep. Sheep's wool you can sell, the dung is good fertilizer, and the meat makes a fine dinner. With a relative to support, you're really up shit creek. He's got no wool, and eating him is too big a risk – who would bail me out if I ended up in the slammer?"
>
> (Yu, 2007, pp. 183–84)

> 孙广才只是经常坐在门槛上，像个上了年纪的女人那样罗嗦着不休，他唉声叹气地自言自语："养人真不如养羊呵，羊毛可以卖钱，羊粪可以肥田，羊肉还可以吃。养着一个人那就倒霉透了。要毛没毛，吃他的肉我又不敢，坐了大牢谁来救我。"
>
> (Yu, 2004, p. 176)

China in Ten Words

In December 2008, knowing that Yu Hua would soon come to the United States to promote the English edition of *Brothers*, I invited him to give a presentation at my college during his book tour the following spring, and he readily agreed. Eager to pin down a title for his talk, I asked him what he would like to talk about. He suggested a couple of options: either literature or contemporary China. Both these topics seemed too broad to be viable lecture titles, and I wondered if there was a way his talk could link the two. Recalling that on my shelves at home I had a book entitled *A Writer's Britain* (by the English novelist Margaret Drabble), I tendered a suggestion: "Why don't we call the talk 'A Writer's China'?"

Yu Hua liked this idea, but I'm not sure he gave much thought to what he was going to say until after he arrived in California. A few hours before he was due to speak, he confided that he was going to tell stories related to two words in modern Chinese, *renmin* 人民 (people) and *lingxiu* 领袖 (leader). The talk was a resounding success, and by the following afternoon, as I drove him to the Los Angeles Airport, he had realized that he could build a whole book around a series of words that carried particular meaning for him. He flew on to his next destination fired with enthusiasm for this new project.

In the months that followed, reading each new chapter of Yu Hua's manuscript as it arrived in my inbox, I was infected with that same excitement. The book was chock-full of vivid anecdotes and memorable situations, sometimes amusing, sometimes shocking, but always highly engaging. It was my pleasant task as translator to bring out all these qualities to fullest effect.

One new challenge with *China in Ten Words* was the task of rendering in English the various verses and jingles that Yu Hua incorporates into his book. In the chapter entitled "Revolution," for example, Yu Hua quotes a jingle that enjoyed wide currency during the Great Leap Forward, and in my translation I tried both to convey its meaning and spirit and also to reproduce to some degree its infectious rhyme scheme (Yu, 2011, p. 115). In the final chapter, "Bamboozle," where Yu Hua references a famous skit by the Chinese comedian Zhao Benshan, I again tried to capture the spirit – not necessarily the letter – of the original Chinese. I was aided in this effort by a happy twist of fate: the key word at the end of Zhao Benshan's last sentence – *que* 瘸 – translates in English as "lame," a word which offers multiple rhyming opportunities:

> I can bamboozle the tough into acting tame,
> Bamboozle the gent into dumping the dame,
> Bamboozle the innocent into taking the blame,
> Bamboozle the winner into conceding the game,
> I'm selling crutches today, so this is my aim:
> I'll bamboozle a man into thinking he's lame.

(Yu, 2011, p. 204)

> 我能把正的忽悠斜了，
> 能把 蔫 的忽悠 谑 了，
> 能把尖人忽悠 嗯 了，
> 能把小 两 口 过 的挺好，
> 我 给 他忽悠分 别 了，
> 今天 卖 拐，
> 一 双 好腿我能 给 他忽悠 瘸 了！

(Yu, 2010, p. 282)

With the title of his talk at Pomona still in his mind, Yu Hua at first thought of entitling the book *Shige cihui: yige zuojia de Zhongguo* 《十个词汇：一个作家的中国》 ("Ten Words: a Writer's China"). But after mulling over this slightly awkward formulation, I proposed to Yu Hua a snappier and somewhat brasher title: *Shige cihui li de Zhongguo (China in Ten Words)*. Although he himself might not have chosen this title, Yu Hua appreciated its pithiness, and his American publisher embraced it unreservedly. The title has not pleased everyone, of course: some readers, seeing it and expecting the book to deliver a comprehensive introduction to contemporary China, are disappointed to find that so much of the book focuses on Yu Hua's personal experiences.

By coincidence, just as Yu Hua was putting the finishing touches on the book's first chapter, "Renmin," the *New York Times* invited him to write an article to mark the twentieth anniversary of the June 4, 1989 crackdown. At Yu Hua's request I sent the newspaper my translation of the "People" chapter, which was duly trimmed down to length appropriate for publication. It appeared in the *New York Times* on May 30, 2009, enjoying pride of place in a full-page feature that included contributions from other Chinese authors whose lives had been altered by the events of 1989. In the years that followed, Yu Hua and I went on to publish some twenty-odd op-ed pieces in Western newspapers. Working to a strict word-limit was, I found, excellent training in conveying ideas with maximum verbal economy.

In terms of impact and sales, *China in Ten Words* is the most successful of my translations. The Pantheon editors recognized the book's potential very early on and lavished a lot of care on it, accordingly. Some details – such as the dates of composition that were originally attached to each chapter – were deleted, and others – such as explanatory descriptions of culture-specific features such as "big-character posters" – were added by Yu Hua at the editors' suggestion. Special attention was given to the book's cover, a visually striking array of red characters and words on a yellow background.

In Yu Hua's original manuscript, *Shige cihui li de Zhongguo* has both an introduction (前言) and a postscript (后记). The introduction is heavy on literary allusions (Homer, Mencius, Dante) and also includes elements that one might associate with an acknowledgements page rather than an introduction (Yu Hua thanks me, for instance, for inviting him to give the talk that inspired this book). The book's postscript, on the other hand, simply tells a story – a touching and revealing anecdote about Yu Hua's early experiences in the healthcare profession and its impact on him as a writer. Why not move the postscript story, the Pantheon editors suggested, to the very start of the introduction, in order to make the most of Yu Hua's storytelling strengths and grip the reader right from the word go? Yu Hua and I could see the advantage of this, and the English edition was revised accordingly.

The seventh day

In the spring of 2013, Yu Hua sent me an electronic file of a newly completed novel, *Diqi tian*, still a couple of months away from being published in China. During that summer I set to work translating it, and the English edition was published by Pantheon in January 2015 (Yu Hua, 2015).

Diqi tian, written in Yu Hua's trademark unadorned language, was not a particularly difficult book to translate. The most controversial aspect of my translation appears to be my omission of the epigraph that is found at the beginning of the Chinese edition. It quotes Genesis 2.2: "And on the seventh day God ended his work which he had made; and he rested on the seventh day from all the work which he had made" (Huang, 2016).

This epigraph, absent from Yu Hua's manuscript, was inserted into the Chinese edition at the prompting of his publisher – presumably on the assumption that the biblical reference would enhance the book's appeal to contemporary Chinese readers (Yu, 2018a, p. 200). From a Western point of view, however, it seems unnecessary – and possibly undesirable – for the novel to claim an affinity with biblical narrative. The quoted lines from Genesis focus the spotlight on the seventh day, sure enough, and to this extent the biblical reference forges a link to Yu Hua's book. In the biblical story, however, the main significance of the seventh day is that this is when God gives himself a rest after his labors. To highlight Genesis 2.2 at the start of the novel might give the unfortunate and misleading impression that Yu Hua is using the epigraph to draw attention to his own god-like role in creating a fictional world of the afterlife. To my mind, the biblical story of the world's creation in seven days is so familiar to Western readers that they do not need reminding of it at the beginning of a book entitled *The Seventh Day* and organized, like the opening of Genesis, into a day-by-day account of events from Day 1 to Day 7. Western readers, on the other hand, might well be interested to know that in China there has long been a folk notion of *tou qi* 头七 (the first seven days after death), when the souls of the dead are thought to linger close to their former home. But nowhere in the book is this point explicitly made, and it is not essential to know this in order to appreciate the novel.

"The April 3rd Incident"

In September 2015, Yu Hua wrote to me to propose a new project: the translation of seven short stories written early in his career. I liked this idea: four of these stories had never been translated into English, and I felt there was room for a new translation of the other three; together they could form a companion volume to *The Past and the Punishments*, the notable collection of early stories by Yu Hua – his first book-length publication in English – translated by Andrew Jones and published in 1996.

Although Yu Hua selected this set of seven stories, he left it to me to organize them as I saw fit, and so I arranged them by date of publication, which had the benefit that the book started off strongly with "As the North Wind Howled" and "The April 3rd Incident," and saved for last the most challenging story, "Summer Typhoon."

As I worked on these pieces, two issues came to the forefront. The first consisted of concrete details: Yu Hua's use of particular words and their precise connotations. A combination of vagueness and detail is a hallmark of Yu Hua's narrative style, and precisely because details are relatively sparse, I am always keen to know just how Yu Hua visualizes the things that do make an appearance in his stories. For example, in both *Zai xiyu zhong huhan* and *Huozhe* we encounter the simple word *yang* 羊. Potentially this could mean "sheep," or maybe "lamb," or possibly "goat." Which is it? Also, the narrators in these two novels regularly mention a *xiaolu* 小路 (narrow road). Just how narrow a road is this? Is it a footpath, or a dirt road? In "Love Story," one of the characters is attracted by a *xuesheng qun* 学生裙 (literally, "student dress") in a shop window. What exactly is a "student dress"? In "In Memory of Willow Yang," the narrator talks of guests changing the position of *yizi* 椅子 (chair) in his house: is that one chair, or several chairs? In all these cases, I asked Yu Hua for clarification, so that I had a clearer picture in my mind as I translated.[3]

Another question came up in two longer stories, "The April 3rd Incident" and "Summer Typhoon." In the Chinese version of "The April 3rd Incident," a blending of the third-person narrative with the mental imaginings of the story's protagonist at times generates a certain amount of confusion. In "Summer Typhoon," likewise, the storyline is studded with brief interludes that give us direct access to characters' memories and musings; in the absence of cues, the reader is often left unclear as to just where we are veering off into internal monologue and where we are following the main storyline. While both stories gain a certain intrigue and mystery from this kind of blurring of edges, they also run a risk of appearing incoherent and becoming hard to follow. I suggested to Yu Hua that in the English edition we might want to consider following the practice adopted by William Faulkner in many of his books – using one typeface for basic narrative and a different one for internal monologues, to make things easier for the reader. Yu Hua thought this a good idea, and so in the English edition changes in font are used to signpost changes in the pattern of expression. This works particularly well, I think, in "Summer Typhoon," where fragmentary memories and musings – often strikingly lyrical – stand out on the page, juxtaposed with the conventional narrative thread, as here:

The boy began to move around the room cautiously. It was indeed quiet here. A long sliver of light hung from the window. *He had once walked alone in a forest, and with the branches interlocking above his head and the leaves covering one another, the sky had looked tattered and disjointed.* The boy seemed to have opened the door – he could see it too. *Sunlight had flitted about, hopping from one leaf to another.* The boy was going downstairs, hopping from one step to the next. *From beneath his feet had come the faint sound of leaves crackling, as soft as freshly tilled earth.*

(Yu, 2018b, p. 177)

孩子开始在屋内小心翼翼地走动。这里确实安静。光亮长长一条挂在窗户上。他曾经在森林里独自行走，头顶的树枝交叉在一起，树叶相互覆盖，天空显得支离破碎。孩子好像打开了屋门，他连门也看到了。阳光在上面跳跃，从一张树叶跳到另一张树叶上。孩子正在下楼，从这一台阶跳到另一台阶上。脚下有树叶轻微的断裂声，松软如新翻耕的泥土。

(Yu, 1995, pp. I, 248)

What next?

Since the early 1990s, when Yu Hua published his first three novels in quick succession, his pace of production has slowed dramatically: he has published only two novels since 1996, and no new short stories since 1999. But he has several books in progress. When I met him for the first time in 2001, he told me he was writing an immensely long novel – much longer than he had ever imagined he could write. Now, almost twenty years have passed, and this novel has yet to see the light of day. But I remain hopeful that this book – and Yu Hua's other projects – will sooner or later be completed.

Notes

1 For one example, see Barr (2011, pp. 33–34).
2 In his review of *The Seventh Day*, Ken Kalfus remarked: "*The Seventh Day* contains many instances of macabre comedy, though Allan H. Barr's workmanlike translation is too wordy to deliver its best potential laugh lines." See Kalfus (2015).
3 For more on this, see Meyer (2019).

References

Barr, A. H. (白亚仁). (2011). "Yiwei yeyu fanyijia de zibaishu" 一位业余翻译家的自白书, *Fanyijia de duihua* 翻译家的对话. Zuojia chubanshe.

Calvert, D. (2014). Exploring the hidden China. *Boston Review*. Retrieved from http://bostonreview.net/books-ideas/calvert-boy-twilight-stories-hidden-china

Huang, Y. (2016, July). Ghosts and the contemporary return: The case of Yu Hua's "The Seventh Day." *Neohelicon*, *43*(1).

Kalfus, K. (2015, March 21). Broke souls. *The New York Times Book Review*.

Leonard, E. (2001, July 16). Writers on writing: Easy on adverbs, exclamation points and especially hooptedoodle. *The New York Times*.

Meyer, L. (2019). What it takes to write, and translate, some of China's most famous stories. *Electric Literature*. Retrieved from https://electricliterature.com/what-it-takes-to-write-and-translate-some-of-chinas-most-famous-stories/

Wang, J. (2006, March). Personal communication.

Yu Hua 余华. (1995). *Yu Hua zuopin ji* 余华作品集. Zhongguo shehui kexueyuan chubanshe.

Yu Hua 余华. (1999). *Huanghun li de nanhai* 黄昏里的男孩. Xin shijie chubanshe.

Yu Hua 余华. (2004). *Zai xiyu zhong huhan* 在细雨中呼喊. Shanghai wenyi chubanshe.

Yu Hua 余华. (2007). *Cries in the Drizzle* (A. H. Barr, Trans.). Anchor.

Yu Hua 余华. (2010). *Shige cihui li de Zhongguo* 十个词汇里的中国. Maitian.

Yu Hua 余华. (2011). *China in Ten Words* (A. H. Barr, Trans.). Pantheon.

Yu Hua 余华. (2014). *Boy in the Twilight* (A. H. Barr, Trans.). Pantheon.

Yu Hua 余华. (2015). *The Seventh Day* (A. H. Barr, Trans.). Pantheon.

Yu Hua 余华. (2018a). Zonglun rensheng, zonglun ziwo 纵论人生，纵论自我, *Wo zhi zhidao ren shi shenme* 我只知道人是什么. Yilin chubanshe.

Yu Hua 余华. (2018b). *The April 3rd Incident: Stories* (A. H. Barr, Trans.). Pantheon.

Index

For Product Safety Concerns and Information please contact our EU
representative GPSR@taylorandfrancis.com
Taylor & Francis Verlag GmbH, Kaufingerstraße 24, 80331 München, Germany

www.ingramcontent.com/pod-product-compliance
Lightning Source LLC
Chambersburg PA
CBHW071412100726
47908CB00004B/1145